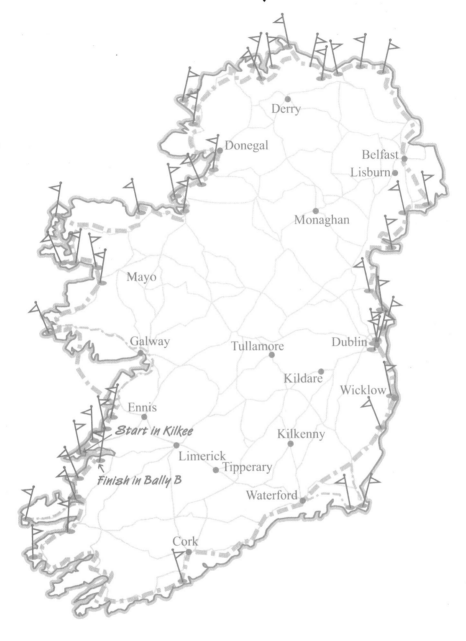

Derry

Donegal

Belfast
Lisburn

Monaghan

Mayo

Galway   Tullamore   Dublin

Kildare

Wicklow

Ennis

Start in Kilkee   Kilkenny

Limerick
Tipperary

Finish in Bally B

Waterford

Cork

A
Course
Called
IRELAND

A Course *Called* IRELAND

*A Long Walk
in Search of a Country, a Pint,
and the Next Tee*

TOM COYNE

GOTHAM BOOKS

Published by Penguin Group (USA) Inc.
375 Hudson Street, New York, New York 10014, U.S.A.
Penguin Group (Canada), 90 Eglinton Avenue East, Suite 700, Toronto, Ontario
M4P 2Y3, Canada (a division of Pearson Penguin Canada Inc.); Penguin Books
Ltd, 80 Strand, London WC2R 0RL, England; Penguin Ireland, 25 St Stephen's
Green, Dublin 2, Ireland (a division of Penguin Books Ltd); Penguin Group
(Australia), 250 Camberwell Road, Camberwell, Victoria 3124, Australia
(a division of Pearson Australia Group Pty Ltd); Penguin Books India Pvt Ltd,
11 Community Centre, Panchsheel Park, New Delhi – 110 017, India; Penguin
Group (NZ), 67 Apollo Drive, Rosedale, North Shore 0632, New Zealand
(a division of Pearson New Zealand Ltd); Penguin Books (South Africa) (Pty) Ltd,
24 Sturdee Avenue, Rosebank, Johannesburg 2196, South Africa

Penguin Books Ltd, Registered Offices: 80 Strand, London WC2R 0RL, England

Published by Gotham Books, a member of Penguin Group (USA) Inc.

First printing, February 2009
1 3 5 7 9 10 8 6 4 2

All photos courtesy of the author.
Maps created by Virginia Norey.

Gotham Books and the skyscraper logo are trademarks of Penguin Group (USA) Inc.

LIBRARY OF CONGRESS CATALOGING-IN-PUBLICATION DATA
Coyne, Tom.
A course called Ireland: a long walk in search of a country, a pint, and the next
tee / Tom Coyne.
p. cm.
ISBN 978-1-592-40424-7 (hardcover)
1. Golf—Ireland. 2. Golf courses—Ireland. 3. Coyne, Tom. I. Title.
GV984.I73C69 2009
796.35209417—dc22 2008042769

Printed in the United States of America
Set in Sabon
Designed by Sabrina Bowers

While the author has made every effort to provide accurate telephone numbers and
Internet addresses at the time of publication, neither the publisher nor the author
assumes any responsibility for errors, or for changes that occur after publication.
Further, the publisher does not have any control over and does not assume any responsibility for author or third-party Web sites or their content.

For the friends who
walked a hole with me

Think you're escaping and run into yourself.
Longest way round is the shortest way home.
James Joyce, *Ulysses*

It's no simple business being mad.
Paddy from Westport

THE DOG WAS GOING TO BE A PROBLEM.

I had already faced off against a gang of galloping live-stock, gone toe to hoof with a mountain goat, and narrowly escaped the nip of a mother swan. I had climbed my way out of sandy pits and thorny ditches, scrambled up stone walls, splashed my way through deep and icy waters. I had felt speeding cars brush the hair on my knuckles. I had lowered my chin into a month-long rain, peeled the blisters off my blisters, watched my feet turn to piles of soggy porridge. I had chafed. Over the last four months, I had encountered quick and flying fists, smelled the sour breath of a hundred lost men, fought my damndest not to become one of them. I took on the British Army. I dodged the police. And I felt the despair of every man who ever chose to walk alone, then found himself dreaming he could go back and choose differently.

But with just a few hours to go, and just a few paces left on my journey, I met a growl in the middle of a quiet country road, and it sounded just like the last thing a person might ever hear.

The dog was tall as a Harley with paws the size of pancakes. His skin was taut and caked in mud as if he'd been resurrected from a bog, and a winding scar cut up his face like a map. A redness leaked from his eyes, and in his stare I recognized a disquieting certainty about how the next few minutes were going to proceed. This wasn't an animal I was looking at, I told myself. This was an inevitability.

I hadn't seen a car for twenty minutes when I rounded a bend and found this dog lying in the middle of the asphalt, unnatural—it was as if I'd left the car road and come upon his. It was like the automobiles knew, and they knew better. I watched the dog lift himself off the gravel, peeling back his lips to bare a craggy ridge of yellow teeth. He dropped his right paw in front of his left, moving in my direction. The low rumbling growl— I could feel it in my feet.

Loping like an elephant, the dog slowly drew closer. I inched backward, my feet endeavoring an about-face, but my back refused to show itself to what was coming. The dog's stride was twice my shuffle, and a separation of thirty yards quickly became twenty, twenty paces turning to fifteen, and soon I was close enough to see frothy brown gums where his mouth was torn at the corners. I turned around, and when I did, he barked. And when he barked, I felt a spontaneous warmth in my high-performance, quick-wicking boxer briefs. Tears squirted from my eyes like juice from cocktail fruit. That bark didn't sound like nature. If I was going to have to sacrifice an ankle, so be it. I tossed my bag and turned around and I ran like a dog. If only.

Behind me came a frenzied scratch of long nails on gravel as the dog scrambled its way up to speed, and I estimated another twelve strides before I would be curled up on the pavement, begging mercy from a dog whose breath smelled of my shin bone. But just then, like a cart girl driving toward you in the midst of a six-hour round, a miraculous vision appeared on the horizon. A blue Nissan was headed my way. The dog pulled up at the sight of the car, and I hopped and flailed like a drunken ballerina, bringing the car to a reluctant halt. The driver's side window cracked an inch. A teenager with prickly black hair sat behind the wheel, a girl sitting next to him, smoking a cigarette. They both eyed me with predictable suspicion.

"You have to help me," I pleaded. "I can't get past this dog. I'm stuck out here—the thing chased me down the road. I need a lift, just until it's out of sight."

The driver looked to his passenger, and his passenger looked at him, their faces screaming *step on it.*

"Please, I'm desperate, I haven't seen another car in an hour," I protested. I abandoned bravery, and put all my chips on hopeless cowardice. "I'll pay you. I'm serious. This is dangerous, this dog is not well."

Meanwhile, the growl started up again, and the roadblock resumed his steps. The girl put down her cigarette and, evidently some sort of dog whisperer for the barmy, she rolled down her window and said, "Shoo. Go on, you dog. Get out of here."

For her contribution to the crisis, I could not have been less thankful. I began to question the caliber of this miracle. This was an obvious open-the-door-to-a-stranger situation, and not only had this couple failed to do so, but one of them tried to shoo Cujo. Could they not see that this was not a shooing sort of dog, that this was a maiming, tearing, saving-the-torso-for-breakfast breed of canine?

The driver looked ahead to where my gear was lying in the road.

"Is that yours?"

"Yeah. The dog was chasing me."

"Are those golf clubs?" he said.

"Yes."

For the first time in our short and heretofore one-sided relationship, the kid with the locked blue Nissan looked me straight in the eyes.

"What in the hell are you doing out here with golf clubs?"

It wasn't the time for that particular question. But it was still a pretty damn good one.

———

Golf trip. Years after *spring break* and *bachelor party* had lost their promise, *golf trip* still tingled with possibility in the minds of so many. For millions of like-minded men, the golf getaway remained one of the few excuses for husbands and dads to get giggly about bunking up with one another in modest accommodations, forking over thousands to lose golf balls and sip canned beer and feast on meals from a Myrtle Beach fryer. If your interest wasn't piqued by blasting venison, if you were able to see camping for the non-vacation that it was, then golf remained your last bit of glue, holding former roommates and old neighbors together. Rare was the chance for men to make dinner reservations for one another, then share a pleasant nightcap where even a fleeting reference to the opposite sex played as a betrayal of their own. It was an opportunity to feel athletic, manly, even, before taking a steam with the brother-in-law you never really liked. Not until that week at Pinehurst, of course, after which you continued to call him *bro*, sans the dripping sarcasm.

In the dozens of failed and wonderful and yet-to-materialize golf trips I had been a part of, all the swaying palms of Florida, all those dollops of green icing in the Arizona desert—it all seemed sleepy when considered against the links of Europe. Golf played elsewhere was but a limp imitation of the battles being fought along the edges of Europe's western isles, where golfers forsook the safety of the clubhouse and embarked upon character-rattling slogs, where it was not about playing perfect, but having played at all. If you had ever leaned sideways into the breeze with a sand wedge in your hands, staring through windblown tears at a golf ball entombed in four feet of fanged thistle, clothes soaked through to the skin, fingers like an overworked fishmonger, and yet you couldn't bring yourself to stop smiling—then you got it. And you might soon understand how I found myself on that road, hauling golf clubs and contemplating a hospital stay, in a quiet and wooded corner of Ireland.

I took my first golf trip to Ireland when I was nineteen years old. Growing up outside Philadelphia as the youngest of five, I had a vague sense of my Irish roots. I knew that my great-grandparents hailed from towns in County Mayo, that they settled in Scranton, Pennsylvania, before the turn of the century, and that none of them ever went back. I wore a green KISS ME, I'M IRISH pin on my Catholic school uniform on March 17, and I suffered through corned beef and cabbage once a year, but that was the extent to which Ireland was celebrated in our house. The only other time I remember hearing about our heritage was when my mother would accuse my father or one of my brothers (and even myself from time to time) of being a damn Irishman. I took it as a compliment, though it never quite sounded like one.

We were Americans, Catholics, golfers, Phillies fans, shore-goers, Wiffle-ballers—even as a redhead, *Irish* ranked low on my list of labels. The potential of my heritage never occurred to me until I graduated high school and my father took me on a golf tour of Ireland, where we spent a week discovering the Irish countryside through a bus window and I first began to wonder—what were my great-grandparents thinking? How was Lackawanna County an upgrade from County Mayo? My family came from a postcard where everyone laughed and danced and the air smelled of turf and sea. How could they have pulled up their roots out of so much soft green and gold?

My father and I spent ten days bouncing around Ireland in that bus, from golf course to hotel and hotel to golf course, and I don't think I've ever enjoyed golf, or my father, or a bouncing bus, for that matter, quite so much. It was the golf trip against which all others would be measured, a few days from that time when a father first starts to look and act like a buddy.

Teeing up that first ball in Ballybunion, as we looked out over an ebb and flow of dunes giving way to green strips of fairway, beach grasses spinning in the breeze, a white-tipped ocean just a three-wood away, I felt an understanding for how this strange game came to be, how a contest of knocking pebbles around a field survived through the centuries. Because those first golfers were knocking pebbles around fields like these. My first round in Ballybunion left me red-cheeked and wide-eyed, sitting straight up in my chair in the clubhouse, recounting hole after hole in a way that somehow wasn't boring. Dad and I replayed all our shots, and then we were quiet for what felt like a week as he slid me my first pint of Guinness (at least the first one he knew about). And just like that original trip to Ireland, all subsequent pints haven't quite lived up to the first, the one after golf with Dad, the one Mom would have so disapproved of. In his introduction to the Ballybunion links, Tom Watson wrote, "After playing Bally-bunion for the first time, a man would think that the game of golf originated here." For me, I think it kind of did.

The golf that week wasn't perfect or great or pretty—it was something we both seemed unequipped to gauge. Golf as I'd known it was a game of explanations and excuses, strategies for future improvements. Yet that didn't seem the language being spoken in places like Ballybunion and Tralee and Rosses Point, places that simply weren't looking for suggestions. Any vocabulary we might have used to rate or judge or quantify a golf vacation elsewhere—those words didn't seem to translate in Ireland. The best description seemed the simplest, the one word the Irish used for everything, and it always seemed to fit. Ireland was grand. Just *grand*.

Many years later, I began devising a golf trip of my own, where I would prove to my unwashed friends why golf played against the Irish Sea was the greatest and truest expression of the game. I started by printing out a map of Irish golf courses, a green island ringed with red flags, each flag denoting the next must-play links. It looked like an old man's birthday cake, green icing crowded with red candles, and I focused in on which slice my friends and I might attempt.

It wasn't easy. How could we skip golf holes deemed unskip-pable by golf pundits the world over? How many holes might we squeeze in before friends were extradited home by their wives, their children, their Mastercard? Should we play it safe with a sampling of old Irish standards, take a chance on an itinerary of best buys, or seek out the bevy of new arrivals? There was only one rule—Ballybunion—but one rule had many offshoots to con-sider, because you couldn't play Ballybunion and skip Tralee, which meant you weren't far from Lahinch, which brought you too close to Connemara to cross it off the list, and made that course in Belmullet an easy temptation, which meant Enniscrone and Rosses Point were a must. We would be close enough to Donegal that we'd have to squeeze it in, which gave us no excuse to skip Northern Ireland, or Dublin, or the whole damn thing.

As I plotted our trip, I learned that Ireland possessed some 40 percent of the true links courses in the world—for a country the size of Indiana, it seemed an absurd statistic. Loosely defined, a links is a seaside course with few, if any, trees. Wind + ocean + ball-gobbling grasses = links. The name referred to the linksland upon which the courses were laid—land that linked the beach with arable turf.* Dunes, essentially, but a complicated ecosystem with properties uniquely suited to a particular style of golf. Soil rife with shell allows links courses to drain like colanders, making for firm, fast conditions that lend themselves to a more along-the-ground style of play than the air attack of modern golf. True links are covered with beach grasses of a hardiness that can only be found in such nutrient-strapped soil, and their tumultuous topography can't be built by blueprint, only by centuries of sea-blown sand.

The golf courses we are accustomed to in America—on television or on a Saturday morning—are almost invariably parkland tracks, tree-lined layouts with tightly cropped edges, fairways defined against carefully tiered cuts of rough. Parkland golf is handsome, convenient, and often obvious, while links golf is unapologetic, unpretentious, and wonderfully unrefined—parkland is the cover girl, lovely and forgettable; linksland is the girl who doesn't bother with makeup but still turns your head, authentic and irresistible, the one you'd travel all the way to Ireland to spend a few more hours with.

The GPS-guided game we play in benign breezes over unblemished fairways allows us to take on a course with one golf shot in our bag—high and deep—knocking the ball over bunkers and over water and thusly being rewarded. Links golf, with its

---

* The Tralee Golf Club website, with credit to Paul Daley's *Links Golf—The Inside Story*, traces the expression *links* to the old English word for lean, *hlinc*, lean terrain formed by receding seas that carved channels into the sand. Over the centuries, winds transformed the channels into gullies and dunes. Rabbit runs that were eventually widened by foxes, then hunters, suggested golf's first fairways. And the hollows used by rabbits for "their feeding halls and dancing floors" were natural sites for a putting surface.

sea winds and lumpy fairways rolling their way into kinked putting surfaces, is not about knocking your ball over and above a
golf course, but rather playing your ball *through* one. It's less like
darts and more like, well, golf, and it can leave you lightheaded
with options as you stand in a heaving fairway and consider your
own definition of fair. For anyone with a golf imagination, playing a links is an all-out indulgence, and it makes one understand
that golf isn't about striking the perfect seven-iron or hitting x number of greens. A good day on a links reminds you that golf is
about one thing, and one thing only—stuffing your ball into the
hole as quickly as you damn well can.

Golf historians trace the game's origin to ancient stick-
whacks-ball pursuits in Holland, Rome, and even China, but
there is no debate that seaside Scots grew golf into the game we
play today, and that the first lost golf balls in Scotland went missing along the margins of authentic links courses—unsuitable for
growing crops, linkslands were left to sportsmen and their pursuits, and the dunes thus became the venue for golf's original
whiff. And that's why there exists such passion about links golf—
we might not know exactly who invented golf, but on a true
links, you get to spend an afternoon with them. By strict definition, there is not one genuine, complete links layout in the entire
United States (recalling so many KEEP OFF DUNES admonishments
by the Jersey shore, I can imagine why), but judging from my
map of Ireland, it looked like you couldn't go ten steps without
tripping over one.

As I studied the courses and pondered our trajectory, the itinerary grew, transforming from a golf trip into something else.
Each flag on the map pushed my imagination along to the next
until I found my trip back where it began, one long round of golf
with no clear beginning, no conspicuous finish line. And soon, I
wasn't looking at a map of Irish golf courses on my bulletin
board. I was looking at *the* Irish golf course. In the caddy par-
lance of my youth, I was looking at the world's ultimate loop.

When you played golf in Ireland, you walked. So I would
walk. I would set out with golf clubs and a good pair of shoes,
invite all my golfing friends to join me, and I would play Ireland
until Ireland was done. The walk to my next tee box might be a

few yards in some cases, a few days in others, but in the end it might add up to the golf trip to end all golf trips, the one without compromises or detours, a round of golf that truly went around.

I had spent most of 2003 and all of 2004 chasing every golfer's dream, dedicating all my dollars and hours to the pursuit of playing professional golf. After teeing it up for 546 consecutive days under the watchful tutelage of the most accomplished instructors, mind-shrinkers, and body-shapers in golf, I became thoroughly convinced that professional bowling would have been a better dream for me. Saddled with a +1 handicap that grew impossible to play to, I had become just good enough at golf to quit it, and I probably would have if it weren't for the possibility of Ballybunion. So Ireland wasn't just a trip or a challenge, it was a mulligan for my golf career. In all those months spent trying to play with the pros, I might have never played *my* greatest round of golf, but what if I could still play *the* greatest round of golf? I would never play the Open, and the only way I was getting on Augusta was with wire snips and night-vision goggles in my bag. But if I could play a course called Ireland, I thought, Tiger would have nothing on me.

I bought a larger map of Ireland that covered half my office wall. I filled it with pins and Post-its, and I began drawing a red line from course to course and town to town, a line that I would find myself standing upon many months later in the Irish southwest, trying to explain to a couple of teenagers how I had arrived at this particular circumstance, struggling to convey to them that not only was my life in grave jeopardy, but worse, I was late for my next tee time.

"I'm from the States, I'm here playing golf all over the country . . ."

The girl leaned across her boyfriend, eyeing me through the cracked window. "Are you the American that's walking around Ireland?"

There was hope. "That's me," I said, the warmth of a satisfied ego washing over me. I was saved. They were fans.

"Yer fuckin' mad," she said.

There hadn't been much doubt up to that point, but it was now confirmed—these two weren't golfers. When the un-golfed got word of my endeavor, they questioned my sanity. But when golfers heard about how I was spending my summer, they questioned my wife's. I was either crazy or the luckiest bastard on the planet, depending on your handicap.

I watched tires spit pebbles in my direction as their car sped down the road without me. And as I looked to my loyal friend who hadn't left my side, a dog who was eyeing me like I was wearing an EAT ME, I'M IRISH pin, I wasn't crazy, and I wasn't lucky. To borrow an old Irish expression, I was fucked.

OUT

hole 1
Level par

ONE HUNDRED AND FIFTY YEARS AGO, A DOZEN YOUNG MEN and women set out from towns in the west of Ireland, traveling by cart and by foot, headed for ports in Ballina and Westport, County Mayo. They bundled up their lives and stepped onto crowded ships pointed toward a place they had never seen before. One of those young women carried with her a mahogany cupboard with delicate glass doors, flowers hand-carved into the panels. Today it hangs in my parents' living room, next to a fifty-two-inch flat-screen television.

The names of those people, why they came, or precisely where they came from, had been lost in my family's shuffle. It had been my experience that the one thing Irish families did better than talk was whisper, and generations of whispers—*who was unlucky and who was ungrateful, who drank too much, died too young, who was a good daughter, a lazy son, who never married and, more quietly now, why not*—blended into a collective hush. I found myself looking at that cupboard from time to time, covered with the next generations' macaroni Christmas ornaments, a ceramic teddy bear, last month's Mother's Day cards. There was a golf ball in one of the nooks, a Titleist with a purple-and-red logo on it and the letters BGC: Ballybunion Golf Club. That cupboard came to America in the arms of a woman trying to put Ireland behind her, and now it hung on the wall showcasing a golf ball from County Kerry, reminding some of us how much we wanted to go back. And as I stood on my first tee box in the southwest of Ireland, looking out over golden dunes and black cliffs holding back a frothy sea, I felt certain that over the next 119 days spent walking the longest possible path to Ballybunion, I was going to figure out which one of us had it right.

My friend Denis had children my age, but we'd become good friends over the years as semi-regular golf partners—he divorced, me self-employed, we had high golf availability in common and found ourselves sharing a cart on many a Tuesday afternoon. And over those many Tuesdays, I came to understand that Denis dearly loved two things in the world—golf and Ireland (and his kids, I'm sure, but that wasn't really relevant during twilight golf). For golf in Ireland, his availability was extreme—a grandson of immigrants, he even had an Irish passport. He was packed for the trip before I even got around to inviting him, booking a spot during my first week, a stretch that promised more links than most.

It was widely known among golfing circles in southeastern Pennsylvania that Denis was a golfer who could come up short from almost anywhere on the golf course. We called him Captain Layup. Facing a carry over a lake, a pitch to the green, or a six-footer to the hole, rest assured that Denis had worked out some way in his subconscious to keep his ball from getting there. It wasn't that he couldn't hit it; rather, Denis was perpetually ready for that once-in-a-century five-iron that was going to travel a three-wood's distance. But if it was going to happen this century for Denis, I hoped that it would happen here, on our first hole of the Irish golf course, a 373-yard par-four on a sleepy little seaside course called Kilkee.

Elder linksman of the group, Denis was granted the honor. Standing on the first tee, looking out over the Atlantic Ocean where the water was torn white against the charcoal rocks, Denis stood tall on the tee box and breathed it all in. Pepper-haired with age in his eyes, that day he was a young boy staring into the sea, looking over this land he loved. He placed his three-wood behind his ball with reverence, took one long contemplative pause, and brought his club back, ready to make his golfing mark on one of this planet's most historic bits of rock.

He paused at the top of his backswing, eyes bright with hope—we braced ourselves, waiting for the cannon blasts, the trumpets, the eruption from the gallery. But all we heard was a loud "FORE!" from the window of a passing pickup truck. The yell had been launched at Denis with perfect mid-backswing timing. The rest of his swing looked like he was trying to fend off a swarm of bees, Denis fumbling into his golf ball and knuckling a heel shot into the very nearby weeds.

I had traveled far from home and my head still wasn't sure if this was sunrise or sunset golf we were playing, but as I watched Denis curse himself in Kilkee, the rest of our foursome choking back belly laughs, I felt a warm familiarity come over me. The drive-by-backswing golf shout was a street-side tee-box classic. And Kilkee or Philadelphia or wherever I might find myself tomorrow, it still played funny everywhere.

It had been months since that warm autumn evening back in Philadelphia, where I accomplished a feat that would have envious friends and unbelieving adversaries flummoxed for months to come. Nothing was as unbelievable about what I was about to attempt—not the miles, the cost, the girth of my itinerary—as the fact that I was golfing my way around Ireland while married, with every intention to remain so.

The menu that evening betrayed my objective—homemade crab cakes, buttery filet, the bottle of Australian chardonnay I'd been saving. It was an announcement meal, but my wife, Allyson, didn't show any suspicion, not until I followed up a run-of-the-mill Phillies rant with a half-nimble leap to the topic of golf, and Ireland.

"I'm thinking about taking a trip."

There came a speechless and timeless pause, one of those silent conversations within a conversation during which battle lines are drawn and whole fortresses erected. This first arrow had caught her off guard, but she was back, well in position as she reached for that bottle of wine and inquired, "Haven't you been to Ireland?"

"This is different." And then I launched a rambling litany of irresistible details and air-tight reasoning. *Forty percent of the true links courses in the world! It costs nothing to walk! Ballybunion!* She listened to my case, her expression somewhere between, *Damn, you're an idiot*, and *Damn, I'm an idiot*. And while some husbands would have ducked after telling their wives that they would like to go take a four-month stroll with their golf clubs, Allyson's eyes actually brightened at this time frame (my last golfing bright idea had me planted on a driving range for a year and a half, thus establishing a set of very low expectations). I was also quick to suggest the possibility of her taking a few weeks to travel the most scenic bits of the country with me, and I explained that the excursion might be cheap—again, relative to the last outing—in that I'd be staying in modest accommodations, and begging my way onto the golf courses.

"It's the perfect time to do it," I explained to her, aware that I was abusing a worn-out word. There was nothing perfect about this kind of idea. Now thirtysomething homeowners, living beyond the clutches of our credit cards, we were talking about children as if they weren't just a nuisance in restaurants, but like they might be an okay idea. Per previous negotiations, I knew I had banked a year of wanton selfishness before she would be asking me to paint my office pink and replace the bookshelf with a changing table. For a husband content to count the healthy Lhasa Apso he'd raised as his contribution to the planet, an uncle of fourteen (fifteen?) nephews and nieces who had yet to remember a single birthday (if I just showed up with a present once in a while, I was bound to be right some of the time), and a brother who had watched his once vibrant siblings turn into baggy-eyed binky-chasers—coming to the baby table and participating in talks was a big step, a step that had certainly earned said husband one measly little golf trip.

"The greatest round of golf ever attempted," I explained. "I might end up in the *Guinness Book of World Records.*"

And on a July night behind a small row house near Rocky Balboa's Art Museum steps, history was made in Philadelphia yet again. Generations of husbands would owe their vacations to the golfer who dared, a man whose twisted notion of what constituted a legitimate golf trip would make countless wives grateful for their own spouses, thoughtful heroes in comparison, guys who were only asking for a mere ten days in Vegas. The asshole-threshold moved that night, and swiftly.

You could almost hear the champ a few blocks away, cheering from those steps with fists raised to the sky when Allyson shook her head and said, "You'll end up in the Guinness. That sounds about right."

In preparation for a four-month golf trip where I'd be visiting north of forty courses, you might imagine that I'd have worn out a few mats at the driving range. I didn't. The months between that evening and that tee box in Kilkee were spent almost entirely in an office chair, sticking pins in a giant map of Ireland, ringing hotels and pro shops and bed-and-breakfasts, piecing together a hundred reservations to be coordinated with fortysome odd tee times. The phone bills might have been kinder if most of my conversations weren't spent trying to explain to assistant pros and old ladies with B&Bs that, cost and quality aside, I was in search of the absolute closest pillow to every links course in Ireland.

"We're very close to the golf course. Five minutes down the road."

"Would you happen to know the mileage?"

"Just a few minutes' drive. You can't miss it."

"Actually, I'm not going to be driving."

"Well the bus stops in town," they often explained, and usually offered. "Ring us and we'll come give you a lift."

I should have taken my own hint. How tough was this trip going to be if I could hardly bring myself to admit to a stranger what I was doing? I'd dance around my lack of transport for a while before eventually confessing, "I'll be on foot. I'll be walking."

"Walking?" It came back through the phone sounding almost profane, as if it had been outlawed centuries before, pedestrians cast out of Ireland with the snakes.

"Yes, walking."

"Oh, no. No no no," they would tell me, like I was a four-year-old drawing on the curtains. "You're not walking. I wouldn't recommend that at all."

I spent months convincing innkeepers, golf pros, and most of all myself that there was a grand golf course to be played around Ireland, if only I could find it. There were issues sitting heavy on my horizon, elephants in the office—the walloping cost of a summer on the road, worries about weather and illness and the probability of my expiring in a roadside ditch. Would I have a phone; what would I pack? And what of the fact that I was in crap shape, overweight with high blood pressure and on Lipitor at age thirty? I'd never hiked a step in my life and had viewed trail-mix-munching backpackers as a breed to be mocked at every opportunity. The guy who envied senior citizens for their scooters, who stopped to hit the open-sesame handicap button on his way into the mall, he was going to hump the long road to Ballybunion? Dire as they seemed, they were concerns for the back burner, stuff to sort out over there when it was too late to concede that I shouldn't be doing this at all. First, the matter of where the hell I was headed, and when. I was planning a thousand-mile stroll along a route that no two feet had ever walked, on roads I had never seen, all designed in a cramped office an ocean away. I knew I wanted my round to end in Ballybunion, but the rest was all up for debate. A robust and ironclad itinerary, chockablock with names and confirmation numbers, was the only thing that was going to get my ass on that plane.

This was an itinerary that would have been unimaginable before the Internet. I became a quick study on finding obscure accommodations in Ireland, and I learned the pitfalls of trying to pinpoint a bed in rural counties. Irish phraseology made it a struggle to triangulate a particular location—aside from the major roads, which I was hoping to avoid, route numbers were almost never referenced in an address. Roads were named by the town in which they terminated—*take the Sligo Road; we're on the Foxford Road*—which seemed a fine system, but it rendered my road atlas obsolete, and inspired something of an existential navigational crisis—*I'm walking a circle around Ireland to Ballybunion, so aren't these all the Ballybunion Road? And aren't they all not?* Another worry was that even though a website claimed a bed-and-breakfast was situated in Crossmolina or in Cork, such was merely a reference to the nearest post office. My next bed could be miles outside of the town I was headed to, a noncrisis if you are with wheels, but on foot, these faux addresses smacked of a sinister duplicity, to say you're located in Kilmacthomas when you're really another six miles down the road—and then the six miles back, so make that *twelve* miles off my course. It was a different way of considering the world, a planet where you couldn't pop in your Honda and go grab a sandwich or pick up detergent or a fresh pair of socks, where you were stuck with the world in front of you. I had to choose a path and live with it, which felt romantic and sort of ballsy, at least from the easy-reclining comfort of a leather office chair.

After a winter spent poking holes in that map, staring at a laminated calendar, sniffing dry-erase markers and thinking of Ireland, there were still gaps in my summer that plagued my sleep with nightmares of bedding down in windswept bogs, nothing but a five-iron for company. I was traveling with a twenty-mile leash to each of my days, and within each of those increments, I had to find golf, rest, and food, while adhering to a timetable that wouldn't devastate my body, mind, or the last bit of equity in our house. Selecting a route was like trying to finagle an interstate through Manhattan—the trajectory changed on a daily basis, and when one link moved, so did they all, a month's itinerary undone by an overbooked B&B, a full tee-time sheet, a TripAdvisor warning. What eventually emerged was a three-inch-thick binder of reservations, tee times, and phone numbers. It was my course map. It was my bible. It was a pile of pages that would keep me sane, a book I could shake at the skies in my darkest moments and know that I wasn't lost, I wasn't crazy. Because I had a plan. I had 103 reservations and forty-three tee times that said this all made perfect sense.

On some evenings, Allyson would sit down in the office after work and we would look at the Michelin map on the wall, stuck with too many pins to count. We would just stare at it, both of us wondering about these towns—Gortahork, Inch, Dunfanaghy—that had made the final cut onto the course, places that weren't in any tourist book where I would soon be playing tourist. Would there be a phone in Ballintoy? A place to eat in Dungloe? Were they friendly in Kincasslagh, and how the hell do you even say it? But some days I ignored the map's names and route numbers and just looked at the picture I had pinned over Tipperary, a shot of Ballybunion's eighth hole at sunset. The fairway looked soft enough to sink into, a golden blanket unfurled beside a black sea. Ireland was full of problems for me, but it was full of holes as well. I wasn't trying to conquer Ireland, I reminded myself, I was only trying to play through. Only an idiot would try to walk the whole of Ireland. But if you just thought of it as the road to Ballybunion, I decided that only an idiot would stop.

Best-laid plans laid, I turned my focus to matters of fitness. Only an athlete, such as I once was, at peak levels of strength and stamina, such as I soon would be, could possibly survive the plan stuffed into that binder. In the months leading up to tee off, I would reshape my custard-quality physique into the taut, relentless muscle of a hard-bellied explorer. So I did the research and joined the best gym in the city. And for the next three months, I forgot where it was.

I had worked as a caddy for a dozen summers, but in all those great summer days, all those sunny strolls around the golf course, young with strapping shoulders and lungs full of July air, I hated every step of it. I loved *being* a caddy. It was the *caddying* that was the problem. Waiting around listening to war stories and dirty jokes, hearing who got in a fight or who got laid, stories that were rarely accurate in either case, I was a kid having the best summers of his life. I loved the cash, the satisfied and sweaty exhaustion, the uncommon camaraderie between jocks and drunks, rich kids mixing with hard cases on unemployment. But walking with two suitcases draped on your back, back when golf bags were designed to cause as much damage as possible to the carrier, that part was for the birds, or for someone who wanted forty bucks far more than I did. I gained a particular reputation as a softie in the caddy room when I admitted to walking to the end of my driveway one morning to get the newspaper, deciding it was too hot, and thus skipping the member-guest tournament, the tournament that caddies didn't skip.

It was an excuse I would become associated with for years, as it not only betrayed me as a wimp, but as a spoiled wimp, too, seeing as I defended myself by explaining that I wasn't really lazy, just that my driveway was really quite long. In a room full of folks without driveways, or short ones at best, it played as spoiled then as it still does now. And as I envisioned myself lugging my clubs along the ribbons the Irish called roads, laboring through mile nine and not even being halfway home yet, I began to understand why I wanted to do this in the first place, and do it this way—because this was my chance to not be that kid, the one who threw in the towel at the end of the driveway, as if this loop might absolve me from all those afternoons when I hid behind a bag rack at the first sight of the caddy master. So I avoided the treadmill with vigor, confident in the knowledge that it was pointless to prepare, because no matter how tough things got out there, I was not going to quit. 'Tis better to suffer in the future than in the present and future both, I reasoned. (Note the wisdom of this logic—it would not go unchallenged.)

With a route established and all my beds and tee boxes booked, my planning took on its final phase—a careful deliberation regarding every ounce that would be joining me on the road. The evening before an important round, I had a habit of needlessly obsessing over the contents of my golf bag, as if a pink tee or a cut Titleist or a misplaced tube of sunblock might toss my game asunder. I would carefully lay out my clubs the night before, sharp grooves and tacky grips, bright steel faces spread across the kitchen table like a royal flush. My bag's pockets were emptied and de-linted, ball-markers and Band-Aids were debated; I was convinced that the thing separating me from golf greatness was a mislaid granola bar. But for this particular round, I could not pack too carefully. This was a test that could absolutely be won or lost by a tool too many.

I planned on hauling my sticks in a Mizuno Scratch-Sac, a canvas carry-bag that was closer to a quiver than a golf bag, and the clubs that made the final cut would be my weightiest companions. There would be no chance to switch out wedges or add a five-wood on the road, so it was essential to choose wisely. The driver and three-wood were easy decisions, and the hybrid made a case for itself, as did the five-wood, but considering the yardage you could squeeze out of a low ball on a firm links course, it seemed silly to carry more than two deep clubs. Three-iron was in, as was the five, and I couldn't say no to the seven. Nine-iron seemed like the logical next choice, but this was where the assembly got murky, in the lofted end of the bag. If I carried the nine, would I skip the pitching wedge and go straight to the gap? If I carried a gap wedge, would I still carry my sixty? It was a crisis, a wedge conundrum. Allyson didn't seem nearly worried enough. I blessed myself and decided on the nine, the pitching wedge, and the sixty-degree lob wedge, and to include a slim Bobby Grace putter. I had been putting with a Ping Craz-E for years, but it had a head like a half-eaten sandwich that would fatten up my pack, not to mention that it was a few ounces heavier than the Grace putter. Nine clubs made it into a bag assembled with a logic I wished my erstwhile loops would have considered—clubs picked not by performance, but poundage.

Six balls or less would be my preferred freight. I had a dozen guests signed up to meet up with me along the way, and the plan was to rely upon them to replenish golf balls, sunblock, and energy bars, and take home with them notebooks, logo balls (my lone souvenir indulgence), and any scrap of paper that I might be able to shake loose from a backpack that was going to be bloated by rain gear and windshirts, a camera, and a damned laptop that, having to file stories and photographs from the road, I couldn't figure out a way to ditch.

I would strap my golf bag to a sack I assumed existed somewhere in the shopping universe, one of those shiny-paneled, multi-pocketed, and thoroughly zippered affairs that you saw on adventure television. In pursuit of this pack, we headed to a store where I never imagined myself setting foot, let alone spending gobs of money, a haven for those yuppies on mountain bikes that you hoped went over their handlebars, and home to bearded soap-dodgers wise in the ways of the Appalachian Trail. We took our Visa out of the freezer and went to the outdoor adventure store.

I was somewhat uneasy about paying $130 for "walking shoes," a product whose hook was that they were designed, in-deed, to withstand the rigors of basic human locomotion. (Was there such a thing as a non-walking shoe? Standing-around shoes?) But the pair the salesman sold me on—and yes, he was bearded, and wearing organic wool socks stuffed into those Crocs sandals I saw all over Whole Foods—were waterproof and pretty cool-looking, and a brand I had never heard of, Keen, which meant they were probably a good choice, a shoe for a walker in the know. They were brown leather with important-looking straps, a big black rubber toe that announced their wearer as a person on his way to a place more timid souls didn't go. That, or as a sucker who paid far too much for a pumped-up pair of Dock-siders.

Provisions quickly piled up at the checkout counter. I wanted to travel cotton-free, save for one pair of jeans. I was facing the possibility of daily Irish downpours, and any gear that sucked up water would suck up pounds, so cotton T-shirts and underwear were staying home and quick-wicking, fast-drying polyesters were taking their place. I bought socks that cost more than USDA prime, and the salesman talked me into a fifty-dollar rain hat that would have made Mary Poppins blush—I would keep whole vil-lages dry wearing this satellite dish around. And to garnish my pile of polyester and wool, I added packs of Shot Bloks, gelati-nous energy shaped into Black Cherry-and-Margarita-flavored cubes. I was braced for the whims of Irish cuisine, my pockets stuffed with cola-flavored power goo.

We were handed off to a gentleman in the back of the store, a thinner adventure expert with a more accomplished beard. The resident backpack specialist propped up his elbow on a shelf of carabiners, looked me up and down, and offered an unimpressed, "So what's your load gonna be?"

My load? I was definitely in the right place, a place where questions about one's load were offered and answered with a straight face. I told him I would be carrying three days' worth of clothes, some toiletries, and nine golf clubs.

"Golf clubs?" His eyebrow went up, a mouth somewhere behind that beard pursing into a dubious curl. "Don't you carry those in a golf bag?"

We had a brief discussion about what I was doing—it was me talking, mostly, explaining my summer's plans. It wasn't long before I was giving him the hard sell, eager to win the confidence of this man who might bequeath me a backpack if he found my adventure worthy. His brow stayed ruffled until I explained that I wanted the absolute best pack they had, price be damned.

From the top row, the one he needed a ladder for, out of reach for the common camper or curious snowboarder, he retrieved a sleek navy blue pack. It had molded shoulder straps like something out of a rocket ship, yet it was subdued in its quality, none of the loud colors or superfluous strings of the cheaper models. The last time I had worn a backpack, I was on my way to pre-calculus, but as he strapped me into the Cadillac of backpacks, it was as if I had found my calling, had finally released my inner nomad. And then he put thirty pounds worth of sand in the pack. He tightened and tugged until it felt like the sack had been surgically attached to my scapula, then pulled on a strap that squeezed my chest into a nicely sculpted B-cup.

This blue bastard was heavy.

"Try it out, walk around," he invited me, and I did, taking two brisk laps around the water bottle aisle before returning to my wife. Allyson couldn't help but smile at this strange incarnation of her husband, a well-appointed adventurer who looked like he was being mauled by a blue octopus.

"What do you think?" she said, sounding unsure.

"Actually," I whispered, "it's kind of heavy."

"Already?" She didn't sound surprised as much as disappointed. I had juggled our lives on the gamble that I might pull this journey off, and here I was, whining about my load before I even owned it. I was the nine-year-old who begged to play football until you bought him shoulder pads, then quit before the first practice.

"Let's try another one," she suggested, optimist that she was. But I didn't want another one. I wanted the best one, and dammit, this was the best one. If I wasn't a top-row backpack guy, I was going to have to figure out a way to become one, lickety split.

The salesman returned for the verdict. Allyson almost said something but caught herself. I had just explained to this man that I was going to walk the whole of Ireland, and neither of us was about to admit to him that my shoulders were sore. I thanked him for his help and dropped the blue backpack on the pile.

Good-byes at the airport were artificially quick and easy. With the dog barking from the front seat, Allyson took a "before" picture of me standing outside terminal C, suspecting she might not recognize me when I returned. There's a right way to say good-bye to your spouse before setting off on a thousand-mile round of golf, but on that April afternoon, that right thing escaped me. There were hugs and kisses and even a few tears from the one of us who wasn't consoled by the fact that he would be spending that evening in a quaint Irish town known for its ocean vistas and summer pub scene. After waiting in line at check-in and tossing my backpack onto the conveyor belt, I looked out to the curb where she was still waiting with our dog in her lap, lifting his paw and both of them waving good-bye. I waved and headed for my gate.

I would have been more sentimental if I hadn't been scared shitless. I found a bathroom and splashed water on my face, sucking for breath as the good-times golf trip was about to go wheels-up—I could hear Ireland cracking its knuckles, ready to begin slapping me across the mouth, mile by mile by mile. There I was, wrecked by four months of the unknown. What would my great-grandparents think of this wannabe wild Irishman turned soft by a few generations of Easy Street? Could that really be a Coyne, terrified by the quiet of a long walk?

I left some crackly voice mail for Allyson, but it was a few days before we would speak again. The Euro-friendly cell phone I had invested in had an Estonian phone number (I swear, call + 372 531 67666 and leave me a message) and turned out to be the cellular equivalent of a rusted-out Trabant. (Irish travel tip: Purchase your mobile phone after arriving in Ireland. Phones are inexpensive, they're pay as you go, and it's simple to top off your balance at any grocery store or gas station.) By the time I figured out that I had to call home, wait for the other person to pick up, and then let their phone call me back, it had been three days since I had spoken with Allyson. I had already met up with Denis and his younger brother, Patrick, an ex-pat who had recently relocated his family to the south of Ireland. Patrick was built like a barrel with a smile that filled up every inch of his face—eager to needle and talk golf and trade caddy stories as he drove us from the airport, I could tell Patrick had brought with him to Ireland a personality bigger than his new home county of Cork. We stopped at a train station to pick up my best man, Joe Byrne, who had just arrived from a four-day tour of English soccer stadiums. The shortest but fittest member of our group, Joe piled his bags into the back of Patrick's compact, squeezing himself and his latest stab at facial hair (tightly mowed goatee, unconnected at the corners) between two sets of golf clubs. It was a long shot to get Joe to splurge on a golf trip, but he justified the ticket by mixing in a stop to see his beloved Sunderland football club. To understand Joe Byrne is to know that he's from Saginaw, Michigan, yet he's adopted the least-winning soccer team in England as his life's passion. It would be like meeting an Australian passionate about Temple University football—a mix of confusion and respect.

We were working on our post-round pints in the heart of Kilkee town, soaking in an orange sunset burst over a glassy sea, when I borrowed Patrick's phone and finally found my wife. Ireland was great, I explained. The start had been shaky—stuffing four men and their clubs into the back of Patrick's blue Fiat, my forehead pressed against the windshield as we whipped around roundabouts and tore through County Clare on the wrong side of the road, Patrick cracking a string of one-liners and ain't-Ireland-odd anecdotes—and I was doubting this round of golf before it had even begun. But after arriving in town and showering off the jet lag, the Kilkee links helped turn things around. Stepping onto a golf course, I was doing something familiar on an unfamiliar day, and when that "FORE!" came in Denis's backswing, I was even reminded of something I seemed to forget all the time—when you stopped worrying about it, golf could even be fun.

Kilkee was a tad untidy and a bit bare in spots, the course still coming back to life from what I had heard was a brutal winter, storms and salt water wreaking havoc on holes up and down Ireland's west coast. But even in its plain and scrappy stretches, Kilkee was a seaside walk that felt relentlessly Irish, a good warm-up for the more stout tracks we would be traversing that week. It lacked the waist-high purgatory grasses typical of so many Irish courses, and it played up, down, and back up the seaside slope in a somewhat city-block routing, but the views were all cliffs and white caps, and we got our cuts in without losing too many balls, or too much heart from trying to make numbers with backward body clocks. At last check, my handicap was hovering around 5, so no degree of grogginess could justify my 85, starting off Ireland at 15 over par. But the round was young, and there were plenty of holes left to get the strokes back.

I could make a case that this round of golf began on that tee box in County Clare, or on that gray morning at terminal C, maybe on that evening out on our patio, or maybe back in Ballina, when the first Coynes decided to take a chance on "over there." Maybe this was about a distant son returned to undo the steps that had taken his family elsewhere. I tried to let those winds of silly self-awareness blow only in the pub, reminding myself that I was here to chase a little white ball until there were no holes left to pick it out of, and that chase began at the end of those first eighteen in Kilkee, when I threw my clubs into the back of Patrick's compact, opened the passenger door, and climbed in for the short drive back up the road to our hotel. I sat in the car, tired, but pleasantly so, after four hours in the sun and wind, red-faced and ready for a pint. Denis and Joe were in the backseat, and Patrick in the front. We sat there for a minute, and they were all quiet, as if they were saying a private post-round prayer of thanks, a prayer that none of their scores called for. I didn't want to be rude and tell our host to hurry along, but what was he waiting for? I turned to Patrick, who was smiling with the ignition key between his fingers. I turned around to see Joe and Denis, two wide grins pointed in my direction.

"What?"

They looked at each other, and Denis finally spoke. "Aren't you walking?"

And in a few minutes, as a Fiat with a smiling round American face in the driver's seat passed me by, I was.

bole 19

15 over par

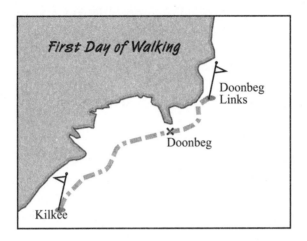

THE NEXT DAY STARTED EARLY, AND IT STARTED WELL. IT BEGAN the way every athlete or explorer was meant to kick off his morning—no yoga or granola or daily affirmations here. Give me the full Irish, a newspaper, and a bathroom with a lock, and I'd march 'til Dublin.

While it sounded like a wrestling move or a courageous salon treatment, the full Irish was the ultimate in breakfast feasts, far predating the Grand Slam, and full in every way—full plate, full stomach, full arteries, an afternoon full of wincing regret. Mainstays of the full Irish included a tall pot of the blackest coffee, two eggs, a tray of toast, lovely Irish sausages and a small pile of rashers (Irish bacon, closer to a New York strip than our meager twigs of pork). To make your Irish truly full, your eggs might share space with sautéed mushrooms and a grilled tomato, a scary slab of blood sausage (a reminder of leaner times, when a pig's blood wasn't wasted, but cooked in casings and portrayed as good eats), and my favorite, a heaping scoop of baked beans.

For such an ostentatious feast, I was always disappointed by the thimble-sized glass of orange juice that accompanied an Irish breakfast, but the careful rationing of OJ offered an insight into the island's staples. Ireland had enough hogs to stop your heart by morning three, but they didn't pick oranges in County Clare.

Sitting down to this morning smorgasbord, you might think your visit to Ireland had coincided with some sort of breakfasting festival, but these feasts for one were being laid out every morning in every hotel and bed-and-breakfast across the country. The way I saw it, I only had 118 of these morning banquets left, so we hustled down to an uncrowded restaurant in our Kilkee hotel and made ourselves full.

It was Joe's first trip to Ireland, and he didn't pretend to know much about the culture, but we both agreed that this breakfast was a meal for those who labored early and hard and long. In this pile of carbs and protein that seemed so foreign to visitors from a coffee-sipping, computer-gazing workforce that came to life sometime before lunch, you could see the thick fingers of hard men digging into their day's biggest meal, not because they were gluttons, but because there were jobs out there that called for these kinds of calories. We had respect for this meal, for the girth of our bacon, and for anyone who could stomach a full Irish and work hard enough to burn it off, maybe even need another toast and sausage come lunchtime. We ate like men that morning, and left the dining room full, but ready to be hungry again.

And for the next ninety minutes, Joe and I took turns inspecting our hotel bathroom from a seated point of view, reading and rereading the backs of our tubes of toothpaste. Unbeknownst to us, when preceded by evening pints of Guinness and a fried-fish dinner, the full Irish breakfast was accompanied by a complimentary cleansing. Our American bellies were no match for the breakfast meats and supercharged java, and we left Kilkee well behind schedule, laboring under our backpacks and vowing to settle for porridge tomorrow. But the sun was warm by ten o'clock and the morning breeze made us impatient to get moving. On the road to Doonbeg, and we were walking Ireland.

Neither of us was too confident with our Celsius, but it felt like the low eighties by late morning. I had planned a short seven-mile jaunt for our first walk of the trip, loosening up our muscles for the larger mileages. My Keens kicked their way along the N67, and we were soon out of the town and into the countryside, where sheep picked up their heads from their nibbling to give us a look, and where curious packs of cattle followed us along stretches of fence line as if they wanted to come along.

I had given plenty of thought as to which side of the road I would take in this country—a simple choice, and all that was at stake was whether or not one of us would end up stuck to a tour-bus windshield. Joe and I both agreed on the right side. Ireland drives on the left, and facing traffic seemed infinitely safer, and as we hailed from a right-side-of-the-road country, it might give a normal feel to an abnormal choice in road transport.

The N67 started off with the promise of a road worthy of a numeral, but as we worked our way deeper into the countryside, it turned into a pebble-covered lane. The road seemed to have magical properties, barely wide enough to fit Joe and I walking side by side, yet suddenly able to accommodate oncoming tractor trailers. We started out dealing with oncoming traffic by stepping aside into the weeds, pressing against a stone wall, then stepping back into the road and starting again. These were quick encounters with drivers who eyed us as they passed. Some gave a short shake of their heads, as if we were doing something naughty. Teenagers in zippy cars honked or pumped a fist, and we took their hollers for applause, their honks for pats on the back. But most of the brief faces we met coming toward us on the road lifted two fingers off their steering wheel to say hello. One after the other, and another. Joe and I started lifting our hands in response—nothing too showy, just a quick hand held hip high as if we knew what we were doing, veteran wanderers who had been saluting folks on the road our whole lives. And after two hours on the road, sweating and our shoulders beginning to protest, the friction making us uncomfortable in places neither of us was ready to admit, it began to feel like we'd been on that road for just that long.

Through the boring stretches with miles of pasture and wire fences, we took heart in a house on the horizon, a pack of buildings that just might be that next town, might even have a gas station with a cooler we might raid. The houses were modest and of a simple design, low and boxy, and you could see through large windows into homes that looked warm and untroubled. A small kitchen, two or three bedrooms, an uncluttered sitting room with a few knickknacks carefully displayed. It was the exteriors that impressed me most. A few hundred square feet and one story, no neighbor for two miles, yet the house would be surrounded by a low stone or cement wall, the partition very carefully constructed, often in better shape than the home itself. Almost all the yards were kept at fairway height, unblemished plots of green with meticulous gardens and yard decorations considerately placed. I remembered how my father talked about his grandparents and their priorities, how their universe revolved around owning their own patch of land, no matter the size. My grandfather called my dad at his fraternity house in 1956 to tell him that he was having a scotch and burning the mortgage. For a people who had been dispossessed throughout their history, property was clearly the thing, and we saw it treated with a tidy sense of pride that I'd never noticed at fifty miles an hour, but that at our snail's pace was impossible to miss.

Our speed was not as robust a clip as I had budgeted for—stepping aside for each approaching vehicle was killing our progress, and it was plain that we were going to have to grow bolder in taking on the traffic. Two hours from Kilkee, we stopped at a crossroads where a brown sign read DOONBEG, pointing us down the road to our right. And next to that sign, another brown placard read DOONBEG, this one pointing irrefutably to the left.

"This is helpful," Joe noted as we sat on our packs and drank our first, second, and third rations of water. Patrick had warned us about the road signs. The distances and directions advertised on the antique black and white signs were famously unreliable, and unclear as to whether they were measured in miles or kilometers. He claimed that Irish kids entertained themselves by twisting around the arrows, so you were better off betting against them most of the time. Joe and I considered this scoop, then opted for the sign that seemed tougher to turn by hand, and headed left. And since we wanted to make our tee time, and I wanted to get around Ireland this decade, we decided to stop getting out of the way of approaching cars and let them get out of ours.

We marched, dreaming of a full Irish and the toast we wished we hadn't left behind, the rhythm of the road lulling us into a mumbling strut, shoulders sloped and eyes cast down at the trail of gravel, gravel, cow shit, gravel. We came around a bend, and from my scout a few paces ahead, a warning:

"Oh, shit."

I looked up and saw a roaring white bus teetering on its wheels, downshifting around a bend, and the metal letters *Van Hool* heading straight for Joe Byrne. I could see the panic in the bus driver's face, lifting up in his seat as if pulling back a stage coach. To our right was a chin-high stone wall topped with a ring of rusted barbed wire. Our minds worked quickly, weighing the cons of a tetanus shot versus the downside of being bounced back to Kilkee off the front of a bus. We opted for the former, grabbing a spot of barbless wire, adrenaline lifting us off the road as our backpacks brushed the bus windows.

We decided to keep our heads up from then on, and we devised a better system for taking on curves, particularly walled curves where it was impossible to see what was hugging the corner ahead of you. For the rest of the morning, one of us would head out to peek around the bend, then wave the other over to the far side of the road while the trailer kept an eye on traffic sneaking up from behind. It slowed us down even more, but it got us alive to another brown sign in the near distance wishing us *Fáilte a Dún Beag.*

There is a quick cure for all the doubt and self-loathing of a long road walk. All the second-guessing about one's choice to deny the ease and accessibility of automated transport goes away fast in the glorious light of arrival.

Joe and I dropped our bags outside the Doonbeg service station. We bought the biggest bottles of water in the store, propped ourselves up on the wall outside and drank. I had just finished my life's first hike, and in the last three hours, I had been transformed.

Sitting in the sun, kneading my shoulders and nodding to passersby, I felt that same satisfaction from when I was a kid, dropping two overloaded golf bags on the bag rail, tired and relieved and ready to be handed a soft pile of cash. But this walk felt even more rich. It wasn't the distance—nine miles wasn't going to win us any medals—but to consider a town that seemed unreasonable to attempt on foot, then to walk into that town having used nothing but our own heart and muscle, filled us with a quiet satisfaction that convinced me, at least for that moment, that we'd get around this course in the end. As hard as the days might get, there would still be an end to each of them that would feel like this.

Doonbeg was a small town with a few shops and a busy restaurant, small even by Kilkee standards, which I found surprising, seeing how Doonbeg was one of Europe's hottest golf destinations, home to Greg Norman's much-blogged-about new links. But standing in the center of town, Joe and I didn't see a flag or fairway anywhere, not a single sign pointing us toward a golf course. Did everyone know about Doonbeg except the people in it?

I walked back into the service station and asked the redheaded shopkeeper (he'd be known as a *ginger* over here—hard G, like *gingham*—and so would I) the way to the golf course.

"Oh, the golf course," the shopkeeper said, a puzzled look about him, as if we'd asked him the quickest way to Karachi. "The golf course is well outside of town. Down the road. Five miles, I'd say."

But this was Doonbeg, I protested. The sign said so! Look, Doonbeg butcher shop, the Doonbeg bus stop. I was standing in the damn Doonbeg gas station! But one ginger explained to another that the entrance to the clubhouse was three miles down the road, and that, for whatever reason, per some planning or permission issues, the driveway to the clubhouse was a good two miles long itself. None of these distances would lift an eyebrow from the typical Yank golfer ensconced in the reclining leather of a luxury bus. But for us, five more miles was like finding out on Christmas Eve that Santa had pushed things back to February. I headed outside and gave Joe the news. We hadn't said ten words to each other since leaving Kilkee, but rested and rehydrated, he was able to muster a proper response to our predicament.

"You've got to be shitting me."

We went back inside, and the shopkeeper confirmed what I had already explained to Joe. It was obvious that we were both crushed. He offered us a ride, offered to ring his friend and give us a lift. He was sure someone in the pro shop would come up to town and pick us up.

"Thank you," I said, "but we want to walk it."

"You want to walk it? Are you serious?" he said.

Our faces glistened with sunburn and our shirts were brown with sweat, the shoulders stretched thin like old socks. We nodded and offered an unconvincing, "We want to walk."

We went outside to stare at our packs lying beside the road, hoping they might have shrunk while we were inside, or disappeared altogether. They hadn't. They were still there, two dinosaur turds tangled with straps. The key to not getting your stuff stolen while traveling abroad, I learned, was to carry it in a bag so bloated that nobody in their right mind would try to pick it up.

As we prepared ourselves to hoist, our friend poked his head out of the shop.

"You're really walking there?"

"Yup," said Joe, swinging his pack across his back, hooking in his right shoulder.

"Well, there is another way. Might save you some time, if you're up for it."

We were.

I had heard rumors of the rigors of bringing the Doonbeg course to life. It was a story I would hear repeated all over Ireland, developers mired in decade-long battles with neighbors, local governments, and what seemed to be enemy number one of anyone in Ireland with a shovel: the dreaded and dastardly environmentalists. The new European Ireland seemed to be catching up fast, from a country with relatively lax environmental protections to one with the most far-reaching.

There was a quiet battle being pitted on this Irish course, invisible to most tourists, a fight they didn't talk about in the pro shops. It was a struggle between the more-golf and enough-golf contingents, those who saw golf dollars as a lifeblood to be nurtured and grown, and those who railed against sacrificing any more of Ireland's coastline to Americans in pleated khakis (try to blend as you might, they will know you by your pleats). Keep Ireland Open was an organization fighting to keep golf courses from cutting off access to the Irish countryside, though in Doonbeg's case, the development of the property was brought to a snail's pace by, well, a snail. A rare and endangered gastropod, *Vertigo angustior,* was discovered in the dunes, rendering acres of land off-limits and forcing Greg Norman to reroute his holes in a curious crisscross fashion in order to squeeze in his eighteen (I've read that the snails are doing well, their population having doubled since Doonbeg opened). The course also had to make concessions to locals and provide them beach access through the property. When the waves were good, the course was traversed by a steady stream of barefoot surfers in wet suits. And there was a modest little house—okay, a shack—that jutted into the golf course, a defiant remnant, I presumed, of a farmer who wouldn't sell.

Let me say that I am pro-snail, and that I applaud a farmer with the courage to say no to piles of euros, holding on to land that might have been in his family for centuries. There was no shortage of tee times in Ireland, and Greg Norman wasn't going to be put out of business by a mollusk. One must carefully weigh the cost and benefits of Ireland's golf explosion—from 248 courses in 1986 to some 450 by 2010—and consider that delicate balance between what it means to play Ireland, and what it is to just play a bunch of Irish golf courses. There's a difference. No one wants Ireland to become Myrtle Beach.

It was a balance Joe and I were forced to consider as we pondered the bureaucracy responsible for the routing of the Doonbeg entranceway. Just a few minutes from the center of town, we could see what we guessed was the Doonbeg clubhouse, a silver stone castle rising out of the dunes, more of a compound than a clubhouse (you didn't have to be an architect to figure out which building was put there by a team of wealthy Americans). This put Doonbeg right there in front of us, a twenty-minute hop at worst. We turned off the main road that wanted to take us miles out of our way, hopped a fence, and started down a dirt path that, had it not been sprinkled with fresh pellets of sheep shit, would have felt like the VIP entrance.

The place was manor house meets modern luxury, a golf kingdom perched above the Atlantic. Stone walls and chimneys by the dozen, with tall glass windows set beneath granite arches. We'd barely gone a mile down that path when Joe and I found ourselves standing in front of the clubhouse, close enough to lob a Titleist through a window. And if either of us could have walked on water, it would have been one of the greatest shortcuts of all time.

Of all the folks who might have played Doonbeg that day, as pristine and impressive a setting for golf as I had ever seen, a playground for golfing millionaires with a greens fee north of $350 per, I could say with confidence that Joe and I were the only ones who arrived there by taking off our shoes and socks, rolling up our pants, wading across a chilly stream, scrambling up the face of a sand dune, then slipping through the rear service gate as a beeping food truck reversed its way in.

We slipped into the regular traffic around the clubhouse, Americans with golf bags strolling to and fro, but only two of them making a squishing sound with each step. We headed into the pro shop where Denis had already arrived and was busy holding court at the counter, impressing a crew of Irish assistants with golf tales from Florida, stories that sounded suspiciously devoid of the words "lay" and "up."

Denis loved Doonbeg. He had already played the course on two previous visits courtesy of a hometown connection on the Doonbeg staff. While a Doonbeg membership wasn't necessarily within his financial stratosphere, as far as anyone in southeastern Pennsylvania was concerned, Denis was a founding member of the place. He wore his Doonbeg sweater in the height of summer,

didn't pick up a club without his Doonbeg glove, slept in Doonbeg underpants. He spoke of the place as if he'd been raised in the
clubhouse, so it was no surprise that he turned crimson when his
brother, Patrick, walked in from the putting green and asked him,
"Hey Denis, you're the member here. Why don't you show your
guests where your locker's at?"

The pro raised an eyebrow, looking down at the tee-time
sheet, and the panic of the price of a foursome started Denis's lips
flapping. "I'm not a member, I never said I was a member, they're
not my guests." He quickly turned everyone's attention to the
wandering golfers who had just arrived—"These two walked
here. From Kilkee!"—and the staff at Doonbeg gave us a warm
welcome, shaking their heads with a mix of pity and disbelief.

Was Doonbeg worth the price? Tough to say, considering the
fact that I was leeching off the munificence of Tourism Ireland,
who had helped to arrange my tee times. I was no expert on
value, but that didn't matter much at Doonbeg, because it wasn't
built for the "How much? *That* much?" crowd. It was a place for
the guys who didn't need the receipt, who traveled a great distance for the purpose of being blown away. And Doonbeg did a
hell of a job at that.

Everything about Doonbeg was impressive. The off-course
accoutrements were immaculate, and it seemed as if the doors to
the clubhouse had just opened yesterday, a sprawling home with
chocolate leather at every turn, billboard-sized portraits framed
in heavy oak showing the windblown white locks of Greg Norman as he stood atop the dunes in his wellies, surveying a seaside
that would become a jaw-dropping links. The fawning service, the
handsome pub and inescapable pro shop, the oceanside castle
that served as the members' private clubhouse, and the view from
the first tee, all so damn impressive, that stunning vista of fairway
running into the cradle of a ten-story dune, a view to pull you out
of your chair in the pub and back onto the golf course.

I wasn't crazy about the bunker in the middle of the green on
twelve (if bound for Doonbeg, remember: There's a bunker in the
middle of the green on twelve). On an older course, the years
might have earned it a quaintness, but on a new design, it just felt
overdressed, one accessory too many. And there was something

tragic about the fact that I spent four hours on such an outrageous property and it was the silly bunker that came to mind first. I was pleased that it gave Patrick another chance to embarrass his older brother—*Denis, you're a member here, you're not gonna tell us there's a bunker in the middle of the freakin' green?* Patrick had found said bunker, and took four thumping chops to resurrect his ball. You could also knock Doonbeg for the fact that it didn't quite feel like Ireland. The resort was its own settlement set off from town, a retreat built by Americans, for Americans. But last time I checked my passport, that gave me nothing to complain about. I just had a certain misgiving about an Irish course with Coors Light on tap in the clubhouse. But this was all nitpicking when one considered the quality of the golf, and the audacity of the Doonbeg landscape.

Winding our way across the sand hills, we played our way in and out of cauldrons of spiny grass and silky fairway, over humps and back down into hollows as we were tossed about a surprisingly fair stretch of holes (short for such a young course, and I was guessing the snails were to thank for that). Bunkering and beer taps aside, the thing Norman got absolutely right in Doonbeg, a site he was said to have visited a shocking twenty-two times during construction (celebrity designers typically make a handful of appearances, at best), was that he let the dunes speak, and they spoke with vigor. It was the sort of links I loved—off the greens, I'd found most of St. Andrews to be flat and the rest of it flatter, but Doonbeg's terrain felt like it had been pounded with a rolling pin until it was all lumps and valleys. The towering dunes ensconcing the first green were the most gorgeous advertisement Norman could have built for the subsequent seventeen, but the fourteenth stood out the most for me—it was perhaps the most beautiful hundred-yard hole I'd ever played, the green stuck into the side of a beach head like a saucer of grass hanging over the ocean.

I was happy enough with my 81, and in the end, Joe and I put eighteen miles on the pedometer from that last hole in Kilkee to our last in Doonbeg. Patrick was undone by his tangle with the twelfth-green bunker, and while Denis did find a number of new and interesting ways to lay up, he played well, the only one of us whose day ended with the same tally of golf balls as it began. The miles hit Joe a little harder. Had he been playing as a twosome with Patrick, their combined 23 on the fourth hole would have been a tough number to overcome. He was an accountant by trade, and his Doonbeg scorecard was going to test his training.

"I should just run down the fairways, throwing golf balls into the weeds," Joe suggested after another five-iron went askew, his Top-Flites replacing the *Vertigo angustior* on the Irish endangered list. Joe's long face on the back nine was testament to the fact that it was impossible to love a golf course if you couldn't keep your ball on it. While I was sold from that first tee box, it would take Joe three pints in the clubhouse afterward to acknowledge that we had just played a pretty special track.

We stayed away from the Coors Light, and Denis denied himself the luxury of the members' quarters to share a pint with us. We sat in the clubhouse bar feeling the way Doonbeg was built to make you feel: grateful. Grateful for the wealth that got you there, for the game that led you to this uncommon corner of the earth. Or, if you were us, sitting there with three-day stubble and bone-tired in a way you hadn't been since high school, you were grateful for a cow path and a low tide. We drank until we all thought we'd played well, and stuck the member with the tab.

ḥoʟє 37

23 over par

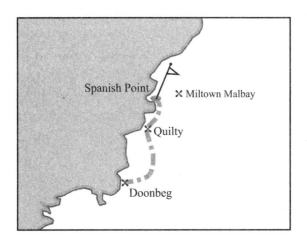

E VEN THE MOST UNQUALIFIED IRISH HISTORIANS COULD STRING together a few conspicuous themes running through the course of Ireland's history. Foremost among those themes appeared to be that this business about the exceptional "luck of the Irish" was a historic load of crap. Irish history was packed with tales of colossal bad breaks and extraordinary misfortune—an Irish king misjudging English intentions, military forces washing up on the wrong beach, armaments arriving a day too late, a liberator arriving fifty years too early, an inconvenient snitch, a rebel who spoke too proudly in the pub—it was a long list of opportunities to be otherwise, chances missed by the smallest of margins. Had the breeze been blowing differently on a few occasions, had the rains let up for an approaching Armada, centuries of Irish history might have had much more to do with the Irish themselves. In American history, Paul Revere got the word out and helped win the war. If it had been Irish history, his horse would have been struck dead by lightning.

As we made our way from Doonbeg, Joe and I walked through some of that bad luck, heading up a coastline that once saw the last remains of the Spanish Armada washed up on its shores. Another undeniable theme to Irish history was Ireland's role as boxing ring for its neighbors. England's beefs with Spain, France, and eventually Germany would be played out in Irish cities and on Irish battlegrounds, just as they were on the coast of Clare, where Catholic Spain had sent ships to battle Crown forces in 1588. But the weather didn't cooperate and hundreds of Spanish were killed, their ships coming apart on the rocks and washing up on a beach that would become known as Spanish Point.

I had been woken that morning in Doonbeg by a strange heat emanating from my boxer briefs. Upon further inspection, I found that my inner thighs had taken on the appearance of a turkey wattle, the bright red flesh bunched up into burning wrinkles. I had scoffed when Allyson threw the anti-chafing stick in my bag back at the adventure store, but she had run a marathon and promised it would earn its spot in my backpack. My wife, travel sage. Coming off an eighteen-mile day and waking to the prospect of another one, I would have given up my passport before that gray stick of lube. I went into the bathroom and applied Body Glide to places a man hopes he'll never need to apply anything, and we headed out for Spanish Point in sunshine and light breezes, Joe and I both walking as if carrying basketballs between our knees (I offered him the rest of my lube stick, but he curtly declined).

As with all such extended adventures, there was nothing quite as exciting as that first day of the journey. There also seemed to be nothing quite as unexciting as the second. It was a quiet and achy walk on day two, the silence only interrupted when Joe stumbled out of the way of a bus, bracing himself against a stone wall that happened to be covered with small, white flowers with sticky thorns. He didn't curse or cry, but as his fingers swelled into bananas, he did inform me, as if to put the blame squarely on my shoulders, that if he should pass out from the poisonous sting of the "Irish Ooga Booga Bush," to please push his carcass off the road.

We left Patrick and Denis in Doonbeg, and I sent them off

with a good 40 percent of my pack, dispensing with the formerly indispensible. Turned monkish by our first road haul, I scuttled every possible gram, passing off to Patrick my jeans, a turtleneck, the extra socks, the pitching wedge (loft was less valuable on a links, and if I couldn't get it done with a choke-down nine-iron, then I just couldn't get it done), and I made the tough call to dispatch my golf shoes. Spikes were a weighty luxury, and the soles of my Keens seemed to have grip enough. I sent back aftershave, wipes for my sunglasses, a box of contact lenses—half a gram on your back for four months had to add up to something. I nearly tossed in the first-aid kit, but my choice to keep it was soon proven wise as I performed an emergency antibacterial procedure on the road to Spanish Point, saving Joe Byrne's fourth digit with a Band-Aid.

Spanish Point didn't feel much like a town, more like a strip of bungalows overlooking a beach where blue waters rolled over a craggy coastline. There were holiday homes and a few hotels and our first Irish trailer park. Referred to as caravan parks, they carried with them none of the stigma attached to their American cousins. It was a regular refrain on American tour buses as they pulled into coastal Irish towns, "Nice view, too bad they ruined it with a trailer park." But in Ireland, more folks than not owned a trailer stationed somewhere near the coastline. It was a nice idea, really, affordable bungalows with beachfront property for all, and caravan parks were full of kids with boogie boards and soccer balls, little summer towns sprung up in parking lots around the country. The Spanish Point clubhouse blended right in with the caravans—we walked past it before we knew we were there, a red flag stuck into a hillside our only clue that a golf course was nearby.

The clubhouse was a one-story, one-room building that was empty when we arrived, save a gentleman covered in plumber's putty—the men's room was under repair, apparently, but he was able to point us toward the first tee. Joe and I went back outside and found a mail slot cut into the clubhouse wall, a sign above it reading GREENS FEES. It was the ultimate honor system. We both pretended we didn't see it and headed for our thirty-seventh hole.

Spanish Point was only eight miles down the road from Doonbeg, but after a three-hour stroll we found ourselves on an altogether different golfing planet. It was nine holes to Doonbeg's
eighteen, and the clubhouse wouldn't have qualified for the Doonbeg maintenance shed. They didn't have any souvenir balls for sale,
no pro shop at all. There was no starter to welcome us and provide
us with more playing advice than we deserved. Rather than being
surrounded by acres of protected and pristine dune lands, we
found ourselves struggling to keep our drives out of somebody's
holiday trailer. And of the three courses we had played thus far,
Spanish Point was the one I knew we'd both head back to first.

There was plenty of discussion about which holes were the
oldest or second-oldest or third-oldest in Ireland, a debate that I
didn't find particularly interesting or important. So many Irish
courses seemed to have been plowed under, relocated, upgraded—
everywhere we went we heard of golf being played on a particular piece of property since the nineteenth century, Victorian
playgrounds that were built, abandoned, rediscovered, courses
that grew from six holes to nine to twelve, back to nine, then
eighteen as communities scratched together the funds and the
know-how. Trying to rank a course by its vintage seemed a fruit-
less exercise.* Wherever it fit on the list, Spanish Point was one of
the old ones, opening in 1896 as a par-27 golf course, now
stretched to a nine-holer with a par of 32 (we went around twice),
a number sure to soothe the egos of golfers who'd been beaten up
down the road. Not as carefully manicured, and somewhat
smashed into the bit of coastline the club commanded, the terrain
had a giddiness about it, the layout filled with quick dips and
wild mounding—it felt like golf played through a mogul course.
We played bump-and-runs from silly distances, tried to drive the
par-fours and paid the price. The 90-yard eighth hole, dubbed
"The Terror," was a punch-wedge played over a pit in the dunes
with the waves crashing white over your shoulder. It wasn't quite

---

* Royal Belfast claims to be the oldest golf club in Ireland (1881), but Curragh in
Kildare claims the oldest golf course, balls having been struck at Curragh back in
1852 on what began as an eleven-hole British soldiers' course. Eleven holes. Love
that.

as dramatic as the fourteenth at Doonbeg, but it had us grabbing for our cameras just the same.

We were headed for the road after playing our eighteen when the gentleman working on the men's room caught us in the parking lot. "If you want to come in and have a pint, we're going to open up the bar." Apparently progress had been made on the bathroom, or at least enough for one day. We took him up on his offer and stepped inside into what felt like a modest fire hall. There were a few dozen empty tables, faded photographs, and dusty trophies lining the walls. Our new friend rolled up a metal partition in front of the bar, and the Spanish Point clubhouse/pro shop/dining room/lounge was open for business.

Over the pints of lager the members slid our way (none of which they would let us pay for), we met members and locals and an American ex-pat who had left the LAPD and was now pulling pints in his retirement in Spanish Point. Kids came into the bar and bought Cokes and candy bars, heading out to play twilight golf in their sneakers with a handful of clubs between them.

The reception an American got in Ireland was not what it was on my first trip, at least not everywhere. Tourism had blossomed to the point where folks seemed slightly less impressed by my accent, and the novelty of a Yank sitting next to you in Ireland hardly seemed a novelty at all. And that's why it was fantastic to find a place like Spanish Point, a nine-holer with a clubhouse that was only open when enough members got thirsty. There were still places where the locals were curious and welcoming to where you'd want to blush, and this was one of them. We met a woman named Maggie who we wanted to come with us the rest of the way—she was married to the bartender, and she had lived in America. We talked golf and sports and even a little politics. She talked frankly about her distaste for the big money behind Doonbeg, and told us how she hated to hear the Irish engaging in a popular new pastime, ripping our president.

"You can say what you want about one man or the war, but I've lived in many different places, and I'll tell you, I think America is the greatest country in the world."

As we watched the light retreat over the ocean, the rocks along the beach going black as the sun went down like another golden pint of Carlsberg, I wondered if Maggie had it right. Joe had broken a hundred that afternoon with golf balls to spare, and on this golf course, that was plenty to make you smile.

It was still light out when we headed for the hotel, back in love with this trip, our bellies lager-lined and ready for whatever fried pile of starch we could afford. It would have been a perfect day if I didn't just then realize that my rain gear was hanging in a closet ten miles back down the road.

ḃoŀe 55

32 over par

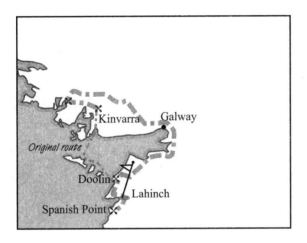

MOST VISITORS ARRIVE IN IRELAND WITH THE SAME CHECK-
list in their heads. Travelers want to see green in a multi-
tude of shades and contours. They want rocks and ruins,
preferably moss-covered and crumbling and set upon an ocean
cliff. They expect plenty of livestock, frolicking sheep, and long-
eared donkeys. They want to hear Irish music played in a pub,
want to engage in genuine conversation with a brogue too thick
to understand, and they want to witness an Act of Uncommon
Irish Hospitality—the man who drove ten miles out of his way to
show you the way to Blarney Castle, the lady at the B&B who did
your wash without even asking—that have made Irish vacations
the stuff of legend.

Ireland was certainly a different place than it had been ten
years ago, but in less than a week, I had experienced all of the
above, the last item on the list checked off when, after a desperate
phone call back to the B&B in Doonbeg, a taxi driver drove
back to Doonbeg, then found Joe and I eating pizzas in a bistro in

Miltown Malbay, my Mizuno rain gear balled up in his arms. It was one of the subtle pleasures of traveling Ireland, the chance to experience attitudes that were truly unbothered. I would typically walk into a hotel or restaurant ready to play by an unwritten list of rules—can't sit outside, can't order from the lunch menu, can't transfer that tab from the bar, no breakfast for dinner, no drinks in the sitting room, no changing the TV. But in Ireland, if it seemed remotely reasonable that you should be able to push together those two tables, or take your soup into the lobby, then you just went ahead and did it. It took me a while to take on this more relaxed posture, to understand that a stranger would gladly go fetch my rain gear ("Of course he'll pick it up for you," our innkeeper told us, "why wouldn't he?"). If I could take on this Irish *why not?* way of life, no doubt it would be smoother going all the way around.

The only disappointing part of the evening was that we didn't stay with that taxi, because my reclaimed rain gear meant my bag was going to be three ounces heavier as we made our way through a stretch of unexpected Irish tropics, wiping sweat out of our eyes on a breezeless, cloudless morning. You don't think sunburn when you think of Ireland, but when the Irish sun does make an appearance, it is surprisingly intense—something to do with Ireland's latitude, I was told—and even after a slathering of Coppertone, I was red-nosed by noon.

Weather was a major topic of conversation in Ireland, a far more significant subject than your typical *nice day* banter. Everybody in Ireland inquired about the weather, and they all had their own theses on the subject, which they were eager to defend. Mediocre weather seemed an Irish given to me, but the way locals fretted about conditions—*miserable day, awful, just awful out there*—you'd think they'd all grown up in Boca Raton. I expected them to be a bit more blasé about another rainy day, but after a few thousand years, the Irish were still holding out for something better. And maybe they were right to—this heat wave was the lead story in every pub and shop, and as a patron in Miltown Malbay explained to Joe and I, "If this is global warming, bring it on."

We eventually made it to Lahinch after learning another valuable road lesson: When it came to the larger towns, a sign welcoming you to that town might be followed by two or three more signs farther down the road, so don't high-five and empty the water bottles when you can only guess that you've arrived. We walked into Lahinch three times before we got there, dropping our bags in the Lahinch Golf Lodge (modest, but good for the money), and, exhausted, awaited the arrival of Steve.

Steve and I were the kind of lifelong friends that could only be made by a university residence lottery. Had we not been thrown together in a vanilla cinder-block cell at Notre Dame, our paths would have probably never crossed. We probably wouldn't have even liked each other, might have traded sneers in the dining hall. I was a gangly, clean-shaven redhead from the East Coast, passionate about golf and football with a suitcase full of whatever had been in the window of The Gap that summer; Steve was the shortish kid with ambitious facial hair, Doc Martens, hip threads from a thrift store, and a cool footlocker full of CDs from bands I'd never heard of. He was proudly Polish from the south side of, as his Midwestern tongue sounded it, *Chicaaahgo*. He wasn't into sports, smoked Winstons semiprofessionally, and cheered for the Fighting Irish with the most dripping sort of sarcasm, only rolling out of bed on Saturdays for the tailgating. He did care about the White Sox, with a passion that seemed as if it needed some sort of diagnosis. But put two guys in a bunk bed, particularly for that first year away from home, and strange bedfellows become best buddies, from shared pizzas and Sega hockey rallies, to years down the road in a golf town in County Clare.

Steve arrived before noon via a bus from Dublin, and rather than let him nap off his jet lag, we quickly put him in front of a Guinness. He compared his first Irish pint to the stout poured in the Irish American Heritage Center in Chicago, quickly bringing to the surface the principal challenge for this next leg of the trip. Steve was a loyal Chicagoan who tended to view the world through Chicago-tinted glasses. I could have taken him to the North Pole to meet Santa Claus, and he would have left the workshop talking about a guy from the South Side with a white beard who was also pretty generous around the holidays. If I could give him an experience that he couldn't compare or counter with an

anecdote from his home city or his beloved country hunting retreat in the wilds of southern Illinois (he already seemed to have
the impression that the Irish countryside was doing a fair Illinois
impression), it would be something of a victory, particularly since
Steve wasn't going to be wooed by the golf courses—he'd never
played a hole in his life. But it wouldn't be a victory for that first
day. Steve brought with him the same pair of Keens I was wearing
(a long way from that first day back in our dorm, when it was my
bucks versus his Chuck Taylors), and his arrival broke the heat
wave. Steve brought the rain.

Lahinch fell on the first page of most global golf course rankings, a links built in 1892 by Limerick golfers looking for a summer track and Scottish soldiers stationed in Lahinch. Golfers had
made pilgrimages to Lahinch's dunes ever since, and even in the
short time I had known the place, it had grown from the two-pub
town of my reminiscing to a coastal Irish resort that had become
a golf stop second, a surfing destination first. The waves beside
the golf course teemed with bobbing heads in wet suits, and in
the town, it seemed as if we were bumping into three surfers for
every golfer. I was unable to find my way back to the pub with
the fireplace where, many summers before, my dad brought the
house down with a rendition of "Irish Eyes" while I sat curled up
under our table, too embarrassed to open my eyes, but Lahinch
still felt like a small enough and nearly perfect place, populated
by an optimal blend of tourists, golfers, surfers, and locals. The
Corner Stone and Kenny's on the main street served up Irish fare
that Steve wanted to take a picture of—he did, making a point to
snap shots of every meal that week—and the seaside promenade
overlooking the beach whetted our appetite for the sand hills below
us, where we couldn't quite make out the pins, but knew they
were there. We didn't see any goats, either, and unlike my mates
who were green to Ireland, I knew that was a bad sign.

The Lahinch Golf Club logo featured a goat kicking up his
hooves, an appropriate emblem seeing as goats once played an
integral role in club operations. As it was told to me in the nineteenth hole, a cracking pub in the center of town, a pair of Lahinch
goats used to be known as the best weathermen in the village. If
the goats were out in the hills nibbling away, rest assured, you

would play your round in good weather. But if you saw the goats heading in from the hills for the safety of the clubhouse, no matter if the sun was blazing, you would soon be fumbling with your umbrella or scrambling back to your car. A club secretary apparently grew tired of fixing a barometer in the clubhouse and famously posted a sign on the busted instrument, instructing golfers curious about the conditions to go and SEE GOATS.

For me, not only did Irish forecasts feel redundant (weatherman had to be the cushiest job in Ireland—*chance of rain, chance of sun,* ad infinitum), but they were irrelevant as well. I didn't have the luxury of waiting for the sun, and neither twister nor typhoon could shake me from an ironclad itinerary. But in the case of Lahinch, if I had spied a goat retreating for the clubhouse, I would have gladly done an about-face and headed back to town. As much as I appreciated the town, as much as I could understand why it was a staple on any Irish golf trip, over the years I had learned to hate—nay, to resent—the links in Lahinch. And not all of them. Just the first one.

Fifteen years ago, our Jerry Quinlan Celtic Golf Tours bus pulled into the parking lot of Lahinch, and I was just barely able to squeeze my head out the door on my way to the tee box. Youngest golfer on the trip, I had wowed my fellow travelers by breaking eighty all over Ireland. I had discovered a surprising kinship with links golf, and I was hitting it well that week. I strolled up to number one at Lahinch, a wide par-four climbing toward a plateau green, and I wondered when Ireland was going to show me something. The rest of the bus was busy licking their wounds; I was busy patting myself on the back, the great American golf hero.

The club was hosting a competition that afternoon, and the first tee box was good and packed. To the right, the pro shop was surrounded by cocksure caddies, skeptical faces eyeing us through the smoke from their cigarettes. To our left, the tall windows of the clubhouse, the glass crowded with faces sipping tea and judging first drives. And behind us, the road from town, where it seemed as if every citizen of Lahinch had abandoned their duties to come lean an elbow on the wall and see what this much-heralded ginger from Philadelphia might do to their links.

The captain of Lahinch came out to the tee to greet our group—an unusual honor, I was told. I tipped my hat to my hosts, teed up my ball, and stepped into that timeless, soundless universe otherwise known as the opening drive. I turned my chin toward the rising fairway in front of me and saw nothing but deep. I almost felt bad for my Titleist—so small, so fresh from the box—did it really deserve this sort of pounding?

The head of my driver snuck up behind the ball. I squeezed the grip, tucked in my bottom lip, and as I watched my driver start to back away from Mr. Titleist, I heard a whisper from behind, our bus driver leaning into the captain's ear:

"Wait'll you see this kid swing."

See me swing, he did. But what the captain, the caddies, the members, every Irishman in Clare did not see, however, was my driver making contact with a golf ball. Spurred on by our bus driver's confidence, I swiped at that ball with the mightiest uppercut my body could muster, swinging with all the grace of a startled gorilla. Somehow, that little white ball had dodged my clubhead. It lay on the ground next to an undisturbed tee, pushed over by the wind from one of Ireland's all-time whiffs.

And then silence, for what felt like the entirety of my golfing life, until the quiet was interrupted by my father's voice, offering his encouragement.

"Jesus Christ. What the hell was that?"

I don't quite remember re-teeing and heel-mashing my next drive into the weeds beside the forward tees. It took nine holes for the blood to leave my cheeks, and I couldn't look my caddy in the eye the whole way around, aware that I'd made him top storyteller for at least a week. I had not only shit the golfing bed, but I had done so in a country that traded stories the way other nations traded oil or radios, a culture dependent upon the telling and retelling of tales of bad luck and squashed hubris. It was more than one stroke. It was a question as to whether I could face Ireland, or a first tee box, ever again.

Drops had just started to fall as we headed down to the bottom of town to revisit the scene—I half expected to find a plaque by the tee box that read, ON JULY 12, 1993, AMERICAN TOM COYNE DISGRACED HIMSELF, HIS FAMILY, AND HIS COUNTRY, PER-

PETRATING THE MOST EXUBERANT WHIFF SINCE THE INTRODUC-
TION OF GOLF TO IRELAND. But there was no mention of that day,
and nobody there to watch us, the gray skies keeping the crowds
away. With Joe pulling rental clubs on a trolley, and non-golfing
Steve in charge of the camera, we took the tee box, and I won the
flip for honors. My golfing soul having already been bared to
Lahinch, aware that I would have to drive my ball backward to
fail to improve on my last effort, I swung as if playing a provisional, nice and easy, and hit the drive I had waited fifteen years
for: straight, center contact, and long.

With my Lahinch demons exorcised, I was at last able to appreciate the course for the joyous dunescape that it was. The
fourth hole, a par-five with a blind second shot aimed at a white
rock atop a swollen sand hill called the Klondyke, was a hole I
remembered being terrified of, a tricked-up travesty that I had
thusly maligned in so many Irish golf debates. But I could now
see it as a risk-reward par-five played through a funnel of cascading green, that Klondyke a remembrance of golf before bulldoz-
ers, when the landscape was allowed to get in your way. It was a
hole unique in the world, reachable with two good three-irons.
The fifth, another aim-for-the-rock-atop-the-dune hole, was the
only 150-yarder I'd ever attempted where you couldn't see the
pin, or the green for that matter. It was like trying to lob your ball
into a basket behind the dunes, and if you didn't mind the fact
that you could make a pretty good swing and still make double
(which I did), you just had to love it.

We got soaked and stuck behind two foursomes of Americans
who wouldn't let the twosome behind them through, not even as
they waited for cans of lager to be carted out to them on the tenth
green. (Sending for roadies at Lahinch? Sacrilege! Are you that
bad a golfer, or that good a drunk?)

"Aren't they supposed to let you through?" Steve noted as we
stood in the middle of the fairway, rethinking my suggestion to
leave the umbrellas home (I stand by my decision—they are useless in Irish wind, and a good rain suit should take their place).

"They should have let us through four holes ago," I said,
impressed with Steve's knowledge of golf etiquette, considering
he'd never stepped foot on a course before.

Steve shook the rain from his glasses. "Buffoons."

But the buffoons before us and the puddles gathering around our feet couldn't spoil the day. It was a shame that the rain kept the camera in its case, aside from the forty-seven shots Steve was able to snap of me stuck chin-high in sand traps. I only remembered being in three bunkers all day, but each seemed such a hilarious photo-op to newcomer Steve—*look at Coyne, he's climbing into the sand again!*—that he couldn't help himself. There was one other picture in my camera, a snapshot of three damp friends sitting around a table in the Lahinch clubhouse, short glasses of whiskey in front of us, all of us with smiles that said we would soon be warm. We toasted one another and Lahinch, and I made a silent apology to the mounds and fairways in the windows all around us. You couldn't judge a course by your misses.

It was a "soft" morning as Steve and I put Joe on the bus for the airport and started down the road to Doolin (*soft* being the Irish expression for a relentless, soggy misery, so-called for the softening effect it could have on your spirit, your resolve, the Snickers in your backpack). I recounted my score as we passed the course— an 82 that could have been a 68, certainly, if it weren't for the regular slew of bad breaks—while Steve tallied his pint total from the previous twenty-four hours. He started counting on the fingers of his right hand, then his left. And back to his right hand. "Seventeen pints?" he asked himself. "Is that possible? I'm not even hungover." He sounded frightened but a little proud, a guy who didn't get out as much as he used to, dispatching beers like he was a kid cracking Old Styles at a Sox game.

I had met a black sheepdog back in town, a sickly animal with a nervous twitter. I found him picking through trash the evening before, and missing my own dog, I showed him some attention as we strolled the main street. Soon the dog was my shadow, turning up at my side throughout the evening, the sad smell of his matted coat following Steve and I past the golf course as we headed out of town, through the thickest traffic we had battled yet. The dog led us down the road like a crazed crossing guard, running out ahead of us, then quickly dropping to his haunches and waiting for us to catch up, instincts from a former life as a shepherd's helper. We did our best to shoo him back to town, but each time we thought he'd left us, minutes later he was back nipping at our heels.

A mile out of Lahinch, our friend was still there, jogging ahead of us and looking back to check that we were still coming, and I began to wonder how far this dog was prepared to go. Long after Steve was back in Chicago, might I still have a partner on the road? Granted, this was an unwell animal that had chosen us over a leaking Dumpster, but I felt a bond as I watched him lope his way along the road. We were two wanderers, looking for a bite and a bed, and people thought us both crazy, no doubt. It felt poetic, perhaps, a bit of loyal companionship to see me on my way, a Lassie to fetch help if need be, and it brought to mind a story from one of that week's pubs, a tale told to me of a loving dog and an ailing sister.

She was on death's door, she was. So I packed up my things, and I took my dog, Max, and we drove ourselves to Dublin to see my sister. We weren't a day in town when Max up and ran away.

On Monday, I searched the city high and low, looking for my Max. I didn't find him anywhere. On Tuesday, I put up notices all over the city, but I didn't hear a word. On Wednesday, I put an ad in the paper, and Thursday I did the same, but there was no sign of him. On Friday, I walked the soles off my shoes, but I never found my Max. Saturday came, and I said good-bye to my sister who'd taken a turn for the better, and I got in my car and headed for home.

And when I got home that evening, would you ever guess what was waiting for me on my front step? Six bottles of milk. I forgot to tell the milkman I was away.

We put our heads down into the rain, vans and buses blowing puddles into our rain pants, but our Max kept up, undaunted. A Land Rover approached, driving too fast for my taste—at such intimate range, all the cars seemed too fast, but something about the boxy black grill made us step aside into the brush, turning our heads away as the tire-splash hit us at shoulder height. And then we heard a long skid, locked wheels slipping across the road, and a hard thump that turned my stomach. The dog had been knocked across the road, into the far shoulder. Like a blindsided boxer, it struggled to its feet, then darted into the brush. The Land Rover's brake lights eventually dimmed, and it continued down the road.

Steve and I looked for the dog, but didn't find it. We covered up as best we could and took our time, careful, heads up the rest of the way.

I had heard Doolin described as the unofficial capital of traditional Irish music. I was expecting something of a Memphis, would settle for a Branson. What we got was a quaint street set along a quiet river, a few music shops and a pub, Gus O'Connor's, that seemed as popular with tourists as that black stuff with the tan collar.

The walk into town felt impossibly uphill. Inclines were part of the course, but for every up, you should be indulged by a little bit of down. The way to Doolin was a steady, shin-splitting ascent, two hours upward during which our entire conversation consisted of, "Uphill sucks." And, "It does."

We fought our way to a horizon where the road finally went flat, narrowing into little more than a winding footpath, and through the clouds in front of us saw coast again, white waves pushing for the shore. A few hundred yards below us, an ancient stone tower looked black in the mist, and a few more miles down the road, a cluster of buildings that had to be Doolin. And a few steps to our left, pulled off the road into a spot where it would have been perfectly safe from any passersby had it not been for an itinerant American golfer, was a white Toyota bouncing on its wheels, a foglike white icing covering the windows. Having returned to downhill and to civilization and to sex, there was bounce back in our heels for the descent into Doolin, coughing noisily as we passed the car, giggling like the assholes we were.

We headed down to the main street and pushed our way through the crowds in O'Connor's, elbowing ourselves into a spot between a gaggle of American girls on summer break and an unthreatening gang of French bikers, close to where I guessed the musicians would eventually appear, a square table in the center of the room with a RESERVED sign upon it. The traditional Irish music session (or *seisiún*) was, by definition, a spontaneous event where someone would start strumming a guitar or blowing a tin whistle and others would join in as they wished, ripping through jigs (6/8 time) and reels (4/4 time) that had been played thus for centuries. A good session could make you love Ireland on its most miserable day, exuberant notes cut with a touch of sadness. They were songs to pound your fist to, ditties to make even the likes of Steve wistful for his love gone sailing across the white Atlantic foam. So we sat there in a quiet pack, waiting for something spontaneous to go ahead and happen.

And soon, with no announcement or introduction, a guy from the back of the bar picked up a black case, walked over to the empty table and sat down. As if someone had given the secret wink, all over the pub folks started standing up, making their way through the crowd to the table. A girl sitting on a stool in front of us, twentysomething with long brown hair and a hard-traveled backpack, pulled a violin case from her bag, and suddenly she was part of the show as well. I had never felt so untalented. I half expected Steve to whip out a jaw harp and start plucking away.

We watched as the players assembled themselves—a fiddler, a drummer, a flute from the far back corner—and a table full of ten strangers began to play as if they'd been jamming since high school, everyone's eyes stuck on that guitar player's fingers, looking for changes and cues. This was special beyond the music, which was loud and lively and irresistibly foot-stomping. A teenager could play a banjo. A man not thirty years old was playing a mean squeezebox. That girl sitting in front of us had traveled considerable distance on a Sunday afternoon to try to follow the chords in O'Connor's pub in Doolin. These were old instruments and old songs, being played by young and eager players. We listened for an hour or so, and I caught the guy who introduced me to the Smashing Pumpkins tapping his fingers to the music, though he quickly stopped when I pointed that out.

In routing my Irish golf course, I had deemed it acceptable to travel via the occasional passenger ferry. With Ireland's coastline as crannied as it was, there were spots where a five-minute ferry could save my shoes a week, and since I'd still technically be on my feet, it seemed a small cheat. If you were playing a golf course and came to a stream, would you walk off the course to find a way around it, or step over the bridge in front of you? With a ferry to take us from Doolin through the Aran Islands and up into Connemara, I had made the tough decision to sacrifice Galway, a thriving and thoroughly pubbed college town, and budgeted for a boat that would carry us across Galway Bay.

We woke up that morning in Doolin, looked out the window, and wondered if our B&B had been transported overnight to some far away mountaintop. The fog was up against the glass. We couldn't see the sea or the ferry dock or the town. Hell, we couldn't see the driveway.

The binder stuffed with reservations had been doing its job, keeping me confident and sheltered, and with each passing morning, I ripped one more page free from the itinerary, looking forward to the day when the stack was reduced to a single photocopy of a one night's booking in Ballybunion. But my Ireland bible couldn't help us that morning, not after our host called down to the pier and discovered that for the first time all year, the ferries wouldn't be running. If the weather stayed the same, there was no guarantee they would be back tomorrow, either. We were faced with a choice—take a bus, or hit the road and spend ten days hiking to a destination I had anticipated reaching by day's end. I put the choice to Steve, confident he'd make the right decision.

"Don't be a jackass," he told me. "We're taking the bus."

I had set off on this golf course with a list of local rules to abide by. Of course, motor transport was out—it was a walking course—but there were a small number of exceptions and indulgences to be noted, such as illness or injury, emergency detours in search of the Internet (filing weekly stories had me on a regular deadline), or a juggling of the itinerary necessitated by unexpected golf. An act of God certainly seemed to qualify—I'd put up with rain, but we agreed that fogged-in ferries were beyond anyone's control, and so we headed for the Galway bus.

Ten minutes into our bus ride, I was a pudding-faced mess sucking for air, my brain spinning loose in my skull, and that morning's smoked salmon creeping its way toward the light. The bus was hot and crowded, and the snoring stranger next to me smelled as if he had spent the holiday weekend bobbing for cigarette butts in a tub of stale lager. The route into Galway hairpinned back and forth for an hour, and for someone who hadn't been in a car in two weeks, my sea legs were shot. I learned my lesson, and became convinced that it wasn't dangerous to walk Ireland. It was damn dangerous not to.

With a few hours to catch my breath in Galway, I showed Steve around a town I hardly recognized from my visit back in college. I remembered the main square, the street down to the waterfront, a kebab shop on the corner—Abrekebabra, home to the greatest piles of food ever wrapped in foil, and blessedly still in business—but Galway now had continental shops and a cosmopolitan crowd, as well as a dozen phone stores where I finally reconnected with the cellular world.

Steve wasn't terribly impressed with Galway. He hadn't been blown away by Doolin or Lahinch, either. He wanted to see something other than guidebook fare, Ireland off the tourist route. The proud Pole was pleasantly surprised by the eastern European twang heard all over Galway. Indeed, one of the most conspicuous side effects of the new, prosperous, European Ireland was the fact that the pint-pulling, hammer-swinging segment of the workforce appeared to be largely Polish, Ireland now being an importer of citizens after centuries of the opposite.

We witnessed another by-product of Ireland's affluence in Galway, one of the culprits I had heard blamed for a decline in tee times around the country. After recovering from the downturn following 9/11, tourist golf in Ireland seemed to be as hot as ever, but rounds played by the Irish themselves were flat or worse, according to managers with whom I'd spoken. Down cycles for golf in the States usually coincided with economic blues, but not so in Ireland—it wasn't that the Irish weren't doing well enough. They were doing *too* well, it seemed.* Where eighteen holes with one's spouse was once a popular way to spend a Sunday afternoon, it was evident as we walked around Galway, pushing through crowds saddled with shopping bags, SUVs packed to the windows with credit-card booty, that a new Irish pastime had emerged: shopping. Riding into town to snap up phones and hooded sweatshirts and flat-screen TVs was all the rage, and the local golf society was suffering for it.

We made our way back to the bus station, where we learned that we would have ended up begging a ride by day's end, fog or no fog. Had we taken the ferry through the Aran Islands and up into the closest town on the other side, a pin on my map stuck into tiny-fonted Kinvarra, we would have walked into town and quickly discovered that there were two Kinvarras in County Galway. There was the Kinvarra we would be standing in, the one without food or accommodation, and there was the one thirty miles in the opposite direction where I had made our reservation four months ago.

I had made a terrible gaffe in font judgment. Interpreting map font sizes was a vital traveler's survival skill, particularly in a country as rural as Ireland. Choosing the right font could be the difference between tucking into room service at a Ramada, or supping on a bag of potato chips with damp socks for a pillow. I would eventually become fluent in map fonts, able to surmise from the girth of the letters whether a town might have a hotel (typically nine points or larger, and more likely if bold or underlined), if I could expect a burger shop or a Laundromat (rare for any town that required my glasses). I had expected to find a bed in a town that required the magnifying glass on my Swiss army knife, a mistake I wouldn't make again. But I still put some of the

---

* Ireland boasts one of the highest per capita GDP's in the world and the second highest in Europe, ahead of Great Britain—an astonishing development when one considers that during the 1980s, as much as 18 percent of the population was unemployed.

blame for our bungled reservations on Ireland's shoulders. Springfield, Lincoln, you could see how they might get reused in a country of 300 million people. But to rerun Kinvarra in the same county? The land of Joyce and Yeats, and they couldn't come up with another name? *West Kinvarra, Kinvarraville,* maybe? Better yet, *Not the Kinvarra with the Bed-and-Breakfast* would have been a huge help. We were lucky to uncover my miscalculation while in a bus station, where we could do something about it, and we came up with a new reason for being allowed to take the bus—reservations snafu—and fast-forwarded our way to the next reservation on the itinerary, a night of luxury that felt well earned.

Choices in accommodations would be growing thin as we worked our way out toward the edges of civilization and the Connemara links, so we were forced to splurge for the Cashel House, a four-star, nineteenth-century country home surrounded by sprawling gardens and rose hedges, the house covered with a soft blanket of ivy. The estate was founded by seaweed tycoons (seriously), and after being turned into a hotel, it was visited by the likes of de Gaulle and his wife, and years later a dirty-fingered redhead and stubble-chinned Steve.

That evening, we slurped lobster bisque and dined on buttery lamb chops in the atrium dining room, the late-day sun warming the gardens all around us. No matter that we were both wearing wet hiking shoes, that our pants were nylon and beltless, that the Canadians to our right could probably smell that O'Connor's session still on us—we were kings in our polyester T-shirts. We were class, and as if to prove it, I lifted our silver wine caddy to pour my dining partner the last glass of cabernet, and I watched as the bottle slipped through the wine caddy and crashed through Steve's crystal goblet, blasting his glass into a thousand shards and transforming our table of lace and white linen into a blood-soaked crime scene. Red was pooling everywhere. Thankfully, an irreplaceable oriental carpet was there to catch most of the spill, a once delicate shade of chartreuse turned a soggy pink.

I decided to skip dessert. I'm not sure when Steve stopped chuckling to himself, but it was after I fell asleep.

At breakfast the next morning we met the lady of the house.

She was in her sixties with a big smile and a spring in her step as she bounced from table to table, and as she stepped up to ours, she inquired, "Did you have a nice rest, boys? Or were you up all night throwing wine bottles around your room?"

She flailed her arms about to imitate my gracefulness, and Steve laughed along with her. Confident that she had a sense of humor about her carpet, I felt safe to ask her to have a look at our map and point us toward our next tee outside Ballyconneely.

She directed us to take the coastal road through the town of Roundstone. I was sure Roundstone would be a lovely spot to stop for lunch, but the main road would take us the long way around, winding us along the edge of Cashel Bay. There seemed a more direct route.

"Is this a road?" I asked her, pointing to what might have been a hair stuck to the map, a slim black line cutting across Connemara and taking us almost directly from Cashel House to Ballyconneely.

She shook her head. "You don't want to go that way. You want the Roundstone road."

But she didn't know what we wanted. She was a driver, I presumed, blind to the plight of the footslogger, no doubt softened by years behind the wheel. We knew better. So we took the bog road.

Tbe BOG ROAD

Mile 14

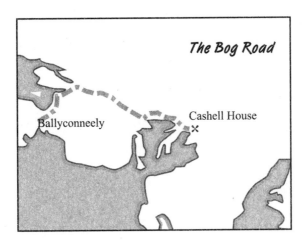

R OAD. PAIN. ROCK. STEVE.
   "Are we there yet?"
Shallow lakes and yellow grasses. Oily turf, softened mountains. Sheep.
   No signs. No buildings. No civilization in any direction.
   "Yes. We're here, Steve. Welcome to Ballyconneely."
   Quiet.
   "Screw you, smart ass."
   Mile fourteen, and close to nothing.

hole 73

42 over par

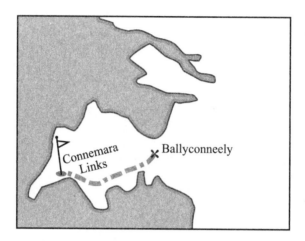

TWO LUMPS IN BLACK RAIN GEAR LAY HUNCHED OVER PICNIC
benches in front of a gas station, struggling to match their
water bottles up with their mouths. They had left the Cashel
House six hours before, setting off across the bog road, which
turned out to be a gravel pathway through the most lonesome
terrain in the Western Hemisphere. They came out the other side
changed, two whistling explorers reduced to mumbling fools.

It had been hours since I lost touch with my brain, somewhere around the time Steve started up his marching chorus of
Tom Coyne's an asshole, Tom Coyne's an asshole, and some
time before I squared off against a mountain goat. I'd already
been ignored by a few thousand hungry Irish sheep, but it was
unusual to see them lying in the middle of the road, no fences
to hold them back, and more strange that they didn't seem
wary of us as we passed. We had walked into some sort of Irish
Amazon where the native lambs had never before seen a human, and where a goat with persuasive looking horns would

step out in front of us, lower his head, and dare us to take one more step.

"Dude," came Steve's call to arms. "Gimme one of your golf clubs."

Forty pounds of future stew had brought us to a dead halt. But when you were alone with no phone signal, not even the comfort of a road sign or a chimney anywhere on your horizon, the rules changed quickly. Faced with a seemingly endless isolation, everything we knew about our day and how we expected it to unfold went hazy. Exposed to so much space, it was impossible to not feel insignificant, and it made us scared shitless of anything that was tough enough to live out here. So we assumed an apologetic stance—sort of a half crouch, avoiding eye contact—and waited for the goat to get bored with us.

Somewhere after the goat my mind went on standby. I had recalled a vision of two men encased in rain gear and wool hats and gloves, wind blowing tears into their sideburns, but my sitting in front of a gas station in Ballyconneely was my only evidence that I had been one of them.

Steve had been clamoring for authentic Ireland since day one, eager for something distinct from the Ireland that had been packed up and shipped over to the pubs in Chicago. Whether we were up for a pint or not (we were), the pub was the town's only diversion, so we hobbled into Keogh's pub (one of a handful of businesses in Ballyconneely, the others including a Keogh's gas station, a Keogh's food shop, and a Keogh's bed-and-breakfast). Maybe it was the weight of the door, or the four wide-bodies perched at the bar that looked like the place had been built around them, but I had the sense that Steve was going to get what he was looking for, and maybe more than he wanted.

We took up two spots at the end of the bar, ordered pints of Lucozade (Irish Gatorade, with fizz and an unusual citrusy tang), and waited for a conversation to eavesdrop on. The pool table was surrounded by kids just off from school, come to the pub for Cokes and bags of crisps (potato chips with flavors like roast chicken and prawn cocktail), and the poker machine in the corner was being monopolized by a woman with a Russian accent who plopped down a tenner on the bar every five or ten minutes and asked for change. The regulars eventually grew indifferent to our presence, and we observed them like anthropologists sent to study the habits of the Irish publican, our eyes peeled for the *craic.*

Craic meant "fun," "good times," "goings on"—pronounced crack, a la the cocaine derivative, it raised American eyebrows when used in expressions like, "So where's the craic?" Everyday terminology like, "What's the craic?" and "How's the craic?" roughly translated to "What's up?" or, in some instances, "Are there girls there, and do you think any of them will talk to me?" And if there had been, the next day you might be telling your friends, "The craic was mighty." Each of the four gentlemen seated at the bar had their roles in establishing and sustaining the craic. I could discern their parts and places—there was the solid one who drank the light lager and looked like he'd arrived from a jobsite that, guessing from his work boots and collared shirt, he must have been in charge of. There was the old man loyal to his Guinness, dressed in a threadbare brown suit that was frayed at every hem but in the pub looked dressy enough. There was a blow-in from the capital city, a retired Dubliner with a home by the beach who had just popped in and was waiting for the craic. And there was the laugher, a gentleman with an ambiguous set of teeth who wasn't working on his day's first pint, or its last, whose role it seemed to be to ensure that the craic stayed afloat. He dutifully added quick, semi-humorous suffixes to all new anecdotes or information, turning even the most benign comment into an occasion to roar with laughter. The accents were speedy in Ballyconneely, but we knew a story was finished when the laugher added a comment like, "Talking in my sleep again," after which we all knew to chuckle, even the Yanks blown in from the Cashel House.

By our second round, we had become enough of a fixture for the Dubliner to ask us where we were from.

"He's from Philly. I'm from Chicago," Steve said.

The Dublin man nodded. "South Side or North Side?"

Our swollen feet were spilling out of our Keens like muffin tops. My Achilles felt like it had been sawed with a steak knife, and I wasn't sure if I was going to be able to get up from my stool without the aid of a forklift. But with that question, Steve looked like he was floating. His face—I hadn't seen him that excited since he quit ROTC.

"South Side, baby, South Side!"

Something perfect had happened. We'd found a place that felt authentic well beyond its Guinness posters and Mason jars. And we'd found a spot where Steve could preach White Sox—"World Champion Chicago White Sox," he reminded them, a room of men who didn't know a Chicago White Sock from a Michigan Blue Berry. But they were all quick converts when he handed them his business card, which read, "I'd rather have a sister in a whorehouse than a brother who's a Cubs fan." (Seriously, it does.)

The responsible-looking lad piped up from behind his Harp, "Only been to O'Hare. Never been to Chicago."

"Actually," Steve started, and he didn't stop for a while, launching into a civics lecture on the annexation of a thin strip of land connecting O'Hare to the city of Chicago that kept the airport under Mayor Daley's control when it was, get this, "actually part of Roseland."

His history lesson hung there in the air above the bar, the Irish faces all turned to Steve as they waited for the punch line. It had been a miscalculation on Steve's part to offer such an involved anecdote without an easy payoff, but the laugher finally stepped in to rescue us from the quiet with a "Well that'll show 'em" that cued up a reassuring chorus of chuckles.

Satisfied, Steve lipped his pint. "Guy knows the South Side, man. Write that down."

We hobbled back and forth to the bathroom like peg-legs home from a hip replacement. Our geriatric shuffle brought on some questions about our condition, and Steve and I came clean about how we had traveled to Ballyconneely.

"The bog road? You can't be serious. You didn't walk the bog road."

"We did."

The lad in work boots turned to the old man in brown lapels.

"Did you hear that, Michael? These lads walked the bog road here from Cashel House. Would you ever do the bog road on foot?"

Michael didn't look up from his jar of stout. "I wouldn't do it in a car."

The rest of the night was spent trading rounds with the locals. We listened to opinions on an upcoming election that I had yet to make heads or tails of (there seemed more political parties than Irish voters), and we took notes during a stout-fueled lecture on the plight of the rural Irish pub. As it was explained (and probably exaggerated) to me, a pub was closing every day in Ireland, a travesty that had been pinned on two perpetrators: the smoking ban, and the new drunk-driving laws (apparently, until recently, you could step out for a few dozen quiet pints, get back in your car, and drive home without breaking the law—if you weren't driving erratically, you couldn't be pulled over).

It was hard to rail against a smoking ban once you had breathed the clean bar air it had won. And as a summer-long resident of Ireland's roads and highways, I said a prayer of thanks for those new laws with each passing Daihatsu. But it was obvious that the out-of-the-way pub was under assault, and it seemed a shame. The pub was once an anchor of rural life, a place where you'd buy your groceries and medicines, a stop on your way home where you'd learn the price of sheep. But every day I was walking past pubs with boarded-up windows and paint peeling off the FOR SALE signs. The most stringent drunk-driving laws (or drink-driving as the Irish called it) in Europe had lowered traffic deaths in Ireland, but the leading cause of driving fatalities remained excessive speed, and I had yet to see a radar gun aimed at any of the roadsters blowing us into the weeds. As it was suggested to me, the farmer who emptied a few glasses and drove home at twenty miles per hour wasn't going to kill anyone, but he was the one being penalized. Rather than drive to the pub, folks were content to buy their cans at the supermarket and get sotted in front of the telly. Fortunately for Steve and I, that wasn't yet the case in Ballyconneely.

We learned an important lesson that night about pitching your tent in a one-pub town. Even if you weren't hungry at the time, it was essential to secure dinner arrangements upon arrival. Just because a town had beer taps didn't mean that it had food. It turned out that the pub's chef had left the day before for a trip home to Romania. Lucky for us, the bartender was kind enough to open up the shop next door, where we bought a loaf of bread, a plastic tub of deli ham, and a tube of decongestant English mustard.

Steve and I headed back to our beds waiting a few hundred yards down the road in a dark and empty house that seemed to sway in the Connemara wind. The lady of the house lived elsewhere, so it was just us, knocking around a dark kitchen, scrounging for two plates and a knife. Up in our room, I laid newspaper over the bedspread and got to the task of preparing our dinner.

When you spend the day filling your lungs with fresh air, you not only hit your pillow like you've been shot, but there's something about a day on your feet that makes you a more tolerant, more patient individual. Leaving the car and living out of a backpack—I had no experience with this kind of life. I might have even resented the bony longhairs who found some phony enlightenment on that road less traveled, but now I had to concede that the hemp and hiking boots crowd was onto something. Traveling modestly forced you to start your day open to anything, without the burden of expectations, and the next thing you knew, a little sunshine or a smiling stranger could make you feel uncommonly content. When your whole life was stuffed into a duffel bag, there was so much less crap to whine about. So while we usually would have complained about our skinny beds or missing television set, or made cracks about the purple feather pillows that looked like botched Muppets, we sat in our boxer shorts, eating ham sandwiches in the quiet. Steve said it best through a mouthful of bread and mustard.

"This is good."

My high school history had skipped Alcock and Brown and headed straight for Lindbergh and Earhart, but I would learn from framed clippings on the pub walls in nearby Clifden town that this team of Brits deserved a brighter spotlight. John Alcock and Arthur Brown crossed the Atlantic eight years ahead of Lindbergh, spending sixteen hours in an open cockpit, deicing their wings the old-fashioned way—climbing out of their seats and hanging above a black ocean to hack away the frozen layers before ditching their plane in the bogland near Ballyconneely. I didn't consider myself an Alcock, and Steve was no Brown, but we felt a certain kinship with the explorers as we passed markers commemorating their landing, signs pointing to a memorial we didn't have the time to inspect. They had probably looked at the miles ahead of them and wondered, *How the hell is this going to happen?* Yet they had gone ahead and got there after risking more than I would ever have to bargain. It had been an easy round of golf so far, pneumonia-free and devoid of any fisticuffs, but I'd put their trip in my back pocket, to think of them when the bad times came. They'd get here eventually. But that morning, the sun was bright and the soft brown fields of Connemara looked like a pretty fine place to crash.

We made quick work of the four miles from the B&B to our next hole, Steve excited for his first-ever round of golf. He had been warned that golf in Ireland was post-graduate stuff, and making your life's first swing beside a churning ocean was an absurd proposition. But he hadn't walked that damn bog just to take pictures. Steve was going to golf. We turned up the drive to the clubhouse and Ireland tested that resolve, the sun disappearing from the sky and the raindrops popping on the brims of our hats.

We rented clubs for Steve in the temporary pro shop (a gorgeous slate clubhouse overlooking the waves was not quite finished) and wrapped ourselves in Gore-Tex. This was a course I had been looking forward to for years, a track prized by those who had made the effort to find it. It was designed by Eddie Hackett, one of Irish golf's patron saints, whose philosophy on course design I admired as much as any other: "Nature is the best architect . . . I just try to dress up what the good Lord provides."*

---

* From an interview on the helpful Links of Heaven website, www.irishgolf.com.

Mr. Hackett passed away in 1996, around the time I was making my first trip around the links of Ireland with my father. Along with Connemara, he was the man behind Carne, Dingle, Waterville, Donegal, and Enniscrone, and he had touched up countless other courses along the way (eighty-five in total, and every last one of them in Ireland). He was a self-taught architect, a pro at the Portmarnock links near Dublin who believed golf could give Ireland a lift, breathing life into depressed rural communities and winning Ireland some positive PR after so much political turmoil. It's said that he worked for next to nothing, and that he could lay out a quality links with little more than a spade and his imagination. Much was owed, by the buyers and sellers of Irish golf alike, to the pair of eyes that, as described in the history of Connemara, looked over an empty field of wild grasses and told the local priest that he could give them something that would bring pride to their town. It was clear that he was onto something as we stepped on the property, a wavy stretch of unspoiled green set on the ocean's edge. The rain wasn't keeping me off it, and it hadn't washed Steve away, either, who ponied up for two dozen of the cheapest balls in the house.

Watching Steve dig a golf ball out of his rain pants on the first tee in Connemara, I couldn't help but think how far we had come from that freshman dorm room and feel a little proud, watching him take practice cuts on that tee box. It was sort of a jerky move, a tad stiff—imagine a landscaper raking leaves with his feet stuck in cement. But he stepped up to his Dunlop and shocked the golfing world, knocking his ball off the tee and in a mostly forward direction.

"Look at you!" I couldn't help it. I wondered if he realized the weight of his accomplishment, not whiffing his first tee ball. And maybe he did. He was certainly smiling, Steve, the golfing machine.

Four steps into that opening dogleg, the fairway hugging a long dune as it turned away from the beach, Steve's smile flipped over fast as an Irish shower turned into our first all-out soaker, a rain-suit-compromising, spirit-sapping, how-did-water-get-in-there downpour. A storm like this at home, you'd grab your kids and run for the basement. And there we were, kicking around the weeds for golf balls. I can't tell you much about those first few holes or what they looked like. To me they all looked like drowning.

"Having fun?" I asked Steve as he trudged down number four, head down, the wheels on his rental trolley barely moving.

Glasses fogged like they'd been dipped in buttermilk, water cascading off his sharp Polish nose, Steve looked at me and said, "Worst experience ever," as if they were the last three words he had in him.

I had planned to offer Steve a few uninvited golf tips throughout his round, but the weather turned our golf into a match of find it, whack it, find it again. Steve had been stopping to take three, four practice swings before I explained to him that it was against the rules of golf to take practice swings in the rain. We played as fast as we could, which wasn't very fast at all.

I stayed ahead of him, willing him along, and on the seventh hole he dribbled one in my direction, his ball rolling into the greenside bunker at my feet. I watched Steve tow his trolley through the slop, waiting for him to come climb into the bunker and learn why they called them traps. But he stopped a good twenty yards short of the sand, grabbed a club from his bag, and took his stance—perhaps a too-wide stance. He looked like he was waiting to be patted down.

"What are you doing?"

"Hitting my ball."

"Your ball's up here," I said.

"No, it's not. It's here."

I walked toward him. He had his nine-iron set square behind something white in the rough.

"Dude, that's a bottle cap."

Steve shook the raindrops from his glasses. He looked down at the plastic bottle top.

"Shit."

He stood there for a moment, as if it might be easier to just go ahead and play the bottle cap anyway. Steve eventually grabbed his trolley and pulled it up to the bunker, climbed in, and proceeded to have a fight with his golf ball.

The ninth hole somehow came and went, and we ran for the

trailers serving as an ad hoc clubhouse. We sat there dripping dry in front of warm bowls of vegetable soup, silently reevaluating our day, our trip, and our ill-chosen religious affiliations that hadn't been able to save us from the last two hours of our lives. We tallied up Steve's scorecard for the front nine, and we were both well impressed with his 78, Steve learning one of the keys to good golf scores—playing fewer holes.

This was an early test of my commitment. There were undoubtedly ample roadblocks lurking among the 700 holes ahead of me, but they couldn't be much taller than this one. After finally warming enough to feel my fingertips, the prospect of donning that dripping cold suit and stepping back into the monsoon felt like a violation of natural law.

An inflexible itinerary can make a man do crazy things. I licked my bowl clean, draped myself in wet waterproofs, and marched to the tenth tee while Steve headed for the phone in the pro shop, armed with the number of a taxi service. The official scoring decision on his unfinished round of golf was not the traditional DNC (Did Not Card) or DNF (Did Not Finish). Steve's first round ended CAB.

As impossible as the game can feel at times, golf does have its own sense of karma, the golf course ever in tune with a cosmic yin and yang. Behind every birdie, a double bogey awaits. Blast one into the lumberyard, watch how your provisional splits the fairway like a bagel. Every time I've had to call upon my resolve to not walk off a course, golf has rewarded me with an unearned putt, a pin-rattling five-iron, a chip-in that was a dollop of cool whipped cream atop a round that was otherwise warm horseshit. And thus far, this course called Ireland had its own sense of give and take. For every hill I'd trudged up, there was a gentle slope behind it to cruise down. The heavier the load on our shoulders, the lighter we felt at the end of the day. For every spot of rain, there was almost always a patch of sunshine waiting to take its place. And for every merciless seaside storm, a bit of mercy, and a glorious afternoon of sun and rainbows like the one I experienced on the back nine at Connemara.

Later that evening, I found Steve asleep in our room, paperback splayed on his chest, half-eaten ham-and-cheese on the nightstand. I told him he didn't miss much, and considering that he had taken up and abandoned golf in the space of nine holes, maybe that was true. But if it was me in that bed, so much would have been missed. Shortly after hitting my drive off the tenth tee on an absolutely deserted golf course, the clouds seemed to run away, pushed aside by a blazing sun and a whisper of wind. The course dried out as if made from the same stuff as my thirty-dollar underpants—it was bone dry in minutes—and I played a magic nine holes.

It wasn't just about the sunshine, though peeling off my rain gear did feel absolutely decadent. The back nine at Connemara was a special stretch of holes, a very different feeling links from the outward half, which seemed a tad tame in comparison. The back nine had me working up and down the dunes, blasting tee balls off plateaus overlooking a vast countryside. Seventeen and eighteen were favorites, two par-fives that played first up into the dunes and then back out of them. As if being rewarded for my commitment, a blast of wind hurled my last drive some 380 yards down the fairway (it was downhill, too), putting an eight-iron in my hands for my second shot. After a divine bounce off a green-side mound, my first eagle wasn't fifteen feet away on this, my ninetieth hole.

Poetry, I thought. The wet made dry, the big scores made low. The test would be passed, capped off with a panacea greater than anything that came in a pint glass, those two circles surrounding a three on your scorecard. I wished Steve was there to witness it—I wished all of Ireland was there to see me can this putt so they could hoist me atop their shoulders and deliver me down the road. Struggling to come to grips with my greatness, I stepped up to my ball and knocked it eight feet past the hole. I then went ahead and accomplished one of the saddest feats in golf, the three-putt-par.

Ireland and I, back to even. The wind was at my back the whole walk home.

hole 91

55 over par

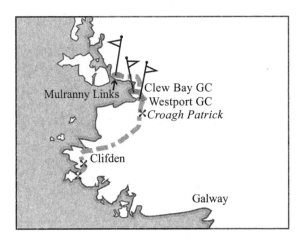

"THE THINGS THAT HAVE BEEN DONE IN THE NAME OF GOLF in this country are criminal. People should be put in jail for it."

Being able to talk golf was almost as important as being able to play it. Golf chatter had turned countless strangers into new friends, salvaged silent dinner parties, and made madras-clad dullards interesting, at least for the space of a wedding reception. But standing in Matt Molloy's pub in Westport, County Mayo, my new friend, Seamus, didn't want to talk golf, quickly making me the most boring guy in the bar. We could talk walking, I guessed, but that was what I was in Molloy's to forget about in the first place.

Westport seemed to be the perfect Irish town. I wasn't the only traveler of that opinion—the sidewalks were shoulder to shoulder with tourists—but crowds seemed a small price for the glassy stream running through the center of town, the lovely tree-lined mall and the Georgian architecture that led you from one perfect pub to another. I had booked three nights at a guesthouse on the river's edge and planned to drop out for a while, regrouping after a tough few days.

Steve and I had worked our way out of Ballyconneely and up through Clifden (a lively hillside town overlooking a salmon river) and then into Letterfrack, where we booked a room behind a dark, paint-flaked pub, our digs as luxurious as that sounds. I gave our accommodations a solid seven on the "How many pints am I going to have to drink before I can sleep in this room?" scale. There was something novel about a bathroom in which you could sit on the toilet, brush your teeth in the sink, and wash your feet in the shower, all at the same time, but after leaving Steve at a bus stop and hiking the hills through Leenane with only a fresh batch of blisters to accompany me, I arrived in Westport ready to stand still and get to know a town beyond a pub and a pillow. So I headed to a pub.

Matt Molloy's was famous for its eponymous owner who played flute for the world-renowned Irish musical group The Chieftains, but the bar stood on its own as an Irish treasure. The first thing that struck me in Molloy's, aside from the blend of Japanese tourists, Americans in Red Sox hats (come on, countrymen, hats off in the pub!), and locals in their Sunday suits, was that, incredibly, there wasn't a television in sight. I felt like Diogenes trying to find a pub in Ireland where there wasn't horse racing blasting out of a television, but in Molloy's, the *craic* was all about the music.

On the Sunday I visited, I found an old man the size of a furnace planted on a stool by the doorway with an accordion in his lap. At the table next to him, white-haired men in dark suits took their turns singing songs from memory. I watched from the corner, next to a guy in a leather jacket who was nodding at each new tune, each selection evidently a better choice than the last.

"Enjoying the music?" he asked me during a break. His accent was Irish, but he was on holiday himself from the other side of the country. "County Meath," he explained. "Ancient seat of the High Kings of Ireland."

"Philadelphia," I replied. "You ever see *Rocky?*"

His name was Seamus, and he seemed younger than his platinum hair. He was here for the music, and between songs explained to me that some of the tunes were reels, some were ceilis, and that they were played in a loop, three times around, specific to a particular dance, which gave a sense of design and purpose to what, to my untrained ears, sounded like a runaway string of diddly-dees. We listened that afternoon as men walked into the bar and launched into a song, then headed back down the road while we were still applauding for these roaming carolers on a pub crawl.

A man with slick black hair and watery eyes walked into Molloy's and settled in at the corner of the bar. The locals turned their attention to him, as if they had all been waiting for him to come tell them a secret. They were trying to pry something out of him, and he looked like he'd rather be left to his pint, but he finally gave in, and in his dusty black shoes and gray wool, he stepped to the center of the room. He breathed deep to fill his lungs, then pursed his lips and pushed out a long note that seemed to float across the pub. The place went church-quiet. Even the baseball hat crowd could tell this was something special, watching a man with closed eyes whistle a sad, soaring tune, the sound from one pair of lips filling up a crowded room. The place roared with applause when he finished, and Seamus turned to me, "That is very, very rare. I haven't seen that since I was a child." He explained that a whistling tradition harkened back to leaner times in Ireland, when there wasn't money for instruments. I had entertainment, I was getting an education, and they weren't running out of Guinness anytime soon. It was a perfect afternoon until Seamus got around to asking what I was doing in Ireland.

"You're a golfer?" he said in a tone that had me wondering if I'd missed an Irish travel advisory—*don't change money in Irish alleyways; don't make fun of guys named Fergus; don't order the battered burger from the chip shop menu* (I wish I had been so warned); *don't mention that you're a golfer in Matt Molloy's.*

"I am. I'm here to write about your golf courses."

Seamus wasn't a fan.

"Well this is one Irishman who is very anti-golf." And quick as an Irish reel, Seamus unleashed a rant that he'd likely been rehearsing on golfers in Meath. He claimed that rolling Irish countryside had been bulldozed flat, farmers pushed off their land, communities cut off from their coastline, and that my favorite pastime was to blame. He even claimed firsthand knowledge of a cairn (a pre-Christian Celtic tomb) being moved to make way for a golf course.

"They deny moving it, but I've seen it. It was there, and then it wasn't. Now you tell me why? All in the name of a quick buck," he said, looking at me as if had the displaced relics in my back pocket.

So there I was, helpless without a "So what do you think of Doonbeg?" to lean on. The other things the Irish seemed keen to talk about—Disney World, Bush, Beckham in America—felt like non sequiturs, and I was pretty sure we'd already covered the weather. I lipped my pint and smiled and Seamus apologized for his passion, which I told him was unnecessary. Growing up in Meath, he explained, a county with an abundance of old ghosts, he felt especially tied to the lore of ancient Ireland. To disturb sacred turf for profit, to move Irish soil for a British game (golf was thusly disparaged in front of me on more than one occasion), it was enough to get him arguing over the accordion. Which he was.

There would always be Irish grumblers at the end of the bar who turned sour at the faintest whiff of success—my mother described the Irish she grew up with as champions at commiserating over failure, but real failures at celebrating someone else's good fortune. It was not surprising to meet an Irishman who resented golf the same way soccer and rugby were still resisted by some Gaelic games devotees,* but I didn't expect to encounter one in the heart of Irish tourism, where, frankly, he was far outnumbered by Titleist-chasers like myself.

I was one pint away from challenging him on almost all his

---

* While Ireland seemed as soccer-obsessed as the rest of Europe, it was hard to believe that soccer and rugby were not played in Ireland's national stadium, Croke Park in Dublin, until 2007, and only because the soccer stadium was being rehabbed. Prior to 1970, rules stated that a member of the Gaelic Athletic Association (GAA, you'll hear more about them) could be banned if discovered playing soccer, rugby, or cricket. The only non-Gaelic sport to be played in Croke had been American football ("lads in pads" they called it): a Steelers-Bears contest and a Notre Dame–Navy game (44–16, go Irish).

arguments. First, no hill was ever bulldozed flat in the construction of any golf course worth its salt. Shopping malls wrecked landscapes, golf courses helped to preserve them. It was clear from my first three weeks on the road that the Irish countryside was under assault by its carpenters and an unchecked explosion of development that had me thinking of Florida, 2004. You couldn't swing a sand wedge without hitting a backhoe or scaffolding or a cement bucket; holiday homes were being thrown up around Ireland by the thousands. Not suburban sprawl, but second-home sprawl, tax breaks and cheap money making it impossible for Irish builders to stand still. In some holiday towns, the only spot of green left was the golf course, so if Seamus really cared about the countryside, he should have invested in a beginner's set and taken some lessons. I considered giving him pointers on an overlapping grip but thought better of it. Nor did I explain to Seamus that tourism was a nine-billion-dollar business in Ireland (for a country of four million, that's a handsome and vital sum), and golf tourists spend nearly 30 percent more than average visitors (you could count on a guilty golfer to overshop for his spouse). I didn't expect him to build a shrine to the white ball in his backyard, but a proud Irishman should have been proud of golf in Ireland—they did it so damn well.

Links golf in Ireland was stunning and pure, but what was most sublime about playing golf in Ireland was the fact that you could actually play it. Such an idea! The consequences of such a golfing culture—weren't they afraid?

Augusta boasted more security than Sing Sing. Pine Valley existed on a floating cloud somewhere, visible only to bank presidents and amateur champions when the moon was half full. But when I played St. Andrews, I had to back off a shot for a guy walking his dog. While greatness for an American golf course was granted according to how many people you could keep off it, a course's quality in Europe was determined by how many people wanted on. When it came to the top ten courses in Ireland, with a handicap card and an Amex, you could play them all. Only two of the best ten tracks in America were willing to take Joe Public's money, and as for membership at the other eight, you'd have an easier time getting into the Senate. And it wasn't just grown-ups who got to play. Junior golf in Ireland seemed a model for our own. Youth memberships at many European clubs were affordable on a paper boy's salary, and the first tee was open to children on weekday afternoons while mom and dad were at work. I couldn't help but marvel at the number of Irish children hanging around the pro shops and the clubhouses—*youngsters at a golf club! Obscene!*—kids by the dozen pulling their fathers' hand-me-downs along the fairways. The putting green sometimes felt like *Romper Room,* but it seemed a small price for such an open, youthful golf culture that was cranking out talent at a pace out of step with its size. Folks found it a mystery that America struggled so mightily in the Ryder Cup, but those kids out on the practice green putting for Cokes until dark probably weren't so surprised.

But I just bobbed my head to a song about Spancil Hill and let Seamus buy me a Guinness, and saved my fancy arguments for my journal.

The room suddenly broke into applause as a little old man with white hair and Harry Caray's glasses stepped into the pub. It was like Fonzie walking into Arnold's, and this was the guy Seamus was waiting for, Mick Lavelle, a Westport celebrity and a human iPod with, legend had it, a thousand different songs cued up and ready. Scanning the room through his coaster-sized lenses, he would point out all the newcomers, asking us where we were from. A guy at the bar said New York and got a few verses of Sinatra; Mick asked where I was from, and before I got to *delphia,* he was singing, "Philadelphia, Here I Come." The room went quiet as he leaned on the table next to me, and with a younger man's tenor, sang to us a song about his dear brother, newly elected to the Irish parliament, known as the Dáil (rhymes with ball, at least at Molly's in Westport).

> *Twas at the last election, me brother he went in.*
> *He was always fond of politics, we knew he'd surely win.*
> *He went around, he canvassed hard, he wandered round about.*
> *He said he'd raise the price of milk and bring down the price of*
>   *stout.*

We are the one-horse farmers and you know that means damn all.
But now they raise their hats for him, he's a member of the Dáil.
We have a brand-new house, you know, we let the old one fall.
For a tigian wasn't good enough for a member of the Dáil.

Well me brother doesn't know A from Zed, he never went to
  school.
But as you know in Irish politics it doesn't matter as a rule.
He goes into pubs, he drinks all night, he never comes home at all.
And the police will never throw him out, he's a member of the
  Dáil.

On one of his trips to Dublin he brought home a brand-new wife.
She was the finest bit of stuff I ever saw in all me life.
And the three of us sleep together and they put me next to the
  wall.
Still when it's dark she doesn't know who's a member of the Dáil.

Me brother is T.D., me boys, me brother is a T.D.
He got me Dad a pension, he was only forty-three.
Me brother is T.D., me boys, me brother is a T.D.
And when he's up in Dublin there's plenty of the other for me.*

Westport owed a special debt to St. Patrick who, in the year 441, took a walk up one of her neighboring mountains. The story goes that he prayed and fasted at the peak for forty days, casting the serpents out of Ireland from a summit that would become known as Croagh Patrick. Known locally as "the reek," it was the most important pilgrimage site in Ireland, and every year thousands of the faithful and the curious followed Patrick's footsteps, making the two-hour trek up the rocky mountainside to visit the small chapel at the top. Some folks did the hike barefoot; some of the penitent did it on their knees. I thought it better to appreciate the beauty of the summit from a more comfortable distance, taking pictures from the generous fairways of the Westport Golf Club.

---

* "Me Brother Is a T.D." by Mick Fitzgerald

Westport was not a links course and it wasn't on the itinerary, but after motivating at a steady clip for the last three weeks, on my second down day in Westport, I found myself itching for the road. So I threw my sticks over my shoulder and followed the arrows pointing to GOLF COURSE, and I soon found myself standing on the first tee of a tidy parkland course that looked wonderfully benign, a fangless alternative to the ball-greedy links I had been battling. Westport woke up on its second nine as the holes turned toward Clew Bay and the fairways started falling off the hill at the heart of the course. I had lovely views of Croagh Patrick from all over the Westport course, its sharp peak rising like a volcano above the gentle mountaintops around it. On the far side of the property, as I worked my way down to the water's edge on eleven, twelve, and fourteen—where Croagh Patrick's pointed crest was the perfect target for my seven-iron—the mountain seemed to erupt in size, the reek casting a long shadow across the bay. After so much links golf, I expected to dispatch Westport with ease, a course that looked as open as a driving range compared to the gorse of Connemara. But I succeeded in adding 89 strokes to my scorecard, once again proving a golf truth that I had yet to accept, that the more room you have to spray it, the more likely you will.

The next afternoon, I sampled another nearby layout that didn't make the original cut. I hadn't heard of it at all until I noticed a small advertisement on the back of a tourist map of Westport. I didn't know what to call Clew Bay—a nine-holer for sure, but was it a links? Parkland? It was farther away than my hostess had described it (*about five miles* means something so very different to a walker), situated at the end of a road guarded by a red-eyed hound dog that I scrambled over a fence to avoid.

Ankles sprinkled with dog slobber, I arrived at Clew Bay Golf Club eager for a quick shower and a bowl of soup to fix me after my haul. I wept a little bit (on the inside) to find that the Clew Bay clubhouse was a half-trailer on blocks, and an empty one at that. I was back on the greens fee honor system, apparently (see the appendix for my top ten courses for Americans without a conscience). I poked around the eight-car parking lot for a little while until the father of the course owner appeared from the house next door, invited me into the minimalist clubhouse—a desk, a chair, and a bathroom—loaded me up with experienced yellow golf balls and a scorecard, and kindly sent me on my way.

Westport Golf Club was a fine diversion, but it didn't command space on a touring golfer's rotation for a reason. If you wanted to play a park course, the best in the world were in America. Croagh Patrick was lovely, but if I wanted mountain vistas, the Poconos would do. But as for Clew Bay, whether it was good, bad, or silly, it was unlike any course I was going to find on my side of the water—it was part golf course, part cliffside assault, with fairways stuck to hillsides like spaghetti tossed at the wall. The property struck me as turf that had until recently been pasture and had been morphed into a golf course with little more than an imagination and a lawn mower. Along with tales of the dying rural pub, I would regularly hear of the struggles of the small Irish farm as I traveled the country. The little guy was being squeezed by the conglomerates, and more and more farmers couldn't justify the cost of their herd, or ignore the value of their acres. The Clew Bay course looked like something of a rural rescue operation, land that could no longer make it in the grazing business and was taking a crack at a second career. The second hole was like playing back up a ski slope, and a black diamond at that. It was a course that walked the line between absurd and unique, but there was something singular about playing a course void of pomp with no clubhouse to rush back to, no crowd to trouble your pace, no worries about overpaying, and no reason to stop playing after nine or eighteen or twenty-seven. I climbed my way around a hillside, rolling my ball along the edge of Clew Bay's still waters, and I found myself lulled into a state of playfulness that I often found on less glamorous golf courses (and this one was less glamorous in the way that, say, sweatpants were less glamorous). It was worry-free golf played with pleasantly low expectations. I found myself staring up at a four-hundred-yard hill with a green planted on top of it like the last tier of a wedding cake, and I could only laugh as I reached for driver and gave it a whack. Clew Bay wasn't much of a golf course, and that was fine with me.

I had already been charmed by Spanish Point, surprised by Clew Bay, and in a few days, I would be won over by another nine-holer in Mulranny. Nine-holers in Ireland made up a far greater percentage of the course population than in the States, where they were maligned as pitch-and-putts, meek imitations unworthy of a golfer's afternoon. But in Ireland, if you gave them a chance, you might find quirky layouts stuffed into uncommon bits of property ignored by developers for their limited size. Nine-holers also gave you that instant do-over which, playing these links courses with so many hidden bounces and blind tee shots, was a perfect salve for the traveler eager to shake off the double bogeys. The short courses harkened back to an older game when a links might have three, six, maybe twelve holes, and they reminded one that you didn't need a fleet of diggers or CEO bucks to lay out a little space to golf your ball. In the case of the Mulranny links, you don't even need to own the property.

From Clew Bay I headed for a night in Newport, collapsing on a picnic bench alongside a wide, rippling river at the bottom of town. I had expected the shoulder and back pain, and I accepted sore legs as a reality of the road, but I was not prepared for the disappearance of my ankles—my Achilles had swollen up thick as pipe, leaving me with two ugly and unbending stumps below the knee. Resting my feet allowed them to tighten up into a state of rigor mortis, but it was worth clomping my way into the Grainne Uaile pub for the best bar food I'd found yet (*gran-ya-wail*, the Irish name of Grace O'Malley, the sixteenth-century Irish pirate queen from County Mayo, immortalized in Irish legend and now, thankfully, a musical). The next morning, it was into Mulranny, a two-pub town set above Clew Bay, where I stayed at an updated country house overlooking the water and the strand and a small patch of green that didn't look like a golf course, but had to be.

I had played rounds of golf where it felt as if the greens were surrounded by some sort of impenetrable barrier, a force-field built of my own ball-striking shortcomings. Some days, the greens looked the size of English muffins, encircled by sticky moats of sorrow. But it wasn't until I teed it up Mulranny Golf Links in County Mayo that I understood that some greens truly were harder to get to than others. Because some greens were surrounded by barbed wire.

Mulranny was a lovely and natural setting for a game of golf, set directly on the water, a plot of wind-lashing links fun. When I showed up at the golf course that morning with a photographer from the *Sunday Tribune* (word of my adventure was slowly spreading, and a camera came from Dublin to document my folly), the greenskeeper asked us to please not shoot pictures of the greenside fences or the resident donkeys. We nodded and told him of course, no fences or donkeys for us, feeling half bad about not admitting that the photographer's camera bag was full of donkey-baiting carrots and that in the course of the photo shoot we would use every one of them.

I was interested to find that a number of courses in Ireland currently or formerly sat upon what is known as "commenage," which in my limited, overheard-it-in-the-pub understanding, was land that had not been walled in when the land acts came into being, i.e., property that was utilized by many with no one rightful owner. Such lands were shared between a number of shareholders (how they decided who the shareholders would be, and how many there would be, no one seemed able to explain). The Mulranny Links resided upon a stretch of land owned and utilized by more than twenty shareholders, the golf club itself holding only one of those shares. So the next time you found yourself complaining about the way things were done at your own club, imagine how board meetings would go if 90 percent of your bondholders were farmers who couldn't give a sheep about golf. You'd be putting up barbed wire, too.

As unexcited as the Mulranny members might have been about their links possessing greenside hazards that might require a tetanus shot, I didn't mind them a bit. To knock your ball along a stretch of seaside turf that you are sharing with donkeys, sheep, cows, and horses was an absolute treat, a throwback to the way the game was originally played, on pastures shared with one's herd, where that first ruling was made and the first relief taken from a steamy horse-made hazard. I sampled the Achill Island nine-holer a few days before, and found it to be pretty much overrun by lambs and their left-behinds—the seaside cliffs on

Achill were lovely to look at, but the sheep had nibbled the entire course down to the roots, forcing the folks at Achill to lay out white stones outlining where the fairways might be. Mulranny didn't seem to have such problems, each hole well-defined and cunningly routed, with just a few sheep deposits to be negotiated. The greens were thankfully devoid of any such obstructions, rolling fair and true, nary a hoofprint to be found anywhere. Thus, the fences.

While the sheep and the donkeys seemed to be tolerated, even enjoyed by the members (not so much the Titleist-stealing resident sheep dog—I heard that you could hit a fairway-splitting drive at Mulranny, only to find that drive an hour later in the parking lot), it was the horses that made the fences a necessity, as hooves on damp turf could turn the lovely links into a pocked and pitted disaster. So three rings of barbed wire were posted to protect each putting surface. Play to the green, open the gate, go on in and putt, don't forget to close the gate on your way out. And if you hit the wires or the fence posts, local rule said you had the choice to play your shot again. Which I was surprised that I never actually did, chipping cleanly through the wires a dozen times. Unlike trees, it seemed that with barbed wire the 90-percent-air rule held true.

As I continued my trek through the less obvious Ireland, I was learning plenty. I learned that sidewalks were called pavements, when they really should have been called nowheres, because in three weeks that was the only place I had found them. I learned that the Irish were just as untrusting of politicians as Americans, the papers awash with outrage and accusation regarding the upcoming election, and when it came to their democracy, I discovered that the Irish electorate was surprisingly vain. I began to think elections were being held to bolster the Irish head-shot industry—on every pole and at every intersection I was met by another broad smiling face, a Cavanagh or an O'Leary asking for my vote. A land of faceless political posters sort of felt like the menu at Denny's, but the candidates soon became my road buddies, new smiles to greet me with each passing constituency (on further reflection, I could guess at the inefficacy of campaign banners that simply read VOTE FOR MURPHY, which in Ireland would be slightly less specific than VOTE FOR HIM). But politics aside, and of more personal importance, I had learned that I should never refer to any sort of weather as the "worst yet" in my journal. Each time I became convinced that I had braved Ireland's best shot, she seemed quick to challenge me on that point. So I noted that I played the front nine in Mulranny in less than ideal conditions. The rain blowing off the sea felt like flaming needles being blow-darted into my face. My rain gloves turned to soggy leather sponges, my grips were as tacky as a greased kielbasa, and my resolve to play on through Ireland was once again challenged. I was playing alongside a Mulranny member who had taken the afternoon off to guide me around his course, which meant that we were both going to be polite and keep up the charade that we were actually enjoying ourselves rather than admitting to our misery and heading for the pub. But as we finished the fifth hole and spotted a rain shelter made of aluminum siding, I again felt Ireland giving a tacit, cosmic bit of reassurance, that there would be shelter in the storm, that the road around Ireland would indeed rise up to meet me.

Until we came around the front of the shelter and saw that our safe haven from the wind and rain was currently occupied. Not by golfers—we were the only players crazy enough to test the course in this weather—but by four unbothered horses. They gave us a sort of equine, "So what are you going to do about it?" look. They weren't going anywhere. Hell, I wouldn't have moved for them, either.

We journeyed on, and as we made the turn to replay Mulranny's nine holes, the weather softened (spirit-crushing shit storm downgraded to miserable dribble), and the course showed itself to be enjoyable enough to stand up to the conditions. And as I sipped a Guinness in Nevin's pub with a new friend named Derek who had braved the winds with me to show me his wonderful little track, I dried my feet by the peat fire and once again felt the potential of this adventure, keenly aware that there was something far greater than the gold at the end of the rainbow—the Guinness at the end of the rain.

ḥоlе 163
98 over par

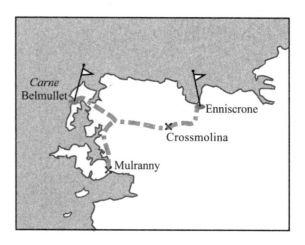

I WAS THE ONLY PATRON IN MOLLOY'S WHO WASN'T LAUGHING.
We'd gone around the room confessing our hometowns to
Mick Lavelle, and when Mick's wagging finger fell upon a young
couple in the corner sharing a bottle of cider, the gentleman answered him, "We're from Belmullet."

Mick's eyes grew wide. "Belmullet,ʔ" he said. "And you almost look human!"

The fact that Belmullet's remoteness was legendary enough to
win laughs in Westport gave me pause. For months, the pin I'd
stuck into Belmullet had been troubling me—it was a town off
the corkboard, a map pin pushed into the drywall. I was tempted
to ignore the little green flag on the far edge of my Michelin map,
but the few people I knew who had played it described it with
unusual praise. A neighbor tried to explain the Belmullet links to
me, a course otherwise known as Carne, but he got tongue-tied
with superlatives before going quiet, shaking his head and telling
me, "Belmullet. Wow." So I would go there. I couldn't spend four

months golfing Ireland and not be the top Irish links expert on my own block. Besides, it was Eddie Hackett's last design, and one that he'd confided was his best. He hadn't let me down in Connemara, so I strapped it up and set out for Carne.

My father was no newcomer to the Irish roadways. He had traversed the country on a half dozen occasions, crossing from south to north and back, no doubt logging miles in the thousands. But he had logged almost all of those miles from the comfort of a reclining pilot's chair in the back of one of those luxury buses, allowing Johnny Whelan, a coach driver of Irish legend, to handle the hairpins for him. So in my quiet hours on the road, an image started to take hold, a vision tough to shake. I could see my parents, now in their seventies, stepping off a plane at the Shannon airport. Mom was wobbly with nerves from a seven-hour flight, and Dad hadn't slept three minutes, his eyes hanging somewhere around his elbows, his last wisps of white hair waving in the breeze as if calling for rescue. And there they were, pouring themselves into a rental car the size of a bassinet and driving for four hours on the wrong side of the road.

I had walked the same roads they would be traveling, and with each sneaky bend and snug stone bridge, with every tractor taking up both sides of the road, I thought of my dad behind the wheel of the Hyundai I had rented for him and wondered: How the hell were they going to survive this? And then, another question: Which one of us got the beach house?

It wouldn't help their cause that Belmullet was tucked in one of the Irish-speaking corners of Mayo (an area designated as Gaeltacht), and I could just imagine my father at the far end of his rope, Mom working on rosaries in the passenger's seat and singing a refrain of *Left, Jim, get left!*, only to arrive in a part of the country where the signs flipped from English into one of the most impenetrable languages on earth. Looking for Belmullet, he'd have to know to follow signs to Béal an Mhuirthead, which was something I don't think he ever learned from the back of that bus.

There were more convenient legs of the journey for my

parents to make their visit, and if he had joined me for a different stretch, Dad might have encountered more golf, but I'd asked them to come do this half of County Mayo with me because we would be visiting the towns where their grandparents came from. A cousin had traced my mother's family to a Mayo village called Pulladoohey that no longer existed on any map, and she'd learned that my great-great-grandfather delivered the mail on horseback from Belmullet through Bangor and on to Ballina—the exact route I would be walking. I expected this history to make the miles a touch shorter, easing the pain of having to walk fifteen miles out to the edge of the Mullet Peninsula, then backtrack the same route inland a day later, but I mostly just spent the hours readjusting my backpack and envying my ancestor for his horse.

I arrived in Belmullet and, by the grace of St. Christopher, found two gray-haired zombies waiting for me in the lobby of our hotel. They were alive, still married by all accounts, and as I suspected, hugs and hellos were followed by a question my dad must have been chewing on for hours: "So where the hell is this Belmullet you said I was looking for?"

Dad did christen the Hyundai on a stone bridge in Galway, and Mom might have taken an ounce too much satisfaction from showing off their modified quarter-panel, vindicated after her four-hour complaint that my father was, indeed, going to hit a wall. But they were there, and more importantly, had sprung for the insurance. The hotel was clean and modern with a pool and a leisure center, and a restaurant where my mother might be tempted to eat more than her dinner roll (travel turned her into a timid diner). All was well, and things could hardly get better. But the following morning, after walking the three miles out to the Carne links and meeting up with Dad by the first tee, they certainly did.

We met an American some days later in my parents' hotel in Ballina, a golfer who was eager for my opinion of Carne. Per his experience, he found the front nine to be rather ordinary, explaining that the course didn't really get interesting until the back. "I've played most of the top courses in the world," he told me, with a good dollop of that Yankee modesty I'd been missing, "and I didn't think the front was anything special." And if it wasn't eight o'clock in the morning, and he wasn't sitting with his wife and daughter, I would have asked him if he was drunk.

Eddie Hackett wasn't a man for frills, so I'll keep my praise as honest as his handiwork. Carne was brilliant. Simply brilliant. Front, back, first hole, last—every mound, every swale, every inch of the place was special. Granted, we played in a light breeze under clear skies with a blazing sun warming our shoulders, and I finally happened to hit the ball like a golfer instead of a tired bag of blisters. But it was more than the conditions that had me understanding what Mr. Hackett was talking about when he called Carne the greatest canvas he'd ever been given. It was dropped smack in the heart of the lovely Irish nowhere. No hotels to catch your eye, no traffic to rattle your focus, no summer homes stuck to the side of a glen like they might crash down upon your fairway. We got lost in Carne, wonderfully so, and for all its blind shots and vanishing fairways, I never felt tricked. I had never played a golf course that felt as wild but played as fair as Carne. There were volumes of characteristics and specs by which I might grade a golf course, but fun and fair pretty much set the curve for me.

A 77 helped dry up some of the blood I'd been spilling on my Irish scorecard, and unlike most scorecards, this one wasn't full of could-haves and should-haves, and I didn't go to bed that night convinced that the golfing planets had lined up against me yet again. In fact, it seemed as if the golfing gods were busy lipping out someone else's putts when I found my tee shot on number eleven, a short par-four that hooked its way around a behemoth sand dune. Having slapped my drive toward a rightward death, I tightened up my bag and set out to scale a bristly dune wall, eventually arriving at a grassy peak from which all the greens and blues of the Belmullet coast were in view. And so was the white of my Titleist, my ball sitting atop a tuft of grass as if the sand hill was simply the tallest tee in Ireland. I'd taken an inadvertent but unbeatable shortcut, the green sitting fifty yards below my feet, and dropping my ball onto it was as easy as hitting the pool from the high dive. But when I hit my second shot on Carne's par-five eighteenth, I knew for certain that Ireland had been my partner today, and that I would make it home safe before Carne could pull the fairway out from under me. A helping wind had batted my drive down the fairway, leaving me 240 to the pin off an up-hill, hooking lie, and a favorable breeze to consider. With my bag whittled down to a team of eight, I was left to choose between a three-wood that might fly the clubhouse, and a three-iron lay-up that would spoil that evening's Guinness, stealing the guts from a good round of golf. Some courses impressed, but Carne inspired, and after four hours in its company, I was teeming with all the imagination this shot might require.

I spent a piece of my life trying to play perfect Florida golf, wooed by sexy, high-soaring golf shots, pursuing a mythical straight ball flight. It felt like magic to give wings to dotted bits of plastic, and so many golfers seemed drunk on the sensation, beating range balls in dry bays, safe in the invariable conditions of our swing studios, tuning our irons to precise distances. We weren't trying to be better golfers; we were stuck on a quest to hit golf's definitive six-iron. We'd taken the bocce out of golf, and it was a shame. My half-empty bag had forced me to rediscover the fun of trying to skip home a seven-iron from 120, watching my ball hop and hurry over knobs and wrinkles, hopefully expiring a few paces from the pin. And those shots gave me a mind's eye to attempt a shot I'd never practiced in any of those studios, a choke-down, cut, up-in-my-stance three-wood. It was a shot I didn't know I had, not until it landed.

I safely two-putted for birdie, and Dad and I retired for a pint and the second half of the Mayo-Galway Gaelic football match (take the best bits of soccer, rugby, and a bar brawl, and you've got Gaelic football—one point for a ball through the posts, three for sticking it in the net). Mayo took a beating, but there were still two bright faces in the pub in Belmullet town. I was still in love with that three-wood, and Dad wasn't too unpleased with his 97, a pretty tidy sum for a seventy-three-year-old carrying his own sticks around the dunes. I could tell his knees were aching, but he didn't say a word about it.

Growing up in an America where multiculturalism was of the moment—Italian-American, German-American, Indian-American, it was all the rage, bigger than Bugle Boy—I was a young teen eager for a hyphen of my own, and I harbored a bitterness about how little my family knew about where we came from. I yearned for the panache of that modifier, and all I really knew was that we were from northeastern Pennsylvania, and that Scranton-American wasn't the panache I was looking for.

My grandmother died when my mother was a child. Her father wasn't able to take care of her, so she left home and went to live with two aunts of legendary work ethic. She went to work in their Scranton dress shop, Timely Styles (if you've heard of it, I hope you're reading this in large print), and for fun on a Saturday afternoon they would take her to the cemetery and let her jump off the tombstones (at least that's what she told me when I whined for a Nintendo). That's what I knew about Mom's side, and only slightly more about Dad's. Mom claimed that she married up when she married my father (she came from a neighborhood called Bone Hill, so upward sounded inevitable) whose family lived on one of Scranton's prestigious avenues. His father had lost every penny he had, and some that he didn't, in the crash in 1932, but he would work his way back into an accounting practice, and would eventually come to own drive-ins and movie theaters all over the northeast, another bit of family history I never fully understood. This was a time when, and a town where, "Irishman" was synonymous with coal miner or trouble, and though they were from different sides of the tracks, these were two families with their eyes set on where they were going, not where they were from. I've heard it called "lace curtain," but that was from the guy grumbling at the end of the bar again. My grandmother had lace curtains, and they were lovely.

I don't know if it was that leprechaun hunting for mising marshmallows, the beer companies turning a holy day into a month-long bender, or the fact that the Irish had scrambled their way out of the mines long enough ago, but at some point during my last twenty years, Irish became cool. The only thing I wanted to be more than Irish was cool, so I studied the literature and the art, learned how to say hello in Irish—*Dia dhuit*—and called myself Irish-American. And I framed a family history that my cousin had brought back from a heritage center in Mayo, the one that told me about my great-great-grandfather and his horse, that pointed us to the place where we weren't just from, but where our family was still living, a town of modest font size called Crossmolina.

As I went googly-eyed on the twenty-one-mile stroll into Crossmolina, mumbling to sheep and counting discarded cigarette packs (there were thousands—as explained to me in Mulranny, open car windows in Ireland were considered legitimate trash receptacles), my parents went ahead to hunt for roots with my newly arrived sister and brother-in-law. I had booked them into an eighteenth-century guest house and asked them to head for the heritage center behind it, armed with that list of names from my cousin.

There were more than old packs of Benson & Hedges to count as I made my way to town. The roadsides around Ireland are dotted with Madonnas and religious shrines, and I'd stumbled upon a half dozen grottoes tucked into the woods where a statue of the Virgin Mary had been placed at the edge of a lake. My father's Catholicism was particularly devoted to the Blessed Mother, a devotion he said came from his grandmother, and as I traveled the country snapping shots of roadside statues and grottoes to Mary, I was struck by the understanding that something Irish had endured in our family, aside from that cupboard in the living room. Those holy places hadn't been put there for the purpose of giving a sweaty backpacker a chance to rest his feet, but they served well in that capacity, and it was a special thing to walk for three hours in silence, alone, and to find a few flat stones by the side of the road leading me down a pathway to a quiet spot with a bench and a few candles still flickering as if lit for my arrival.

Taking it slow back in Spanish Point had allowed Joe Byrne and I to learn of the Rineen ambush—we dropped our bags beside a roadside monument and listened as a tour guide told his busload of Americans about the 1920 ambush that saw an outnumbered, unequipped group of IRA men score a major victory in the War of Independence. The walker's education continued a few miles up the road when I learned of the "Countess of Irish Freedom," Constance Markievicz, Irish revolutionary, friend to W. B. Yeats, and first woman to ever be elected to British Parliament. She was immortalized in sculpture beside the Sligo road, a woman with pike in hand leading a group of chained peasants through a torn gate. And on my way into Crossmolina, a small stone memorial on the side of the road told me of the North Mayo Fenian Conspiracy, a moment in Irish history skipped by the history book in my bag. The engraving told of seven local men who organized in a Crossmolina castle, where they plotted to fight for tenant rights before being discovered and imprisoned for eight years. Their leader, P. W. Nally, a famed stalwart of the GAA who helped rejuvenate Irish identity through the Gaelic games (a stand in Croke Park still bears his name) died nineteen days before he was to be released from prison.

I couldn't say if it was the memorials or the Madonnas, or the fact that I had been pondering my roots for twenty miles under a cloudless summer sky, to the point where I was waiting for my great-great-grandfather to come clopping by and offer me a lift, but it was easy to envision Crossmolina a hundred years ago. A slow-moving river ran quiet through the center of town, and the main street led up a hill to a central roundabout where an ivory statue of Mary stood atop a tall granite pedestal. I sat on a wall across from the monument, butcher shop and a small town library in front of me, and I thought of unknown relatives walking into Crossmolina town on a Sunday. No doubt they knew that butcher at the top of the street, or perhaps preferred the shop with the red awning down at the bottom. I'm sure they knew The Thatch Pub, but probably didn't know the Polish girl who pulled me a pint. I sat there envisioning ancestors in these streets with faces that looked like mine, until there appeared two faces very much like mine that were about to drive the wrong way around the roundabout in a blue Hyundai. My father swerved back into his lane, missing the Madonna by inches (he claimed yards), and parked crooked in front of the library. Mom jumped out of the passenger side, excited about something other than being freed from her passenger seat.

"You won't believe it," she told me, and she was right. They had found our cousins, and they were coming to dinner.

Some women play tennis. Some ladies summer in the Hamptons. Some scrapbook or crochet. My mother skeeves. To skeeve is to avoid food or accommodations of a suspicious origin or quality. It usually involves telling a waiter, "Thank you, that looks lovely," then pushing food around your plate without biting into anything but the ice cubes from your water glass. Mom was a seasoned skeever. She never left home without her own pillow case and box of peanut butter crackers, and she practiced her art all over the globe. My family had walked out of restaurants from Maui to the West End, so I was careful to keep my parents far away from the I-hope-I-have-my-own-toilet Ireland I had been living in, and had booked them into places like the Mount Falcon in Ballina—a four-star estate on the River Moy, with flat screens and helipads for all—and the Enniscoe House in Crossmolina, which wasn't as luxurious as the Mount Falcon but was certainly as grand. A front door to accommodate a colossus welcomed us into a foyer full of antlers from Victorian expeditions and trout the size of guitars mounted in old glass cases, with sitting rooms off of sitting rooms, warm turf fires, and King Louis sofas that swallowed you up like a beanbag. Centuries of books were piled around the house as if bracing the doors against modernity—no telephones in your room at Enniscoe, and no televisions either. And best of all, Mom could leave her pillow case in her carry-on, at least for now.

Their afternoon had gone thusly: As I could have predicted, my shy mother made best-friends-forever with the woman at the North Mayo Heritage Center behind the Enniscoe House. I had supplied my mother with the name of one Agnes Murray, a distant relative who would be able to introduce us to other more remotely related Murrays. The lady at the heritage center looked up Agnes Murray, only to find that she had passed away in recent years, and that there were no records of her connections or kin. There was no answer at the phone number my mother had, and the family trail had gone cold yet again. My parents were on their way out to the car when the woman came running to catch them—she'd looked up the Murrays in town, and one of their phone numbers matched the digits for Agnes. The woman gave my parents directions and sent them off. They were on the trail. And then quickly, back off it.

After an hour navigating back roads with no names or numbers (Paddy from Kinsale's postal address was, seriously, "The Blue House"), my father finally pulled up beside a home where a man in a suit appeared to be on his way to work. Little did they know they were in for an Act of Uncommon Irish Hospitality as the gentleman spent twenty minutes with Mom and Dad, drawing them a detailed map to the Murray home. (I had found the Irish to be particularly generous in giving directions, often scribbling down maps or repeating the route until you could recite it for an audience, sometimes even grabbing you by the hand and leading you there themselves.) The map served my parents well, and soon they were parked in front of a small farm where Mom and Dad were met in the yard by a young man in old man's clothing.

I would have hauled a few extra miles for the chance to be there for that introduction, when a kid fresh from milking his herd looked up to find two gray-haired Americans in golf shirts and khakis standing in his front yard, my sister and brother-in-law waving from the back seat. I could imagine my Dad's booming voice and firm grip, "Jim Coyne, from America," and Mom more gently, "I'm Alice. Pleased to meet you. We're your cousins."

As with any such bizarre circumstance, I suppose the kid had no choice but to believe them. His name was Eamon and he was nineteen years old. He was gracious and slightly speechless, and he explained that he didn't know much about his family history, and that Agnes Murray didn't ring a bell. It turned out that his family was probably the last subject on which he wanted to be quizzed. As he explained to my parents, his mother had passed away a few years back, and his father had just died that past Christmas. He apologized for not knowing more and said his sisters would really be the ones to ask about the family. He reached into his coveralls for his cell phone and gave his younger sister a call. "Our cousins from America are here," is what he told her.

Eamon was too modest to trouble us for dinner, but he promised he would bring his brother and sister out to see us later that evening. The doorbell at Enniscoe rang just before dessert, and after the host finally convinced them that they should please come join us in the dining room where we had the room to ourselves, in walked the Murrays. There was Eamon, tall with high, bony cheeks, changed from coveralls into a pressed, collared shirt. His sister Celia was next to him, a pretty blonde of college age, and as I shook her hand, I could see the confusion in her eyes, wondering what her brother had gotten her into. And there was Liam, dressed in a Mayo football jersey. Maybe fourteen years old, he was tall as his brother and thin as a whisper, and he didn't take his eyes off his shoes. They were too shy to accept any chocolate cake, but my dad twisted their arms into a round of 7UPs.

The silence in the room was interrupted by brief stabs at conversation. *Have you been to America?* They hadn't. *Do you play soccer?* They preferred Gaelic football. Celia was going to secretary school. Eamon had left school to run the farm full-time. They had a few dozen cattle and the farm didn't make money, but he was just trying to keep it going until a better idea came along. Liam was in seventh grade. We asked him if he ever wanted to visit America, and he shrugged, and it was quiet. And the quiet, it started to scream: *Tell these kids why the hell they are here at eight o'clock in the evening, sitting there as if they'd been summoned to this sprawling estate with twinkling chandeliers and framed fish on the wall, to sit and sip soda pop with strangers.* And worse, on a school night. We were all waiting for Mom to kick in, which, after retiring to one of the sitting rooms to stare at the fire and nod and smile at one another, she finally did, bringing everyone's attention to the illusive Agnes Murray, conspicuous in her absence.

Celia looked to her brothers, to Eamon, then Liam. "I'm sorry, I don't think we know anyone named Agnes Murray."

Mom handed over the family tree from the heritage center, trying to lead her witness. Did any of those names sound familiar? Even one of them? Celia studied the paper, squinted in earnest. Eamon took the sheet and looked even closer, as if names they knew were hidden in the margins. They tried their damndest but nothing rang a bell. "This could be our family," she conceded, "But we didn't really keep up on it. Maybe our aunt would know," she said, and Eamon nodded at that suggestion.

Our tree was shaken but still standing. We couldn't say precisely how they were related to us, but with the phone numbers and the heritage center and the map the gentleman drew for my parents, there was too much evidence to deny a connection. As long as their father was a Murray from Mayo, this was still a family reunion, albeit a subdued one.

"The only thing I really know about our family," Eamon explained, "is that my father came from Tyrone." Which wasn't Mayo, by the way. It wasn't even close.

But we had a map, my mother protested, a phone number, and a $300 family tree.

"You know, there is another family of Murrays down the road from us, not too far at all," Eamon said, looking at his sister as if to apologize.

"That's right. Not very far at all."

Crickets. And not Irish crickets, but crickets from a far away place, as I assumed the fetal position in my mind, imagining myself somewhere safe and nowhere near this room with my parents and three Irish kids who had gotten dressed up on a Tuesday to come sit in a guest house with five Americans to which they were in no possible way related.

We had arrived at that undeniable moment in the evening, the one where you found out that your date was a vegetarian, or thought golf was stupid, or drank mudslides—that deal-breaking, cut-your-losses moment when everything became about finding the exits as quickly as possible. But Mom would have none of it. Along with being into dustcovers and spotless restaurant bathrooms, Mom was also into feelings. More than any person I'd ever met, my mother was genuinely interested in other people— sad what a rare quality that could be, but she possessed it in abundance, the kind of person who could get someone's life story going through a drive-thru. She asked how they were doing— how they were *really* doing, three kids under the age of twenty, left to run a farm and a family. Did they have aunts or uncles, did they have enough to get by, did they need any help? And she didn't offer help as someone who was condescending to their troubles, but as someone who knew what it was like to need it.

Meanwhile, I had taken Liam's approach, my eyes stuck on the tips of my shoes as my cheeks began to burn. From the age of five, I shriveled with embarrassment when Mom spoke to strangers or new acquaintances so frankly, and one thing I had learned in my weeks in Ireland, and in my thirty years with some Irish in me, was that this wasn't a culture that was big on feelings. You didn't go to therapy or do affirmations here. You didn't get to the root of your unhappiness—you didn't admit that you were unhappy. You got up, and got on—they'd been doing it for centuries, so as the three of them stared blankly at my mother, offering one word answers to her questions about their genuine well-being, I wanted to pass her a note. *Get back to soccer*, it would have read. *Please, no more feelings.*

"I lost my mother when I was thirteen years old. My father couldn't take care of me, so when I was your age," my mom said, looking at Liam, waiting for him to look up at her, "I woke up one morning, and I didn't have my parents. I know what you are going through. And I know that it will make you a better person. It's hard to believe that now, I know. But it made me a strong person, and you will grow up to be such strong people. You will. Your parents will be very proud."

I looked up from my feet and saw Celia's eyes locked on my mother's. There were tears running down her face.

We talked for a while longer, about the problem with Mayo football (the lads from Kerry were unstoppable, it seemed), a friend of theirs who'd been to Disney World (Celia wasn't interested in Florida, didn't care for humidity), and why anyone would be walking their way to Ballina tomorrow. We exchanged addresses and e-mails, and promised we would be in touch. My mother hugged each of them as they left, Celia a little longer than her brothers.

We sat in the parlor after they were gone, staring at the fire, smiling and shaking our heads about the last few hours, very aware how strange we must have seemed. But we agreed that it worked out in the end. My parents could have ended up knocking on any door in Mayo that afternoon, but thank God for that map. It had taken them straight to our cousins. We were all convinced of that.

The coast road was always a wise choice for a pedestrian—the camera ops, the less mountainous terrain, the diminished odds of wandering onto a four-lane highway—but in the case of the coastal road from Ballina to Enniscrone, it was a particularly lovely choice. I walked beneath a canopy of heavy branches, the morning sun dappled along an untraveled road. A white horse let me scratch his collar as he munched on some scrub, and I stopped to snap pictures of a small cemetery hidden behind a toppled iron gate, a few crooked headstones barely visible through the weeds with years predating my own country. I passed a charcoal stone church on a hill that was nearby to nothing, where a sign announced that a priest would be there to say mass on every third Sunday. My route almost always felt like more miles than I budgeted for, but the walk to Enniscrone felt shorter.

This was one I had been waiting for, my original Irish gem. Ennsicrone was the first course my father and I played in Ireland. I was fourteen, trapped on a castles-and-graveyards trip with no golf on our itinerary, but Dad and I snuck away for an afternoon at a nearby course that the guy at the hotel heard wasn't half bad. This was eighteen years ago, and it seemed as if the townspeople hardly knew the Enniscrone links were there. Two little girls came out of a modest clubhouse to pull our trolleys around, and after what might be the most boring opening stretch in Ireland—two flat par-fives and a par-four that ran straight down a fence line— Enniscrone rewarded those who pushed past its modest clubhouse and meager beginnings, treating us to a wild rollercoaster in and out of the dunes. On this return trip, we still found the dunes to be the mightiest in Ireland—on the back nine, looking up at the towering walls of beach grass, it felt like you were playing down Park Avenue—and a redesign had pumped life into Enniscrone's opening. It was still a gem, certainly, but by no means a hidden one, which, in my eyes, made it sparkle a bit less brightly.

Enniscrone remained a must-play, and the town was a cozy beach spot for those less interested in the crowds of Westport or Sligo, but I couldn't help but recall that former round with my dad, and that sensation of literally finding Enniscrone, stumbling upon it, that joy in not only golfing a wild links, but that singular contentedness of feeling like you were the only golfer on the planet who knew about it. And when we finished at Enniscrone on our first playing, we worked our way back out of the dunes and down to the clubhouse, looking at nothing but green hills dotted with sheep in the distance. But now, from eighteen tee, we looked at the back of a hotel, and a very unglamorous housing development. A golfer's prayer: that the same thing never happens to Carne.

On past trips to Ireland, Dad and I roamed the country like frenzied golfing vagabonds, a new hotel every night, a new eighteen every morning, our bus driver pouring us into the Shannon airport at week's end. This time around, Dad got to settle down, got to know the people and spend a few solid days walking the streets, breathing the air in the part of the world where his grandparents were born. And he even got some rest, refreshed and ready to take on those dunes. We both knew it was probably his final round in Ireland—touch wood, he's in fine health and has plenty of golf left in him, but at seventy-three, and having already made a half-dozen links pilgrimages to Ireland, he's got other spots to check off his list. If I hadn't been on this adventure, I doubt he could have brought himself to make that damn drive to JFK ever again.

But it was great that he had. Not just to see his son or take a more peaceful tour about the place, but because on the final hole at Enniscrone, he split the fairway with a modest drive, then knocked a low screaming three-wood along the turf, nearly reaching the green. He made a solid chip, six feet short of the hole.

I was away, but when it mattered, I knew Dad was going to putt out. And this one did matter—neither of us said it, but it was a roll significant beyond its six feet. And wouldn't you know it, Dad stepped up and parred his last hole in Ireland. Dead center the whole way.

Tbe Beacb Bar

Seven pints over par

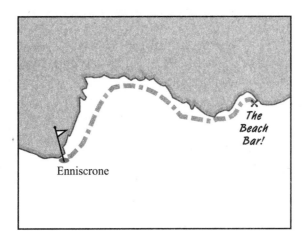

AS A RESULT OF MY DECISION TO SPEND FOUR MONTHS PLAYING
every links course in Ireland, there were two questions I
would now be faced with for the rest of my life. First: Which Irish
course reigned supreme? And second, a question I felt far more
qualified to answer: Which pub?

If I ever made it to Ballybunion, I planned on offering my
final ranking of the Irish courses, a list of the links where I'd be
heading back to first if the cost, the distance, and the chance that
I might be barred from some of them were all nonfactors. Course
rankings always seemed a sham to me, magazine filler for the
purpose of soothing egos or getting greenskeepers fired, so my list
would be entirely and stupidly subjective, prejudiced by nonsci-
entific criteria and nonsense. Did it rain? Did the layout boost my
ego or squash my spirit? Was my head foggy from last evening's
research? Did they make a fuss at reception? Did the caddy master see *A Gentleman's Game*? (One did, earning his course a free
pass into my top five.) Did they offer me a free logo ball, maybe

even the gift of a golf shirt that I couldn't possibly accept, but did anyway? In my journal, my course descriptions had ranged from pretty great to really great to even more great than really, but in the consideration and categorization of the pubs of Ireland, I was a far more discerning critic, a seasoned guru who would not be easily impressed. Pubs would be graded on a stringent four-pint scale, based on ambience, authenticity, and overall *craic*. And with those criteria in mind, I was surprised to find that the best pub in Ireland wasn't called something like The Purple Rose or The Drunken Shamrock, it wasn't some place named Paddy O'McMullicallahan's Traditional Irish Pub. Its name sounded like a place you'd go for happy hour in Cancun, an off-the-map spot called The Beach Bar.

Making my way from Enniscrone, I was heading into a spot on my map that had been covered with a question mark on a Post-it note. The only bed I was able to book along this stretch to Sligo was in an out-of-the way place called Aughris Head, but how far out of the way was the question—Aughris Head appeared to be situated at the end of a windy rural road whose mileage was impossible to discern on paper. It was during those twenty-one lonely miles to Aughris that the image first popped into my sun-softened brain, a picture of me standing atop a tall, black cliff, looking down into a hungry Atlantic, waves fighting the rocks below. A smile on my face, and hoisted above my head like some sort of Mayan sacrifice, a helpless sack of golf clubs. I still had three months and a dozen counties to go, but on the way to Aughris Head, I figured out exactly how this round was going to end.

Day dreams of club-tossing were interrupted by the first sign for The Beach Bar Bed & Breakfast, only eight kilometers away—just four miles to go (rounding off kilometer/mile conversions was another way to boost morale). I rewarded myself for walking in the right direction by dropping the bags and checking the pedometer—thirteen miles gone and at least 1,500 calories burned, I emptied my water bottle and steeled my psyche against a distance I knew couldn't be trusted, eight kilometers per a hand-painted pub sign, an unreliable navigator if ever there was one. But I couldn't help but congratulate myself early, because four miles would be three miles before I knew it, and two miles was a distance I considered just about there.

The sun was warm and a soft breeze helped me along a road that rolled downward toward the sea. Cars crowded with surfers would pass from time to time and send a honk my way, and I would wave in return. The first thirty minutes passed quickly, and I was three miles away before I'd even looked at my pedometer. I came to a crossroads and found another sign for the Beach Bar, an arrow affirming that yes, I was headed in the right direction, and that I only had nine kilometers—let's round up this time, six miles—left to go.

On a previous trip to Ireland, I sat at our mahogany hotel bar in the southwestern town of Killarney, conversing with an Irishman who explained to me that his absolute favorite thing about the United States was the exacting precision of our road signs. Their veracity left him gob-smacked: "There will be a sign telling you there's two miles to the exit. And by god, precisely two miles later, there it is! I thought that was fantastic. You'll see a sign, it says 8/10 of a mile to the next exit. I'd be looking at the dial, and bang, 8/10 of a mile, and not a step further."

I had previously found that conversation to be a little bit country cliché, tipsy Irishman comes to the States and writes home about our indoor plumbing. But as I looked up at that sign for the Beach Bar, the weight of an entire island sitting on my shoulders and the sound of tears splashing all around my feet, I had a whole new respect for the signage fan in Killarney who must have been on vacation from his home in Aughris Head.

And while it managed to remain a few kilometers ahead of me for most of the chase, I eventually caught up to the illusive Beach Bar, cornering it against the edge of the sea. I came to the adjoining B&B first, followed a teenager in surfer shorts up the stairs to a room where I dropped my bag and asked him without an ounce of courtesy, "Where's the pub?"

After making two Guinnesses disappear, my brain ache quieted down to a soft hum, and I was able to soak in my surroundings. I was sitting in a dimly lit room with one window and a fireplace. There was a man at the bar in a twisted up Yankees hat, across from two men seated at a table working on pint bottles of cider. A nine-year-old on a sugar high was bouncing around the room, begging change from his dad for another bag of crisps. There were five of us in the place, six counting the rosy-cheeked girl behind the bar, and the place felt comfortably crowded. The Beach Bar was three hundred years old, so I was told, rumored to have a history as a *sibin* (speakeasy), and that wasn't hard to believe. If I was ever going to smuggle whiskey into the country, or if I craved an unbothered pint, these four walls close to nothing but sand and waves would be the place. I sat there waiting for fishermen to kick open the door and come warm themselves by the fire as they leaned over bowls of stew, or a patch-eyed old man to walk into the room with a barrel of *potcheen* tucked under his arm (moonshine, named for the small pots in which it was distilled).

I stepped outside to make a call home to Allyson, my pint still in tow (another one of those things you don't need permission for—go ahead, take your glass outside, they trust you'll bring it back), and what I had missed on my way in made itself wonderfully clear. The bar was a low, white-walled building with a thatched roof, and it was perched on the edge of a lovely cove of sand and stone, the afternoon water looking black and cold. The beach was strewn with seaweed and puddles from a receding tide, and it was empty except for two dogs, a tubby white Labrador and a busy little terrier that reminded me of my dog back home. I sat on a picnic bench, looking at the afternoon sun skipping off the waves, the slopes of the Sligo mountains far across the bay. I watched the dogs play, the terrier hopping on the back of the old lab, trying to goad him into a chase.

I opened my phone, and found a text from a friend in Kinsale. I hadn't spoken with Patrick since Doonbeg, but he had a copy of my itinerary, and he told me that he'd hung a map on their living room wall where his daughters, seven and ten years old, were following my progress, sketching out my route and playing a sort of *Where in Ireland is the golfer today?* But it was still a bit of a surprise, and then a tremendous sensation of well-being, to not be the only person on the planet who knew where I was.

ON TO SLIGO TMW! ROSSES POINT, PLAY HARD! PADDY

If I had a car at my disposal, I would have spent the afternoon reminding myself to keep left and motored straight for Sligo and the safety of the Radisson by Rosses Point. Finding the Beach Bar was a mistake I would have avoided with a better map in my office, but after all the preparation, it was my accidents that provided what I was trying to plan for, something effortlessly and authentically Irish. It would have been harder to screw up like this in a rental car, and it would have cost me.

The Lab hopped up on the picnic table, his coat matted with wet sand. He walked over and sat down next to me, looking out at the ocean as if to say, *Pretty nice, huh?* I took quick stock of my world as I stood there—thatched pub, clean bed, cool pint of stout, a Labrador—and it was pretty nice, indeed.

ḣole 199

116 over par

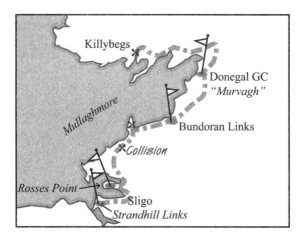

Cast a cold Eye
On life, on Death
Horseman pass by

Four years studying Irish literature, a semester spent working with one of the world's preeminent Yeats scholars from Oxford, and I still didn't know what it meant.

I had kept sightseeing side trips to a minimum, but if some tourist-friendly distraction happened to get in my way en route to the next tee, I might stop and snap a picture. And such was the case with Yeats's grave in Drumcliffe, just outside of Rosses Point. This was Sligo, Yeats country, and that lopped-off volcano up ahead was the Ben Bulben he wrote about, its parabolic slope covered with soft splotches of red and yellow. (I don't believe Yeats described it as parabolic in his verse, but it was.) So we stopped, dropped our packs, and wandered the graveyard and pondered over his epitaph, no matter if it put us behind schedule.

My wife hadn't seen anything but golf courses yet, and she was already on her way to another one.

Four weeks in, and it was something wonderful and surreal to meet Allyson in the Sligo train station. This course was playing far tougher than I had expected—my numbers were more robust than I had hoped, but it was those gaps between holes, the long days with no golf, just miles, where I came to understand that this was a course I might not complete. There were people who could handle six hours alone on roads that were all starting to look the same, who didn't mind another meal with a newspaper for company, and I tried to transform myself into one of those people, staying focused on small trials—one more mile, one more breakfast, *one day at a time*, I told myself, borrowing an AA adage that still held meaning for a guy with a pint glass stuck to his face. I curled myself up in the safety blanket of routine—water breaks on the hour, two pints in the pub with an *Irish Sun*, hunt down a takeout place, pray for a kebab, scarf it in bed, fall asleep to *Big Brother*. It wasn't glamorous, but it was consistent, and the consistent bits were the only thing keeping me moving along my map.

And then Allyson. One morning, there she was, standing in the train station with an army-green backpack on her shoulders. Was this my wife? Or just another backpacker whose bag I envied for its slenderness? It took me a day to get it—she was here, transplanted from some other universe that I had begun to think might not exist anymore. My cocoon of walk, golf, and eat had suddenly split open. The life where I didn't wash my underwear in a sink each night with a bar of hand soap crashed into the life where I did. I had counted the minutes until she got here, and once she had, it was wonderful. But I didn't expect it to be a little bit scary, too.

I hit the road with this blonde with the green backpack and made a short walk from Sligo to Strandhill. This must be my wife, I reasoned, because she followed me the whole way. I wasn't the only one surprised by who I was looking at—Allyson eyed me with a curious smile as we made our way out of town. It had only been a month since she had seen me last, but much had changed since she took that picture of a pale, round face standing outside the airport. Belly fat had somehow climbed its way up into my chest and shoulders, and my face looked as if some of it had melted away, revealing cheek bones and a discernable chin, my skin a healthy shade of summer. If my white shirt hadn't turned the color of dishwater, and if my shoes didn't smell like a flooded basement, I might have even felt sexy.

Allyson didn't quite agree that the seven-mile stroll out to Strandhill was the restful day I had advertised it as. I had tried to ratchet up the level of accommodations for Allyson's first visit, but when she dropped her bag in the quaint surfer town, our 1.5-star hostel was quite good enough. We were there. There could have been mice setting the table for breakfast and it would have been lovely. She wasn't walking another foot.

The Strandhill links was overshadowed by Rosses Point across the bay, but I had a soft spot for Irish courses inhabited by actual Irish golfers, where you saw guys in jeans throwing their bags onto trolleys in the parking lot and heading out with their sons. These were the courses where you witnessed firsthand evidence that golf was a less vain endeavor in Ireland, and largely a self-taught game (I had yet to see a driving range). I found the native Irish golf swing a perfect complement to the wild and untamed Irish landscape. There were some feral lashers roaming the rough of Ireland, unafraid to go out there and stink. On occasion, I'd even find an Irishman driving his golf ball reverse-handed—left hand low, a carryover from the way a hurling player might have gripped his hurley (his stick). We found some of that golf afoot in Strandhill, where the course was a bit rough but absolutely entertaining. Set on the side of a hill with fairways that felt like class-five rapids, the views of the sea and the Sligo mountainscapes were lovely. And the fourteenth hole that played like a hallway, squeezing you along a path between competing dunes, was one of my favorite Irish holes thus far, and not just because local gentleman referred to it as a part of the female anatomy (it wasn't a name they used on the scorecard).

It was a day back into Sligo, and then out to Rosses Point, where we checked into a tidy guesthouse overlooking the bay and the remains of an old farm on Oyster Island. (I loved the fact that the lady of the house wasn't there when we arrived because she'd snuck out for nine holes.) County Sligo Golf Club, or commonly known as Rosses Point, was founded in 1894, the current course laid out by Harry Colt in 1927. Its history was one of the most rich of any Irish links, but my favorite piece of the Rosses Point story, as explained in Jim Finegan's *Where Golf Is Great* (a book I had quite deliberately left at home—it weighs ten pounds), was that it was the childhood course of Pat Ruddy, the renowned Irish course designer who had picked up where Eddie Hackett left off, and who I hoped to bump into at one of his links along my way.

Golf holes were beginning to run together in my imagination, my Keens wandering an endless field of hills, gorse, and heather. Rosses Point proved that a links could be measured by more than the height of its dunes, and that a course laid out on linksland could be bold without having to scream it in your ear. Rosses Point lacked the unruly undulations that Americans came to Ireland to traverse, and it proved me wrong for thinking that a worthy links was nothing more than the sum of its humps. Rosses Point opened with four holes that felt like you were climbing to the top of Ben Bulben, then launched you down the backside of the hill to seaside terrain that, for feeling somewhat flat, was chockablock with intrigue. I loved the water hazards that I'd never seen replicated on another golf course, bottomless trenches like cracks in the earth snaking their way through the fairways and around the greens. The hulking dunes of Carne or Enniscrone would have only interrupted the views at Rosses Point— Ben Bulben seemed to follow you around the course, with water and the Sligo beaches surrounding you on three sides as you golfed your way out to the edge of Ireland. There was an understated grandeur to the course, a century's worth of subtleties locked in its contours. It was special in a way that made me understand why, once in a while, I'd meet a veteran of the Irish links who would tell me that, of all the courses in Ireland, he put Rosses Point at the top.

Allyson had it easy so far. A few sunny strolls, three picturesque golf courses, even a night in the Sligo Radisson, a rare Wi-Fi and satellite TV treat. So when we set off on day four, headed from Rosses Point to Mullaghmore, Ben Bulben looming far ahead of us, I thought it best not to tell her that by the time we sat down, the mountain would be behind us, and completely out of sight.

It was a warm morning and I followed behind, watching Allyson pick wildflowers from the side of the road, putting them in her pockets to be pressed when she got back home. It was smooth going on a road with plenty of shoulder, until we were a few miles past Yeats's grave in Drumcliffe, when the traffic stopped and a long line of cars clogged the N59. A few minutes later, we saw flashing red lights on the horizon and walked toward them to find a detour, officers diverting cars off to the left. We stopped.

"Is this okay?" she asked. She hadn't been in Ireland long enough to master the *give me a good reason why not* approach. So in front of a long line of drivers who were being redirected back where they came from, I was once again thankful for my choice of transport, as we walked past the barricade without a word from the police, and headed down a long, quiet stretch of empty motorway.

Thirty minutes later, there was still no indication of the reason for the detour. There were no cars aside from a few police cruisers roaring past us, and two ambulances headed in our direction, full throttle, returning from whatever it was we were about to see. After the sirens, the four-lane stretch was eerily quiet, cold, like all the world had succumbed to a virus and only the walkers were spared.

"I feel like those kids in *Stand By Me*," Allyson said.

"Like we're going to see a dead body. I know."

You heard stories in the news about "travelers," stories not about tourists, but about a problem. They were called traveling people or gypsies, or less charitably, tinkers, and I had only ever heard of them as the subject of a warning—*Mind your wallet, gypsies up ahead. Watch for that kid begging change, he's a tinker, won't let you alone.* On one afternoon, I was sitting in an empty pub waiting for fish and chips when the phone rang behind the bar. Seconds later, the staff was scrambling for the doors and bolting them shut. It was the police on the phone, I was told. There were travelers in the next village and they were feared to be headed our way, so at two o'clock in the afternoon, every pub in town shut its doors. Once travelers got into a pub, I was told, it was a struggle to get them out, and the damage they left in their wake could be considerable. Somehow a bunch of nomads with Land Rovers had become drunken huns in the Irish conscious-ness. These travelers were either a vicious breed of thieves and con men, or victims of a PR atrocity.

I would pass their camps on the side of the road, a few SUVs or vans with campers in tow, all the windows jammed full of in-discriminate junk. Blankets and pillows, stuffed animals and car-nival crap, the kind of tchotchkes you might pay a kid a buck for outside a rock show. And that was what we found spread over both sides of the N15, stuffed tigers and pink gorillas, knockoff Barbies and blow-up guitars. It was all spilled out of a white van that had been ripped open like a bag of chips. Up ahead, it looked like the van's engine had torn free and tumbled down the road. But the bundle of pipe and wire turned out to be another vehicle, one of those young man's homemade sports cars, folded up into a box of scrap.

A bus had stopped on the other side of the road and a few dozen witnesses were giving statements, watching as a cleanup crew pushed stuffed animals around with their brooms. A man in a leather jacket swung an empty can of Stella from his fingers and told us that two teenagers in the sports car had tried to overtake the bus. When they pulled out into the oncoming lane, they met a van full of travelers head-on. There were fifteen people in the van. They were all rushed away in ambulances, most of them alive, he could tell, but with some, it was tough to say.

I had found the Irish to be curiously preoccupied with speed-ing. There were ubiquitous roadside billboards begging motorists to slow down, and on television, the anti-speeding commercials were as graphic as a Tarantino flick. The whole country seemed to be talking about a recent television spot where a distracted driver pinned a kissing couple against a stone wall, dissecting the lad and leaving his lover's face a mangled web of purple scars. It brought the pub to a hush every time it came on, and it was on all the time. It seemed overkill to me, a small-time, small-town point of worry—must be nice to have time to fret about speeding, I thought, me the hardened Yank from one of America's murder capitals. But the truth was, I had never been so much as pushed in Philadelphia, while I had already come within a breath of dozens of those zipping roadsters. One slippery stone, one uneven ledge—I was an untied shoelace away from something far more serious than double bogey. Twenty-first-century engines and seventeenth-century roads were a toxic combination, and my wife was now here to see for herself what I was up against. She was white as we watched the police snap pictures of blood and gasoline mixed up in the muddy gravel.

"It was easier not knowing what the roads are like. I liked it better not knowing," she said. "This isn't safe, Tom. This isn't smart."

"Can't stop now." And we couldn't. There were still ten miles to Mullaghmore.

Somewhere around mile seventeen, Allyson was no longer worried about the Irish roads. She wasn't extolling me to come home or reminding me how hard it had been, spending her summer alone. She just shuffled her feet forward and mumbled, a few grunts from time to time, breathing like a spent race horse, a slightly lobotomized look on her face. I had walked that time-to-come-home talk right out of her.

You didn't just pass through towns as you logged miles across Ireland, you traversed various mental states. From an initial carpe diem exuberance, to the first quick stab of pain when you learned that you'd only been walking seven minutes, through a blast of confidence and pride, past an outburst of self-directed profanity that lasted until you reached the indomitable forward thrust, that eventually gave way to an infantile self-pity. But as we approached a town at mile eighteen that Allyson believed was Mullaghmore, only to find that it was Cliffony, and Mullaghmore was actually three more miles down the road (I knew it was Cliffony we were approaching, but didn't have the heart to tell her otherwise), she blew right past those latter stages and walked into a new mental landscape.

"If I get hit by a car, I don't think I'd feel it," she explained, somehow managing to move forward without the bottom of her hiking shoes leaving the pavement. "Then I could get in an ambulance. That would be nice."

After a twenty-one-mile day, the visit to Yeats's grave feeling like something we did back in college, we arrived in Mullaghmore. We checked into our hotel and Allyson dropped herself onto the bed and stared at the ceiling fan for a solid twenty minutes, mouth slightly agape, like she was watching a UFO.

"You better be playing golf tomorrow," she said.

Not only had the miles washed away any talk of my ending my journey, but I had inadvertently invented the guilt-proof golf trip, designing a golf getaway that even the most self-centered nudge of a spouse would find it impossible to resent her husband for. If anyone ever found himself afraid to suggest to his wife that she might enjoy spending an afternoon of her vacation sitting in a clubhouse while he played a quick eighteen, I had stumbled upon the solution: Hand her an overstuffed backpack, and ask her to walk to the course. Before you knew it, she'd be pushing you back out there to make it a long thirty-six.

The next morning, Mullaghmore wasn't the stupid sonofabitch, faraway bastard that Allyson had mistaken it for—it was actually a lovely little fishing town with a small harbor, and a long stretch of dunes beside the water that looked like a golf course that just needed pins. A fantastic stone manor atop a hillside seemed to scream *renovate me into a clubhouse* (if there ever comes a Mullaghmore National, I don't need the credit, but would appreciate a membership).

The three hours into Bundoran took us through three counties, from Sligo to twenty minutes crossing a sliver of Leitrim and into Donegal. It was my tradition to snap a picture of the destination town's sign upon arrival, and then visit the first pub in town for a celebratory pint of hydrating sports drink, washed down with a Carlsberg. We took a high-top table in the back of the Celtic bar, where every inch of the place was covered with soccer jerseys, team scarves, team pictures, and player portraits, none of which looked familiar to me. But I did notice that all the memorabilia was celebrating one team, that the posts in the pub were striped green and white, and that this bar wasn't Celtic as in the ancient Hibernian culture, but rather, the Glasgow Celtic soccer team, known because of their ringed green and white jerseys as the Hoops.

This being a Celtic bar was a far more meaningful association than the allegiances of sports bars back home, where one tavern was a Steelers hub while the wing joint across the street was overrun by Packers fans. Glasgow Celtic was considered the Catholic team of Scottish soccer, rivals of the Glasgow Rangers, a team in blue considered the Protestant alternative, and the rivalry between the two was bitter in a way that had no American equivalent. It was about religion and class with a nasty postcolonial hangover to the whole thing, and a closer look at the jerseys in the Celtic bar gave us a pretty strong impression of how complicated an enmity it was. There was a Celtic jersey on the wall for Bobby Sands, an IRA volunteer and famed hunger striker who died in protest of the treatment of Irish prisoners (at Celtic-Rangers games, Rangers fans had been known to sing songs mocking Sands on his deathbed—that's the kind of bitterness we're talking about). There were posters upping the IRA and a T-shirt from the Long Kesh Celtic Supporters, Long Kesh being a prison for Republican paramilitaries. Just outside the pub, we found a small memorial similar to so many of the grottoes or religious shrines that I'd already passed, but this one was a memorial to the Republican hunger strikers, and a flyer advertised a fund-raiser that weekend for the families of imprisoned freedom fighters. And in case I wasn't convinced that Glasgow Celtic loyalty had little to do with being from Glasgow and everything to do with being Catholic, a few more days down the road into Donegal, I would find a tall stone cross on the side of the road marking the spot from which the first piece of sod for the new Celtic stadium had been taken.

I knew that if I ever found myself trying to enjoy myself in a pub and overheard a publican waxing about the Troubles or boasting about the IRA, I could safely guess that they were American. The Irish knew better. Thus far, Ireland was a country on

the move, a population bored with the old grudges, a place content in its liberty and its success. That cause seemed like old history for the roadside monuments—Ireland was about software
companies and property development and world-class resorts,
not car bombs and gun runners. But something changed when we
walked into Bundoran in County Donegal. As we drew closer to
the Northern Ireland border, there was a sense that folks in this
far corner of the country might not be quite as ready, or as able,
to forget about the flag they were waving next door. And it struck
me how far I had actually traveled. Not for the mileage—I tallied
the distance every evening and a new number was just more ink
in my journal—but for the fact that I had walked far enough to
see attitudes change and accents thicken. Ireland was a country
of counties, thirty-two in total, each with its own traditions and
points of pride, and Donegal was the sixth my shoes had visited.
The Irish counties were divided into four provinces, each having
once been controlled by an Irish high king—there was the southwestern province of Munster where my trip had begun, the eastern province of Connacht where I'd just spent a month searching
out my next tee box, and the southeastern province of Leinster
which lurked on the other side of my map, a far-flung destination
I could hope for but couldn't quite believe. And then there was
the province in the north, two syllables that snapped off your
tongue and begged some attention—it didn't occur to me until
the Celtic bar in the county of Donegal that while we were still in
the Republic of Ireland, we had just walked into Ulster.

For a course I had never heard of, a links that hardly made the
flip side of an American golfer's checklist, the history of the Bundoran Golf Club was worth a stop in itself. An 1894 vintage
made Bundoran one of the oldest clubs in Ireland, and like most
courses of that era, it owed its beginning to either the British
Army or to the railroads—in Bundoran's case, the latter. Travel-
happy Victorians saw the rails expanding all over Ireland, and
where there was a train station, there came a hotel followed by a
golf course. This formula led to an Irish golf explosion during the

late nineteenth and early twentieth centuries, and while Colt and Hackett and Ruddy get much of the glow from the game's success in Ireland, a gentleman named George Baillie should have his bust added to the mantel. Baillie designed courses for the Great Northern Railway, and in a short period of time, laid out courses in Lisburn (1891), Larne (1894), Knock (1895), Magilligan (1896), Greenore (1896), Castlerock (1900), Scrabo (1907), Omagh (1910), and in 1894 the links at Bundoran beside the railway's Great Northern Hotel.* Bundoran would get a 1927 redesign by no less than Harry Vardon, and from 1951 through 1957, Christy O'Connor Sr., one of Ireland's all-time greatest golfing sons, served as the club's head pro. More than one linksman in Donegal shared with me the story of Christy O'Connor on Bundoran's thirteenth hole. Christy was playing with a foursome of members one afternoon when he came to the 220-yard par-three, where he proceeded to knock his ball onto the green. One of the members inquired as to what club Christy had used.

"Three-iron," he answered. To which the member replied, "Really? I only needed a four."

Christy walked over to his bag, took out ten golf balls, and proceeded to knock each of those golf balls onto the green, starting with his one-iron, and working his way all the way down to his wedge.

The Bundoran course was short and a plain in spots, lacking the drama and definition of a truly notable links, but it did get interesting as we played our way around the Great Northern Hotel and headed for the water. The eleventh hole, a par-four that stretched along the beach cliff and played toward a long strand ahead of you with surfers sitting atop the waves, was one of the best holes I'd played in weeks. And the reception from the Bundoran staff and membership only bolstered my hypothesis that, at least when traveling with a Yankee twang, there existed an inverse relationship between the warmth of the welcome and the fame of the golf course. It was a theory with exceptions, but it seemed to me that folks at the lesser links were especially ap-

---

* My education on Mr. Baillie and the lost courses of Donegal came courtesy of Tom Plunkett, club historian at Narin & Portnoo Golf Club.

preciative of your patronage, and that was certainly the case in Bundoran, where the assistant pro made a fuss over the American popping in as a single, and did me the favor of matching me up with a pair of members already halfway down the first, thus sparing me from another afternoon of golf for one (Allyson was taking a nap in the hotel—see, the walking works!), saving me from another four hours fighting with myself over what constituted a gimme.

One of the members' names was Michael (his friend pronounced it as the Irish *Me-haul*), a white-haired gentleman with watery eyes. He didn't bring his club back very far, but he kept his ball in front of him and he played fast (if you couldn't play quickly, it was best to stick to your Long Island foursome—the Irish played fast, aware of what the weather could do). He was soft-spoken and grandfatherly, but with fire in his belly yet. In the clubhouse, he showed us a faded photograph of a younger, red-cheeked version of himself and Jack Nicklaus taken back in the age of white belts, the tips of their collars touching their shoulders, and Michael's hair slicked back tight. I nearly fell off my stool when he told me he was a devotee of Jimi Hendrix and Janice Joplin, and that he was headed to a rock festival up the road this weekend. He was a generous host, proud of his club and his town. I had walked through Bundoran on my way to the course, leaving Allyson in the not–so–Grand Hotel, and found streets lined with burger joints and souvenir shops and enough arcades to suck all the change out of Ireland. I had the sense it was a happening spot before everyone started booking two-dollar flights to Ibiza.

"They call Bundoran the Vegas of Donegal," Michael said with a smile. "I've been to Vegas, so I know we're no Vegas. But we do get a crowd."

When word slipped that I had walked into Bundoran from Mullaghmore (as it sometimes slipped when I was thirsty), and into Mullaghmore from Philadelphia, the free pints came quick, two women at the table next to us asking me to stand up and show everyone my shoes. Michael knew Mullaghmore well, and I asked him about that estate overlooking the town, where a tall iron gate guarded the entrance to what looked like a castle sitting

atop a hill. He explained that the house belonged to the great-
uncle of Prince Charles, Lord Mountbatten, who spent his summers in Mullaghmore. He said Mountbatten was popular with
the locals, that he could be seen walking around town and wasn't
against coming down to the village for a pint and a chat. The IRA
blew up his boat in Mullaghmore Harbor in 1979. Three others
were killed in the blast, including a fourteen- and a fifteen-year-
old boy. Michael sounded sadly resigned when he called it, "A
dent in Irish history."

That evening we ate at a restaurant on Michael's recommen-
dation, a fine-dining establishment where Allyson would learn a
few of the tricks of Irish dinner service. First, in the more upscale
restaurants, you ordered your dinner while you sat in the bar or
lounge and didn't go into the dining room until your first course
was waiting for you at your place. I thought it a nice variation on
our routine back home—two rooms for the price of one—but it
tested my dad's patience back in Crossmolina, where he couldn't
help himself from standing up every two minutes and heading for
the dining room, only to be rebuffed by a waiter who assured him
that, no, they still hadn't forgotten about us. Allyson also figured
out that the scale for beef doneness in Ireland ranged from gray
to anthracite. Our steaks were large and lovely, but the only thing
medium about them was their medium shade of brown. European beef had taken its knocks over the years, and I could understand a chef erring on the overcooked side, but if you really
wanted pink in Ireland, you had to be prepared to fight for it.
Dad asked for a burger done medium in Enniscrone, and you
would have thought he had asked for donkey meat. The waitress
returned from the kitchen, terrified. "I'm sorry, sir, but the chef
won't do a burger medium. He just won't do it."

The food at Michael's favorite restaurant was otherwise tasty
and the ambience homey, aside from the table next to us where a
gentleman in short sleeves and a green tie was trying to prove
right centuries worth of ethnic slurs, and putting me off potatoes
for a week. Each table was brought the same sides to share—
along with carrots and greens came a generous helping of au gra-
tin potatoes, a banquet-sized bowl of boiled potatoes, and a
baked potato for each of us. Allyson looked at our table, eyes

The 14th at Doonbeg

Blasting out
at Lahinch

Mile 14 on the Bog Road

The case for sidewalks

The Cliffs of Antrim

In Waterville

The greenskeeper
at Achill Island

Golfing into
the clouds at
Rosses Point

A session at O'Connors in Doolin

The Beach Bar,
Aughris Head

My drinking companions at
the Beach Bar

Dad gives it a lash at Enniscrone

Allyson, desperate for Mullaghmore

Allyson encounters Irish rush hour

The Full Irish

Fine dining on
the road

What Guinness
can make you do

Crossing the
Carrick-a-Rede
Rope Bridge

Holding on
for dear life
in Baltray

Surf's up in Ballycastle

Down 18 to the Ardglass Clubhouse

The first tee at Royal County Down

bunched with confusion, as if we'd been brought someone else's dinner (I knew I'd been in Ireland too long when three sides of potatoes didn't strike me as funny), but in the face of so much starch, the guy next to us stopped his waitress and asked her to please bring him a bowl of French fries. It was enough to make me reach for the carrots. But I didn't.

After dinner, we met up with Michael in a happening pub beside the bridge in the center of town where Allyson enjoyed her first true Irish session. A carpenter with prickly black hair joined our table and tried to pick up Allyson while I was in the bathroom. She was rescued when I returned to the table to prove that she was indeed married, which only inspired the young man to try twice as hard (the lads weren't shy). He was mid-woo when he decided to up his ante by going out to his truck and retrieving a banjo and jumping into the session, joining a fiddle, a guitar, and an accordion. Unfortunately for him, I found his banjo playing more attractive than my wife did—I continued to be amazed that the young Irish could play these songs and these instruments, and that they kept banjos in the backseat, just in case.

We stayed until last call, then tried to slip out during the final song before our friend's banjo was back in its case. We found the front door locked and a bartender with braided hair standing beside it with arms crossed, shaking her head at us like we had just done something very stupid. We turned around to see every person in the bar, even the old man who could hardly lift himself off his stool, standing and signing with hands over their hearts.

"They're playing the anthem," she informed us. "You'll have to wait."

For a wannabe Irishman, it was sad that I didn't know better or even recognize the tune. I didn't recall hearing it anywhere else in Ireland, and I certainly hadn't seen a session end like this one, an entire pub standing at reverent attention at half past midnight. But this was the lost county up in northwest Ulster—not just proud to be Irish, you could tell, but proud to be Ireland.

One of the most obvious indications of Ireland's new prosperity was the fact that the entire country seemed to be taking part in one enormous wedding celebration. Where there was a town, there was a hotel, and where there was a hotel, I would find a wedding, my backpack bumping into full-blast nuptial bacchanalia on a Thursday, Friday, even a Wednesday evening. On any given Saturday, the village sidewalks would be dotted with pink and purple bridesmaids as vintage cars covered in streamers and soapy messages honked their way around the town square.

Weddings were surely less common in a not-too-long-ago Ireland that had watched its population decline for 150 years, its marrying-age citizens shipping off to Boston and Manchester. But that had all changed, and the whole country seemed to be twenty-three years old, under the influence of hair gel and cigarettes and in possession of at least one Liverpool jersey. Packs of kids with ice cream slathered faces roamed the towns and the cities looking for something to do, and hotel breakfasts were beginning to feel like day care, where I would hide myself in the corner, away from the high chairs, dodging projectile porridge. An unpleasant side effect of the laid-back, why-not attitude was that Irish parents were not bashful about bringing their offspring into a restaurant and unleashing them on the room, sticky-fingered sugar bombs bouncing from table to table. You could shoot sideways glances until your eyeballs ached, but if Dad had his cider and Mom her chardonnay, it didn't matter that their kid had your pant leg—the wee ones had run of the room.

I had already walked into the jaws of a dozen weddings or the lobby-strewn remains thereof, and as with children at breakfast I tried to keep my distance. I never saw an actual reception, just the guests floating around the periphery of the festivities. They were there every time I checked in—slack-tied teenagers sipping vodka Red Bulls in the lobby, huddles of groomsmen passing around cigarettes in the parking lot, tipsy bridesmaids cozying up to skinny kids swimming in their dress shirts—and there at every checkout—a hundred hangovers back in the bar at breakfast, bracing themselves with cider and breakfast fry-ups, arguing with one another over their room charges. In sweat-stained nylon and a backpack, crossing paths with a wedding party always made me feel underdressed. And in amazingly good health.

In Donegal Town, Allyson and I counted no less than seven wedding parties honking their way around the town square in ribboned Rolls-Royces. And it was one of those pairs of newly-weds that we had to thank for unknowingly pointing us to St. Ernan's House, a guesthouse just outside the town situated on its own tiny island in Donegal Bay, a spot that Allyson and I agreed was pretty much pure magic.

After leaving Michael in Bundoran, we had traveled through Ballyshannon to the Donegal Golf Club, known locally as Murvagh, an Eddie Hackett design from 1976 with a recent touch-up from Pat Ruddy. Situated at the edge of a pine forest, Murvagh was built on a thumb of sandy soil protruding into the bay. Against a backdrop of rippling mountain peaks with Donegal Bay in the foreground, Murvagh was an unadorned, built-by-an-unapologetic-ocean, discovered-by-a-lawnmower links, lacking the cliffside tee boxes and stinging ocean spray of some of Ireland's top destination courses, but a layout packed with wind-whipped grasses and pleasantly rumpled fairways. A par of 73 made it one of Ireland's longer links, and a weekday rate of 55 made it a special reward for travelers willing to try the north-west.

Overtired before I reached the first tee (walking Ireland had furnished my golf ego with a bevy of excuses), I played Murvagh like I'd just learned about golf in the parking lot, taking 94 strokes to get around the property and hitting enough sideways shots to get my wife wondering aloud, "Is there something wrong with you?" Allyson preferred the front nine for its views of the bay spotted with tiny islands, though it seemed the less dramatic than the back nine. She snapped pictures of one island in particular, a tree-covered plot that wasn't larger than a football field and was surrounded by an old stone wall. Per the girl working in the pro shop, there was a castle at the heart of the island that you could muck your way out to at low tide. Murvagh also won a top rating for coolest club logo—against a golden shield, an outstretched arm held a defiant red cross as if wielding a claymore, the Latin motto *In hoc signo vinces* ("In this sign, you will conquer") inscribed underneath. It was the O'Donnell family crest and it made one want to go out and golf vigorously, and for God.

Ireland's history reads like a thousand-year melee, a new battle or invasion or rebellion with each turning page, and Donegal's place in that history was a particularly bloody one. The northwestern county hosted countless dustups between rival O'Donnell and O'Neill clans, and its chieftains had been doing battle with the English since the thirteenth century. It was explained to me by a trustworthy bartender in Donegal Town that the cross in hand on the O'Donnell shield symbolized the blessing bestowed by priests upon soldiers heading off to fight (while I preferred the pub explanation, further investigation mentioned a legend claiming that the mark of the cross was put on the shield of a converted O'Donnell by St. Patrick himself). It was a proud and defiant image, and thus seemed perfectly suited to the Donegal denizens, with their accents that seemed to peak a few beats earlier than elsewhere, and who I was enjoying as much as any people in the country. But that still didn't mean I wanted to spend my last weekend with Allyson in the hotel at the edge of Donegal Town, where our three-star digs had been overrun by every Irish citizen of marrying and drinking age. We politely pushed our way through the gray suits and empty glasses in the lobby, canceled our reservation (they kindly obliged), and headed for the nearest bookstore, where we pored over the travel section (better than hauling around a Fodor's, I had learned, was to make use of the one waiting for me in the next bookshop along the road), and learned of a guesthouse just outside town that sounded too strange to skip.

A Catholic encyclopedia pointed me to four different St. Ernan's from Ireland, all of which were a thousand years too old to enjoy the house that would bear their name. A taxi driver drove us through what he called the well-to-do side of Donegal (I did allow myself tangential taxi trips to and from restaurants, hotels, restarting my course from where it left off), and I got my first glimpse of American-size suburban spreads overlooking Donegal Bay. It seemed impossible that we were headed toward what the guide book described as a luxury country home set on its own island, but not two miles from Donegal Town, the road ended at a black iron gate, and a one-way stone bridge led us out to a small stamp of an island, not larger than the islands I'd spotted from Murvagh's fourth hole, just enough room for a parking lot and a few gardens and the house itself.

Our room was large with water views from every window (advantage of booking a room in an island hotel: impossible to get stuck with a resort view), and in minutes we were asleep in a bed that felt like a boat, the sound of the bay lapping against the stone banks all around us. St. Ernan's was old without feeling worn, spacious rooms full of soft chairs and delicate veneers, and it was without a doubt the tidiest house floating in Donegal Bay. I didn't want to leave, and not just because we had found the perfect Irish guesthouse, but because leaving St. Ernan's meant putting Allyson on a bus at the crack of dawn and not seeing her for another two months. I'd abandoned my plug-along, keep-swinging spirit back in Sligo, and as I stood there watching her bus pull away in the rain at six in the morning, I needed it back more than ever. Two choices—keep walking toward Killybegs in the downpour, or stay right where I was, content with the miles and holes I'd already covered, and wait for the next bus to the airport.

You would hear fishermen in the pub complain about having nothing to do, and if you didn't know any better, you might tell them to get off their duffs—it's an island, for crying out loud. But after decades of overfishing, fish quotas had been tightened by the European Parliament. Irish waters were now shared with the rest of Europe's fleet, and the biggest kids on the block took the biggest slice of the cake. Spain seemed a popular scapegoat in the pub, enemy number-one of landlocked fishermen who pointed to her huge and supposedly unscrupulous fleet as the root of their problems. Whoever was to blame, in the coastal village of Killybegs, the crisis was clear. It sat larger than a herd of elephants smack in the center of town. Long rows of shiny trawlers the size of battleships were parked in the harbor by the dozens. It was still morning when I arrived in town, but no ships were sailing, no slips were empty, and the docks themselves were devoid of a single crate or net or rubber boot, like a ghost town for old boats if they didn't all look so fresh from the factory. Those bright and towering ships, their condition told a story: that things were going well here, and then quickly, they weren't.

My B&B wasn't ready for me to check in when I arrived, so I found a small park across from the harbor. It was still raining and cold, and I sat on a bench beneath a tree for cover and watched the boats stuck there in the dark water.

I knew they were coming. Four months on the road, even on a golf trip in Ireland, I was sure they'd catch up with me somewhere. And they did in Killybegs, my wife on her way to the airport and me sitting on that bench in the rain, wishing my dad and I had gone fishing in the Keys instead of golfing in Ireland, tired of this game and done with this country. It was the shit times, and they were here.

hole 271

178 over par

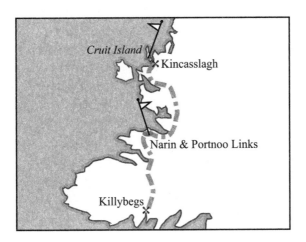

IT WAS ALL UP TO NARIN & PORTNOO. MY INTEREST IN IRELAND flagging, my love of golf fading by the footstep, the momentum in the battle between my mind's reason and my heart's romance was shifting fast, and reason was delivering the blows. My clubs were minutes from being loosened from my back and tossed to a salt-corroded hereafter when a car on the road to Narin pulled up beside me and rolled down the window. I was expecting the offer of a lift, an offer that, in my softened condition, I was ready to take. But I was surprised when a man in glasses and a thick Donegal accent asked, "Mr. Coyne, I presume?"

Not only had the driver and his wife been following my progress online and in the newspapers, but they said the lads at the golf club were waiting for me, and asked if I might stop in for a drink at their home across the street after my round. And in the space of a three-minute conversation, I was slapped out of my endgame fantasies and returned to the business at hand. This wasn't a lost and lonely nightmare—this was again a quest, larger than my growing pile of scorecards. There were readers out there with me. There were friends who'd given their weeks and their calves to this journey, and still more to come. There were husbands the golfing world over counting on my shoulders to prove that there was no such thing as too much golf, too much Ireland, too much Carlsberg. Strangers were following me; they had stopped by the side of the road and called me by name. I felt heroic. I felt like Forrest Gump. And then I felt like an ass not long thereafter, as I stood in the middle of a cow pasture, clubs slung over my shoulder, grass up to my nose and an electric fence separating me from the Narin & Portnoo golf course, wondering if any golf course—even one called Ireland—was really worth this latest, and most unnecessary, kick to my twins.

My friends from the road had pointed me toward a hotel from where I could see red and purple sweaters pulling trolleys across the Narin & Portnoo fairways in the distance, a wide lake beneath my window separating me from the golf course. My options to the golf course were either forty minutes around the water via the road I had already traversed, or the innkeeper's alternative, my favorite two words in Ireland—"short" and "cut"—*aicearra* in Irish, which was how I wished he might have phrased it, because it might have scared me back onto the road.

I believed I was making a wise decision when I headed down the road and hopped a stone wall and started out across a farmer's fallow patch, traipsing toward a golf course just a few hundred yards away, but the problems with the innkeeper's detour presented themselves quickly. First, the field of tangled thistle had not been mowed since the time of St. Patrick, and each step was like pulling my foot out of cement, then sticking it back in. But it wasn't the wasted minutes or missed tee time or the lactic acid sweating out of my thighs that troubled me most—it was the embarrassment. I thought I had left vanity back on a roadside in Kilkee, but it was impossible to feel like anything but an idiot as I stood on the wrong side of a cattle fence trying to look confident with golf clubs hanging from my shoulder, as if I wasn't really lost and trapped, but had chosen to golf my ball around a field of chin-high weeds. I waved to passing foursomes on the other side of the wire, golfers nodding *hello* and *good day* in my direction, all of us taking part in a doomed charade where I wasn't really the biggest ass in Donegal. I trudged the length of the field—two, maybe three holes long, it seemed—looking for a gate or broken bit of fence, finding none, and startling a young couple on the second green who stopped putting when I suddenly appeared at the edge of the brush, some ginger-haired golfing yeti restricted from the golf course by three rungs of electrified wire. They stared for a while, until I finally confessed, "I was looking for a shortcut," hoping they might be able to point me in the right direction. But they just smiled and shrugged and the woman giggled, encouraging me to head back from whence I came.

I climbed back out of the field and discovered the turnoff the innkeeper had spoken of, the one *after* the farmer's driveway, and I found a path that did lead into the heart of the golf course. I was a few hours behind schedule when I arrived at the Narin & Portnoo clubhouse, a cozy, utilitarian building where pro shop, men's grill, women's lounge, and restaurant were all situated in the same simple room. There was something about less-is-more golf clubhouses that seemed to make the membership more fraternal than most, as in Spanish Point, where it didn't matter if you wanted a candy bar or a sleeve of balls or a beer, or if you were there to inquire how John was recovering, or how Mary had faired in her match—it happened around the same handful of tables. In the Narin & Portnoo clubhouse, I sat down with a gentleman named Sean, a solid Donegal man with white hair and a thick build, the kind of Irishman you shook hands with and believed in the benefits of root vegetables. Sean seemed as multi-purpose at Narin & Portnoo as the clubhouse—golf pro, starter, and manager in one. Immensely proud of his club, he told me the first tee was open to me whenever I liked, as long as I remembered to tell everyone that Narin & Portnoo was the best course in Ireland. But before I got into negotiating my rates—soup, sandwich, and a sleeve of balls went a long way toward a warm review—I thought I'd give the course a once-over myself, where I found there would be very little need for bribery at all.

Sean found a spot for me with a threesome of members—Pat, Jimmy, and Frank, who made sure my first round in an Irish four-ball lived up to the billing. Almost as entertaining as the golf

course was my playing partner, Patrick, the jokes falling out of
his pockets like tees.

*So Michael was in the clubhouse talking to anybody who
would listen to him. "Jaysus," he says, "I couldn't make a putt. I
was hitting the corner of the hole all day long." Corner of the
hole, all day long, he says. So I finally go over to him and I draw
a circle on his napkin, and I ask him, "So tell me, Michael, exactly which fucking corner were you hitting?"*

I hated to waste a stunning links and a sunny afternoon on
empty legs, but the farmer's untamed meadow had sapped a tres-
passer's strength. I dragged my clubs around dunes where golf
had been played since 1903, the current course born in 1930 as a
nine-holer, expanded to eighteen holes in 1965, and the original
par of 69 stretched to 73 in 2004. It was clear why golf had flour-
ished on this warren during a century in which courses all over
Donegal had disappeared (Narin's course historian had discovered records of a handful of Narin courses that had vanished by
the start of the Great War). The links possessed a work-your-
way-out, fight-your-way-back layout stretched along the bay, and
after a few pedestrian starters, the course was at a sprint from the
fifth hole onward, a links not so much built through the dunes of
Narin, but simply laid upon them. We rolled our golf balls over
peaks and into gorges, battling a sparsely bunkered course that
let the wind and weeds do the punishing. Classic and under-
worked a la Rosses Point, it was a pleasure to golf one's ball
across lumpy golf holes that could be attacked ten different ways.
Golf was great again—until the back-to-back-to-back par-fives of
thirteen, fourteen, and fifteen, which at the end of that marathon
afternoon felt like death by golf (the sixteenth was a nice reward
for one's perseverance, a lovely downhill flip-wedge of a par-
three). As we played back along the field where I had been quarantined earlier that afternoon, I was pleased enough with Narin
& Portnoo that I didn't weep or swear or try to drive a Titleist
into the side of the tractor that was busy chopping fifteen summers' worth of grass down to fairway height. Apparently the
pointing golfers hadn't been the only ones watching me that afternoon, wondering where in the hell I was going with those golf
clubs.

I had been studying up on my O'Donnells and the high kings of Ireland, had read stories of Niall of the Nine Hostages, who enslaved Saint Patrick and brought him to Ireland, had heard all about the earls who made the famous flight from Rathmullan. But as I made my way from Narin up to Kincasslagh, a pronunciation I've butchered from that afternoon to this, mine were the only ears in Ireland unfamiliar with the O'Donnell of real consequence, Kincasslagh's favorite son, the easy-listening superstar Daniel O'Donnell, whose dreamy gaze greeted me in the foyer of my hotel, the map on the wall telling me I had unknowingly hiked into the heart of "Daniel O'Donnell Country." Fans came from around the world, I was told, to see his home and breathe the air that inspired albums like *Daniel in Blue Jeans* and *From Daniel with Love*, but I had come to this yonder edge of Ireland for something else—an unknown bit of rock called Cruit Island, which no Irishman had ever crooned about before.

After my afternoon plodding along a fence line like a reprobate golfer out for his hour of sun, I was disappointed—rather, I was crushed—to hear that my next course was still a good hour "on the hoof" from my hotel. Cruit Island (prounounced *crutch* or *critch*) was a late itinerary add-on, and I was beginning to wonder why I had circled so many nine-holers on my map. While they were quick and charming, these half-tracks weren't going to compete with grand layouts triple their size. And as the miles piled up, was another nine-hole course really worth the blisters? I was tempted to push off to my next town and get a headstart on the long journey to Rosapenna, when the large man with a buzz cut behind the hotel desk read my frustration and asked, "So you really don't have a car?"

"No, I don't."

"You really walked here? From Narin?"

I couldn't even muster a nod to the *Yer really walking?* inquiry, nary a humph. I dreamt of a waterproof baseball cap that read simply: *Yes, I'm walking. Yes, I'm an eejit.*

"Well if you really want to walk, you don't want the main

road. There is another way, but . . ." He scratched his afternoon stubble, looking out the window at the skies behind us. ". . . the tide's out. You should be all right."

Now I would typically steer clear of shortcuts that were contingent upon the gravitational interaction of the earth and moon. But I was hot and I was cranky and chafed on a steamy afternoon, pissed off to be playing Ireland as a onesome, and just ornery enough to say screw it, I would risk death by rising ocean water to get me off the road four minutes faster.

While the road out to Cruit seemed to take me left, the attendant pointed me right toward an old church in the distance. Behind the church I would find a path down to the beach. And when I came to the beach, there I would see the way out to Cruit. It would easily save me a half hour, he promised.

I stood at the end of the path behind the old church, looking at an endless stretch of shoe-swallowing mud, a wide harbor drained of water and stretching outward for miles. I called the hotel, just to make sure I wasn't about to become the dumbest tourist in Irish history.

"I'm looking at a bunch of sand here," I complained into my mobile phone. "Don't see any golf course."

"Golf course is on the other side of the island. Just follow the road out to the green and white caravan."

The road? Neither in my immediate vision, nor in any of my heat-fired hallucinations did there exist a road, no green and white caravan. But in all fairness to my friend, after giving his advice a chance, I did find a lone pair of tire tracks in the sand heading out into the dry harbor. For twenty minutes, I made shallow footprints across an expanse of uncovered sea-bottom, and I felt a sensation akin to pulling up to the clubhouse at Pine Valley, or passing through the gates at Augusta and eyeing that immaculate white scoreboard that read MASTERS—it was an overwhelming feeling of *cool*. I was walking across sand that would be meters beneath the waves in a few hours, passing small islands of stone and grass that would be unreachable soon, out in the farthest, rockiest, bluest reaches of Donegal. I felt like the only man on the course, the only player on the planet, and for the first time since Killybegs, it didn't bother me a bit. I felt lucky to be alone as I climbed up onto one of the islands dotting the bay, and I found a stone cross atop the rocks, placed there in 1940, with an inscription that read, "May this cairn be a blessing to all who pass, and a beacon to guide them safely back to their homes and loved ones."

The tire tracks eventually led me to a green and white caravan, which led me to a path, which brought me to a road, which saved me a chunk of my trip to Cruit Island. I arrived at Cruit ready to be underwhelmed. I found the course to be entirely inhospitable to a newcomer, with seven out of the nine holes playing blind. Without a clue where I was headed much of the time, I spent most of the afternoon accidentally hitting into locals, and locals retaliated by accidentally hitting into me. Not only did I need a helmet at Cruit Island, but I found that a number of the shrunken greens were of an unreasonable slope. The course was short by any standard, and the whole property was dissected by an ugly string of telephone wires. And for all that, Cruit Island might have been the loveliest little stretch of golf holes in Ireland.

I played a second nine to make up for my first go-round, which was, considering the number of blind tee shots, something of an exploratory venture. A purist might have balked at a design where everything wound its way out of your view. The eighth hole was a weakish par-three, and sure, the phone lines were an eyesore. But if you could play Cruit Island on a clear day and not admit that the *craic* was mighty, then you were surely a golfing curmudgeon, that guy I wished they would have stuck in someone else's cart. At Cruit, the holes dropped off precipices with winding banks like something out of a skateboard park, while all around you the waves of the North Atlantic burst on the black claws of Donegal's coast. And whether you enjoyed the rest of the course or not, whether you spent the other parts of your afternoon wondering why you had wandered so far from Doonbeg, I dared any sighted golfer to deny that the sixth at Cruit Island was, yard for yard, one of the best holes in the world.

Seventeen at Sawgrass? A respite. Pine Valley's Devil's Asshole? A mere pothole in comparison to the abyss of sea-cave and closing tide that separated tee from green on the sixth at Cruit. At

150 yards, it played nine-iron on my front nine, choke-down three-iron into a new wind on the back. You faced a gnarled cavern of eroded ocean tunnels at low tide, with ocean spray licking your toes when the tide turned in. I would have been pleased enough to find this sort of scenery on a helicopter tour or a climbing expedition, let alone have the pleasure of trying to knock down a seven-iron over it.

I found a story about Daniel O'Donnell in a British newspaper where he talked about his passion for golf, and he named his favorite golf course in Ireland. I'd say we had different tastes in music, but when it came to judging a links, the man knew more than most so-called experts. Scores of golfers came to Ireland to cross off names on a list from a magazine, satisfied they had the place covered, but O'Donnell and I both knew why they hadn't. Because they were heading home without ever having mispronounced Kincasslagh, or learning the right way to say Cruit.

hole 307

197 over par

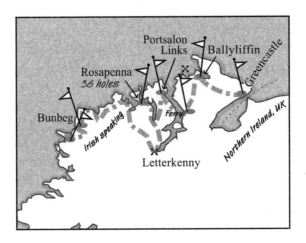

IT WAS A TRIP ABOUT FIRSTS AND ONLYS—FIRST SET OF STICKS humped around Ireland, only golfer in the clubhouse who smelled like a wet bath mat—but I hadn't planned to walk away from the Gweedore golf course knowing that I was, without a doubt, the first and only American golfer who ever traveled to the town of Bunbeg, paid for a hotel room, and even cleaned his clubs the night before, all for the purpose of playing the Gweedore nine-holer. Not to say that the golf course, or, more precisely, the sheep pasture missing nine cup-sized chunks of turf, didn't have its moments—undulating, certainly, it played up, down, and around a crest at the heart of the property, and I had a soft spot for livestock on a links. But Gweedore was so crowded with piles of warm Raisinets left by the wooly flocks roaming the fairways and nibbling the whole place down to the nub, that I spent my morning looking for my next step, instead of soaking in the Bunbeg seaside which, when I noticed it, was gorgeous.

The back side of the golf course rolled its way down to golden

beaches and calm, blue waters, the white cottages across Gweedore
Bay just visible in the distance. If it was my local track, I'd take it
over a boring park course, certainly, and some of the mounding
was true links. But I remembered it most for the attention I had
to give to the soles of my shoes, the signs in front of the closed
clubhouse that were all in Irish, the fact that I played to the wrong
green twice and still wasn't sure if I'd played nine holes, seven, or
maybe thirteen, and that I spent ten minutes watching the greenskeeper chase a stray goat back onto the goat half of the property,
stalking him down the fairway, whooping and waving his arms
and chasing the animal back through a gate that I swore I didn't
leave open, even though I was the only player on, or even near,
the Gweedore course. I had arrived that morning to a closed
clubhouse, the sign by the first tee explaining TAÍLLÍ 20 DEIREADH
SEACHTAINE, and PLASÓIGE 20 GACH LÁ EILE. Which, thanks to
my semester of Irish, I was able to translate as FREE GOLF, and GO
AHEAD, REALLY. So I did.

   I had been told that I was heading into authentic Gaeltacht,
wholly different from the Irish-speaking pockets I had visited
where the only things speaking Irish were the road signs. And the
signs themselves were no small issue—Irish signage was something of a hot controversy, particularly down in the southwest
where protesters had spray-painted the anglicized DINGLE over
the Irish AN DAINGEAN on the road signs, hoping to make the
tourist-loving peninsula more tourist-friendly. It was an argument dating back to Irish independence when the language was
legislated back to life after having been essentially outlawed
by the English. It was still compulsory for all children to learn
Irish in school, and I'd been told it was law that any municipal
employee be a capable speaker. Want to report your car stolen?
You had the right to do so in Irish (also referred to as Gaelic, al-
though Irish was more accurate, as Gaelic applied to variations
spoken in Scotland and the Isle of Man). Some viewed the Irish
language as a vital cog of Irish culture, others as their least favorite class in primary school. Either way, "mulligan" in Irish was
maol-ochón.

   As it was embellished to me back in Bundoran about my upcoming visits to the towns of Bunbeg and Gortahork, "They

never even heard English up there." Donegal was described as the forgotten county tucked up in the farthest corner of Ulster, isolated from the political and economic hubs of Dublin and Cork. It was Ireland's fourth-largest county, but had no rail or national bus service (just buses in and out of Letterkenny and Donegal Town) and felt closest to the Ireland that we Yanks waxed poetic about, unspoiled and unchanged—not quite Colonial Williamsburg, but if outdoor plumbing was on your traveler's checklist, I crossed it off mine in Donegal. Still, it seemed unlikely that a few days walk on an island could take me to a place where the ease and ubiquity of English were replaced by a language that sounded like the Torah read backward. But that was what I heard when I arrived in Gortahork, stepped into a pub for a pint of Lucozade, and found three men sitting in a poorly lit room at noon, dressed in dark wool and drinking stout poured from bottles.

They turned their heads to give me a quick once-over, then went back to their conversation in deep-toned Irish. The words had a fullness to them, a weight, like you could grab onto the syllables and untangle them with your fingers. I sipped my pint of fizzy sugar and eavesdropped for the seven Irish words familiar to me. They were either discussing the weather, I gathered, or having an argument about a bicycle. Surely they were all wondering what I was doing in the corner of their small pub, golf clubs propped beside the door, scribbling away in a journal. They might have been discussing it, might have even been giving the American in the rain suit a sound slagging, but it all sounded pretty good to me.

Letterkenny was almost a city, the largest town in Donegal and a chance for decent pizza and a movie as I awaited the arrival of my next golfing partner, my wife's big little brother, Brian. A weekend in Letterkenny was also a chance to experience another side effect of Ireland's nuptial boom, the siege of stag and hen parties that I had read was wreaking havoc in Dublin, where wedding packs roamed the trendy neighborhoods with heads full of Smirnoff and muscles full of caffeinated mixer. The pre-wedding

MO seemed to be to gather up the lads or lasses (moms and dads tagged along a surprising amount of the time) and head for the biggest town in the county, which meant that Letterkenny was packed on a Saturday night with kids from every far-off corner of deepest Donegal. I met one such thirsty squad in the Wolfe Tone Bar, the most politically unambiguous pub I visited in all of Ireland, named after the Irish revolutionary who was captured in Letterkenny in 1798. It was a sprawling and stylish place, handsomely furnished with polished wood and spot-lit artwork. Posts were ringed with green Glasgow Celtic hoops, and the walls were covered with portraits of Republican heroes and Easter Rising rebels. Lift your glass, and you could toast Wolfe Tone, Michael Collins, or Eamon de Valera. There was James Connelly, Bobby Sands, Gerry Adams, even Nelson Mandela up on the wall (the Arafat photo forced an audible *huh?*). If the IRA had a world in Epcot Center, it would have felt something like this, which gave me pause about where I was and where I was heading. But the fact that something so contentious had been turned into something as commercial as mega-pub decor seemed cause for hope, the last gasp of any headline being the bumper sticker.

Most of the crowd in the Wolfe Tone wasn't there for the politics. Most were there to pound vodka-Cokes and harass the guitar player for more Bon Jovi and toast their mate who was going to be hungover from the following morning to his wedding day, three weeks away. (For a country of such a proud stout and whiskey tradition, it seemed a shame that so many pubs kept five tankards of vodka on the speed-pour while the Jameson bottle collected dust). I had been running back and forth from my seat at the bar to the bookie next door, wagering pittances on the horse races on TV as my Saturday evening entertainment, when I struck up a conversation with a member of a stag party. I knew the guidebook said to avoid eye contact with gangs of teetering twenty-year-olds after nine o'clock, but the kid next to me looked harmless enough, hair buzzed as if for summer camp, round glasses, and a chip-softened physique. He seemed a little overwhelmed by what I correctly guessed was his first stag party. We talked horses, as far as I could tell (his Donegal accent was garbled by what smelled like a Siberian infantryman's ration of

Smirnoff), before he suddenly awoke from a groggy stupor as if he had something very important to ask me. I braced for another interrogation on what I thought about all this Iraq business, but instead, the young man asked me if I liked tractors.

Honestly, just like that. "Do you like tractors?"

I had never really come to any consensus about tractors. I suppose I would have had to call myself undecided on the tractor issue, but it seemed obvious he was fishing for a yes. If he was anti-tractor, he most likely would have propositioned me with, "You don't like tractors, do you?" or maybe, "Tractors, they're the worst, am I right?"

"Sure, I like tractors," I said. It turned out that he was in the tractor-flipping business—not as in rolling them over in a bog, but as in buying old rust buckets, fixing them up with his buddies, and bringing them to shows where they might even sell at a profit. I had no idea there was such an economy out there, and no matter that he was from a tiny town and didn't much care for Letterkenny (didn't like "the big city," he claimed), he was an entrepreneur in a country of tractor owners, on a stag weekend with his mate who fixed up tractors, too. So we talked tractors. I think. All I was certain of was that I never got around to explaining what I was doing in Ireland, not before he was napping, chin-down, on the racing form I'd bought. And that was more than fine with me.

That evening was a good refresher in the ways of the younger crowd as I prepared for the arrival of my twenty-two-year-old brother-in-law. Fresh from his graduation from Loyola College in Baltimore, Brian stepped off the bus in Letterkenny, his pockets stuffed with graduation booty. He was a hockey player, checking-line big. I'd found that he could be quiet around his in-law, a bit buttoned up from time to time, but the next two weeks were expected to change all that, an experiment in bonding that my wife hoped would make up for Brian's having to endure two older sisters for twenty-two years. It was Allyson's intention that I take Brian under my wing, make him wise in the ways of man, but those ways all seemed to boil down to one issue: whether or not I could get him to take off his trucker cap at dinner. Hats were rare enough in Ireland, and indoors an absolute no-no, so the

STP lid stitched to Brian's scalp might indeed rise to the level of a thing.

Brian arrived with an iPod full of bands I'd never heard of and a jug of protein pills—he was into weights and running and amino cocktails, which almost gave us something in common. Three hundred miles of cardio had transformed my body-by-Old-Country-Buffet into something strangely taut, the weeks of sun baking my complexion from clam chowder to a warm and healthy gold. In my six weeks of eating Irish, I had consumed at least one family of swine and ordered enough fried food to alter the global climate, and yet I had lost at least ten pounds. I stopped in a pharmacy to find that my blood pressure was down, even without the meds I'd ditched on day three, and by Letterkenny I was accidentally in the best shape of my life. My calves looked like I had rented them from an infomercial; there were two softball-size knots of muscle in the backs of my thighs that simply could not be accounted for. Hills went unnoticed—I actually came to prefer a steady incline, my new legs carrying me along without pain or hard breath, easy as riding an escalator, and my original three-mile-per-hour pace was now closer to four—all proof that it was possible to eat and drink like a jerk and still lose weight, as long as the pub was seventeen miles away and you didn't mind the walk. I guessed that I might even be in better shape than Brian, whose middle had been softened by a spring semester off the ice and in the Greene Turtle Grille, but he was an athlete, ten years my junior, who would surely have no problem keeping up.

The Rosapenna Hotel was a splurge, modest from the outside but real luxury within. Our room was far too wonderful for two backpackers, thanks to a generous suite upgrade from the gregarious hotel manager who had been following my progress online, and had greeted us at the desk with a, "Mr. Coyne, so how are the feet?" Perhaps Brian started off his trip with the absolute wrong impression of how these next ten days were going to go—we'd be curled up on Styrofoam with popcorn-stuffed pillows soon enough—but I wasn't one to say no to a king-size sleigh bed and a sitting room, complimentary cabernet, and fresh fruit in Waterford crystal.

Brian was the first travelmate to join me in hauling his own golf clubs from course to course, and as I watched him experiment with a dozen strategies for strapping his sticks to his backpack, each arrangement dumping his golf bag on the carpet quicker than the last, I couldn't help but shake my head, smiling with nostalgia at the pile of nonnecessities on his bed. I was looking at myself from not every long ago, a silly, untested me, who thought it would be fine to bring along a gallon water jug, cologne and aftershave, the value-size bottle of lens solution, and no less than twenty-seven packs of citrus-flavored gum.

Brian also unpacked a sack of provisions for me: contact solution (the smallest bottle Allyson could find), sun block, energy eats, and, most importantly, a dozen fresh Titleists. As anyone knew who had ever played Ireland, Irish golf balls were a lousy bunch of runaways. They left you fast. So along with my dozen Pro V1s, Brian had brought a box of thirty Dunlops for himself. He held up his booty of golf balls, laughing, a little cocky, "Think I brought enough for two weeks?"

And as all such proud proclamations turn out, they didn't quite last him two days.

If there's anything I'd found maddening about links golf in Ireland, it was that good golf shots could so quickly, so arbitrarily become gone golf shots. Considering a shot with sound judgment, and executing that particular shot with absolute precision, that was pretty much as good as anyone could do in this game. Such a feat should always be rewarded. But as I made my way around Ireland, I had to bite my tongue from time to time, grin and bear it, when a perfect sweet-spot effort ran through the green and into the hungry weeds. Gone. It happened all the time.

It wouldn't hurt as much if Titleist Pro V1s in Ireland didn't run a debit-card-destroying €18 for a sleeve. That was nine dollars per ball! So I was eager to dig into young Brian's goodie bag and replenish my supply. But two days later, on the thirteenth at Sandy Hills in Rosapenna, Brian was already playing the souvenir logo ball I'd bought in the pro shop—the last ball between us—and I knew this stretch of the trip was going to be expensive in an unexpected way.

Aside from the golf balls, I found Rosapenna to be one of the best values on this trip. Granted, the Rosapenna Hotel wasn't going to get a thumbs-up in your budget travel guide, but compared to its luxury resort peers, it was quite a good deal, particularly with the reduced greens fees for guests. And Pat Ruddy's Sandy Hills links was not to be missed—tough as nails, the course pushed you into deep fairway bowls and tossed you off towering dunes. I had played courses where I felt enveloped by the Irish countryside, but at Sandy Hills, I literally felt lost in it, just rolling landscape and the sea, each hole entirely to itself. And the second shot down to the sixth hole, the blue waters of Sheephaven Bay for a backdrop, the dunes on either side perfectly framing your approach—if you didn't hit the fairway, it was worth dropping one out there for the view, which both Brian and I did.

The Old Tom Morris course was fun, if not as dramatic as the new course. Full of history and the grandfather of golf's footsteps, it was a traditional out-and-back layout on the front, with a slightly incongruous back nine across the street that climbed its way up, over, and around a hillside. With the nearby St. Patrick's links closed for alteration, we left Rosapenna a day early, bellies full and blisters softened (they even threw in a foot massage, which, for my misshapen stumps, was nothing short of orgasmic). Brian was down twenty-five golf balls after two days— twenty-five *gross*, he was quick to point out, having found five balls while hunting for his own, giving him a net tally of twenty. But by either count, his graduation cash was in jeopardy.

Now Brian was a fair enough golfer with sort of a self-taught swing. Hockey slap-shot meets tipsy lumberjack—he'd broken ninety in his golfing life and expected to do the same at some point during his half dozen Irish rounds. But he got a serious case of the rights somewhere on his way to Donegal, and on nearly every tee box, we went through an exercise of hope, hope, hope, then another wild lash and a golf ball soaring in an almost impossibly sideways direction, like a wounded bird in a windstorm, careening out of sight and crashing down into fields of waist-high weeds, into places not previously considered part of the golf course.

"Gone," Brian would announce, defiance in his voice, like he was warning his golf ball, *Go on and tell your friends—I'm gonna lose every last one of you.*

Yet I didn't suppose Brian really minded losing his thirty-eighth golf ball (twenty-eighth net) in Portsalon. The place just had too much going for it. The links was stretched along an award-winning beach, a perfect half crescent of sand cupped by steep slopes and green glens (I had never heard of an award for a beach, but Portsalon's prize-winning was well-advertised). The holes were fast and tight and packed against the coast in a way that gave the sea winds full reign over the course. The links had been redesigned by Pat Ruddy, and fresh from his Sandy Hills layout, I had a sense that Mr. Ruddy possessed little patience for ball-sprayers, and that Brian would have liked the chance to lace up his skates and put Ruddy into the boards. We didn't go down to sample the lovely strand, but my playing partner did send a handful of Dunlops off for some beach time. A scratch player would have had to buy balls at the turn on this afternoon, with category-nine winds off the ocean sending our drives boomeranging back toward us and into the weeds, and a stinging rain that had us abandoning them without much of a fight. We cursed the breezes for blinding us to Porsalon after a two-day haul from Rosapenna, but it was the town of Portsalon, or the lack thereof, that made everything all right.

I'd stayed in one-pub towns that had me weeping for *craic*, desperate for stimulation beyond *Clifford the Big Red Dog* in Irish on channel four. But Portsalon was blessedly boring—golf course, clubhouse, chipper (fast-food joint), and next to the chipper, a pub that, had I not stumbled upon the Beach Bar, would have been the top of my pops. The Stores Pub sat perched above the beach, and on the pub's back patio you could lean against the rail with stout in hand, ocean spray sweetening your Guinness, looking out at the mountains in the distance. (I spent plenty of time eyeing one peak in particular, the tallest one with a ribbon of road crawling back and forth up its slope—I didn't see any way to our next town without having to take it on in the morning.) Inside, the pub was all nooks and crannies with a peat fire and a pool table. But its most sublime feature was what was beneath the pub: an immaculate, newly furnished apartment, three bedrooms and a kitchen and hot showers, with a balcony overlooking the waves and a private bit of beach.

Cooking my own spaghetti provided an uncommon shot of happiness, as it occurred to me that everything I had eaten in the last six weeks had been served to me or slid across the counter in a brown paper bag. Being able to wash our clothes in a real washer felt like rock-star stuff. It wasn't very rock star that we had to get the bartender to come down and show us how to turn it on (starting up a Euro washing machine was like doing Sudoku—pick a number, a letter, try another number until it hums to life, fingers crossed that you haven't just murdered your wardrobe), but the place was a favorite find. Considering that there wasn't a hotel or B&B in the town itself (the only hotel had recently closed, I learned), we felt particularly blessed by our digs beneath the pub. We drank most of the Carlsberg in Portsalon in celebration of the fact that we literally could have—and may have—crawled to our beds. And the next morning, after an evening embarrassing my home country on the pool table, we set off for the town of Rathmullan with heads that felt like we had just cracked our skulls open and poured the pints right in.

We walked that lovely beach toward the glens in the distance, the lazy gulls circling above the waves, the sand covered with unbroken shells that seemed to scoop up the morning sunlight, and Brian's face like a plate of fried eggs—two runny yellow eyes stuck on sweaty white cheeks. I wasn't doing much better. We left the beach and headed for that hill, stopping at the end of each hairpin turn—I counted 407—until we finally reached the top, only to find that the road to Rathmullan went from steep, to still steeper.

Brian fell behind, complaining of a sore ankle, and he insisted on wearing his headphones when I had tried to politely explain that your ears on this course were as good as an extra set of eyes. Perked ears were your only protection against the biggest walking threat in Ireland: overtaking traffic sneaking up on you from behind. Cars would pull out and pass on any sort of road, and when they veered into the right lane and stepped on the gas, a pedestrian might come within a wristwatch of a speeding rear-view mirror that he never saw coming. But Brian was bored and wanted his tunes, even though it meant, as he would later confess, that his fingers had felt the brush of a roadster he couldn't hear. We were three miles to our destination when I made him look up from his shoes and take off the earphones.

"Golf course," I said, pointing to a small road sign pointing to Otway Golf Club, a name I had never heard before and wasn't on either of our maps. But the course was to our left, in the direction of the water, and might be a links to investigate. "Up for it?"

Brian shrugged, not entirely convinced. But this older dog knew there was one true cure for that fog settled behind his eyeballs, better than any aspirin or pillow. Get out there in the fresh air chasing a white ball, and somehow the morning's cobwebs always seemed to blow away. Either that, or you threw up next to the second tee box. But he would feel better either way.

We came to the end of the road and discovered a small beach cove, and around the beach were planted a handful of lush greens, tee boxes perched here and there around the property. It was an intimate nine-holer, like a movie set almost, a golf course in a box. There was no one on the course or in the clubhouse, so we stuffed our best intentions into the greens fees box and headed off number one, a par-three that dropped us a good forty yards down to sea level. We came to the second tee, and after only one hole, I was already glad we'd came—not because it was a great golf course, but because we had accidentally stumbled upon the most confusing golf course in Ireland. On tee box number two, we stood at the bottom of a hill, ready for our next hole. But in front of us, at the top of the hill, a barbed-wire fence not thirty paces away marked the edge of the property. And behind us, the hole we'd just played. Curious.

After a more careful inspection of my surroundings, I counted only five holes in view. There was another chunk of this golf course somewhere, but where? Was there a hatch? An old wardrobe we'd have to open up and play through? Was this a five-holer? We had no scorecard to tell us otherwise. I made an educated guess based on prior run-ins with Irish barbed wire, and I teed up my ball, pointed straight at OB oblivion.

"Where are you aiming?" Brian asked, laughing to say he knew I was only kidding. But instead I put my faith in Otway and made Brian do the same. And wouldn't you know it, as we scrambled up the slope in front of us, we found a gateway in the fence that led to a second beach cove and a new stretch of fairways and greens. No matter that we didn't find either of our drives; more importantly, we'd actually found the golf course.

It wasn't just the faux boundary fence that made Otway a shoo-in for Ireland's most jumbled-up links. It was the fact that one tee box served as teeing ground for two holes, with no way of knowing which hole was which from the tee. *That's three, right? Then where the hell's five?* Number six played across holes one and nine, and number nine played over eight and six. We found a scorecard with a course map after our round and discovered that we hadn't actually played the Otway golf course at all. What we had played was great fun, playing into and out of a lumpy beach cove with greens and tees stuck here and there, almost daring you to make up your own golf course—which we did, hitting from four tee to five green, missing four altogether, then finishing with nine, seven, and eight, in that order. And beside the fifth green, the most protected on the course, tucked in a hollow of granite and moss, we found an old stone cross and altar marking the location of a mass rock, a place where Catholic mass was celebrated in secret during the seventeenth century. The hole was blessed, indeed—Brian one-putted for what might have been the first time in Ireland, and we headed back up the road, not sure what we had just played, but glad that we did.

An hour later we found Rathmullan, a town that was most famous for the folks who left it some four hundred years ago. The Flight of the Earls from Rathmullan made official the end of Ireland's old Gaelic order, as the chieftains of Ireland, O'Neill and O'Donnell among them, fled Ireland for Spain. As a Catholic country, and the biggest thorn in England's side, Spain had been a destination for generations of Irish ex-patriots. Still today, Madrid has a thriving Irish culture with its own Gaelic football club. There was even a town in Spain called Coyne (couldn't find it on the map, but Dad had a picture to prove it). Reading up on Rathmullan, I couldn't help but think of history's sense of irony, the Irish having set sail for Spain for centuries, and now the Spanish in return sailing for Irish waters, their boats and nets receiving, I gathered, a very different reception.

The next morning, Brian and I too set sail from Rathmullan,

taking the Lough Swilly ferry across to Buncrana, a town where we hadn't planned to stop, hoping to keep pushing into Ireland's northernmost peninsula and on to Ballyliffin. But as the ferry drew closer to the shore, we eyed the land on our horizon, two explorers sniffing out that which we had come for. Golf course, ho.

It turned out that we were looking at the North West Golf Club, a solid eighteen-hole blend of links and parkland, flat and treeless without dunes to blow up Brian's nagging ankle. It was also void of the dune grasses to steal his balls, the fairways manicured and defined in a style that felt American. It was a nice break, to be honest, and Brian played his best golf yet, making it around with the five balls he bought in the pro shop with cobbled-together pocket change.

It turned out that what we thought was one sprawling golf course from the ferry, was actually the North West course plus a nine-holer closer to the ferry pier, the Buncrana Golf Club, which made our day's detour feel well justified. I would have hated to come all that way and have missed the chance to tee it up on the most dangerous golf course on the planet.

The Buncrana nine holes were squashed into a field the size of a soccer pitch, making for some entertaining golf shots, if you happened to be playing the course alone. My best drive of the day was accidentally played by a passing foursome, and another drive ended up in a pocket in the group in front of us (they all denied it, but the grin of a guilty ball thief is the most unmistakable of all smiles). The fifth hole was my favorite—called Calamity, the most aptly labeled hole in Ireland—a par-four that actually shared the same fairway with the next hole, the par-four sixth. I thought we were lost again, but there it was on the course map on the scorecard—two greens, two tees, one fairway. It was like there had been an accident in the other lane, so all the traffic had to share this one. I almost killed a teenager in the group in front of me, who in turn teed off on six and returned fire, not ten yards wide of his target. But all in all, and not counting the ball I knew was going home in that pasty bastard's pocket, I shot my best round of the trip at Buncrana, coming in at even par. After all these years, I finally figured it out. I didn't need easier golf courses. I needed more perilous ones.

As we made our way to Ballyliffin, a golf town at the absolute tippity top of the island, I had the feeling that Brian's luck was going to change as well. Ballyliffin had what Brian needed more than anything else: a driving range. And not for the practice, but for the bullets. Brian was down forty-two balls at last count—$300 worth at Irish prices—so I believed him when he told me he procured those dozen balls with black stripes in the pro shop. After a front nine on the old course where it was once again in question as to whether Brian would have enough balls for the back, he somehow started to straighten it out, started to see his tee shots actually bounce in the distance, leaping up from the turf as if to say, *I'm here, I'm still alive!*

Brian put together a solid 50 on the back nine. Previously brought to a silent moping through the weeds, he now pepped up, and started offering more on-course criticism than Johnny Miller—*D'you mean to hit it there? Hey Coyne, did I tie you on that hole? Bogey? Yeah, me too.* And as we walked our way out of Ballyliffin, not too bothered about the two miles back to the hotel, I noted Brian's good play, congratulated him on his efforts, encouraging him that the next day's round on the new course would be his chance to get back at Ireland.

"Even got a ball left," he explained. "Just need to hit the driving range tomorrow, I'll be all set."

We both knew he wasn't going to the range to work on his swing, but after two months and five hundred miles, whatever it took to keep you swinging worked for me.

We hated to leave Ballyliffin. Not just because it was a perfect links lover's retreat—handsome clubhouse and two formidable eighteen-hole layouts dropped onto a vast and remote dune landscape where there wasn't a level lie to be found on the property—but because it meant we were on our way to Greencastle, two long days of walking ahead of us, during which Brian's ankle decided to go ahead and die.

He stopped talking somewhere after mile two. It was quiet for a few hours, me turning around every once in a while to see Brian's face twisted up with pain, backpack sagging down around his knees, golf clubs flopping sideways and ready to spill into the road. You could see the questions burning behind those eyes: *What the hell am I doing out here? Why'd I bring so much damn gum?*

We stopped every twenty minutes or so, allowing Brian to hurl his pack to the pavement, limp over to a property wall, and sit down to rub his ankle for a moment while I stood there feeling good about myself. Not that I took any pleasure from his misery. I had struggled through the same Achilles anguish earlier in the trip, and I knew the pain that had him clomping around flat-footed like a sun-burnt Frankenstein. It was no fun, but his feet would break themselves in, I assured Brian, and stopping to let the tendons tighten up was the worst thing he could do. So we arrived in Greencastle, my last town in Donegal after what felt like a lifetime in the forgotten county. I hadn't planned on spending the night in Greencastle, but with Brian's hobbling and a sign pointing me toward a Greencastle golf course that I figured I should investigate, I headed toward the harbor, looking for a room for the night.

There weren't any. So we went into the pub, to seek local counsel.

It was just past two in the afternoon on a Tuesday, but Sean sitting at the bar looked like he had been there since breakfast. A gathering of foam-lined pint glasses crowded the bar in front of him, and he looked tired and in need of a sandwich. He pinned me for an American when I asked the barmaid if there were any rooms available upstairs (in some pubs, there were), and we got to talking about the Yankees and a brother of his who lived in Brooklyn. He was thin, with the wispiness of a day-drinker, and his accent was more Dublin than Donegal. But he knew a place where we could stay.

"Right up the road from here," he explained. Brian and I looked at each other and shrugged, *why not*. As long as the next words out of his mouth weren't, "My place," we were in.

"Come on, I'll give you a lift," he said. I smiled and thanked him and prepared to once again explain why we would really rather walk, but before I could say "DUI," our friend was out the door and throwing our bags in the back of his Volkswagen. I looked at Brian.

"Good idea?"

He shrugged. "Beats walking."

"Dying? You sure?"

So in Greencastle we witnessed yet another Act of Uncommon Irish Hospitality, one that could have won the doer of said deed two months in the pokey. If there was any doubt that he'd been hard at work on his day-load, aside from the beer on his breath, or the fact that he was looking at me instead of the windshield as we sped up the road, I was pretty much convinced when Sean explained to me that one of the great things about living in an out-of-the-way town like Greencastle was that the Garda (the police) didn't bother you about the drinking and the driving.

"It's right around here. We're close, very close," he said as we drove up the road, then back down. The problem with this particular road, it seemed to me, was that it was full of plain, one-story homes with no bed-and-breakfasts in sight, no signs advertising any vacancy, just quaint Irish households, one of which I suspected was going to be very confused in a few minutes when Sean started knocking on their door, asking if his American friends could sleep over.

"Got to be this one," he said, pulling into the driveway. "Better check." Sean hopped out, and, as predicted, began banging on the door. It finally cracked open.

We sat in the car.

"This isn't a bed-and-breakfast. What the hell is he doing?"

Brian looked numb in the back seat. "Are we going to have to walk back to town?"

But in a moment, Sean turned around and headed back to the car, giving us the thumbs-up.

"I knew she had rooms," he told us. "You're in."

A gray-haired lady met us at the door. She was bent with age, and she looked cautiously at our backpacks and golf clubs. Her voice was booming, the batteries dead in a hearing aid some-where in the house.

"There's an empty room in the back, but I haven't been doing the bed-and-breakfast since last April. So I can't offer you any breakfast, maybe just some juice and cereal."

And suddenly, all was good. All was great. Where I had pre-pared myself to spend a night curled up beneath Sean's cot, Stella cans for my pillow, now I would be bedding down in a place I had been dreaming about for weeks, the Irish bed-and-no-breakfast.

My love affair with the full Irish breakfast had simmered down to a casual interest, casual interest turned into a begrudging accep-tance, and recently, reduced to an unshakeable horror. Bed-and-breakfasting wasn't just wearing on my stomach, it was beating up my soul. This was a participatory sort of lodging that, as an Ameri-can accustomed to the anonymity of hotels and do-not-disturbs, had become overwhelming, particularly at the end of a long walking day. At a B&B, you were expected to bring something to the table—a chat, a few questions, and certainly some manners. *This ain't the Ramada, that lady raised her kids here!* I had the arrival routine down pretty well, seeing as I went through it every afternoon: *Knock knock, hello, I'm the American, there's my room, there's the toilet, there's the key to the front door, and there's that antique key to my room that I'll be jangling in my room's door for a good twenty min-utes come midnight.* And then the unavoidable question, "What time would you like breakfast?" This was where I got a little dizzy. And a little sheepish. "Thanks, but I don't want breakfast."

I doubted you could utter a more profane sentence in an Irish B&B.

"No breakfast?" The panic in my host's voice, as if I'd told her there was a dirty bomb in my backpack.

"Well, maybe just some cereal."

This was even more offensive. Now I had admitted that I would be hungry come morning, but that I wanted absolutely no part of what the lady of the house might be preparing for me—which was, inevitably, her finest full Irish. In her eyes, this was my first and only night in Ireland, and it was her duty to her town, her nation, the tourist board, to stuff me full of eggs and sausage, to prove that

Ireland's ultimate breakfast lived in her home county. But gobbling down hefty slabs of bacon every morning for forty-eight days in a row, it was getting a little scary (if I could have found some barbecue sauce, I might have taken a bite out of myself). So the fact that I wasn't going to have to go through any of that, that I could sleep in peace, eyes not popping open at seven o'clock to the sound of banging frying pans—Sean had done a bang-up job. I just about ran through the front door. Brian soaked his feet in the tub, and I watched HBO in her living room, and all was good. It felt like home.

I made my way out to the Greencastle course for a late-afternoon round, just a few miles out of town, walking past the ruins of a thirteenth-century castle that gave the town its name. The manager was waiting for me outside the clubhouse, a gentleman named Billy who was further proof that the Irish weren't anywhere more affable than in Donegal. He introduced me around the clubhouse, then took me into his office to fill me in on Greencastle's recent makeover. After the club's centenary in 1992, their nine holes were stretched to eighteen, and good thing, because the rest of my afternoon at the Greencastle Golf Club was as pleasant as its beginning. Set into the cliffs above Lough Foyle, Greencastle was my absolute favorite thing in a golf course—unexpected. It was an uneven track, not a surprise considering that one nine was a hundred years older than the other, but for the handful of sluggish, parkland holes that felt like I might be golfing in Ohio, the holes perched on the coastline were stunners, with sea-cliff tee boxes and a blind dogleg that wound you along the water's edge to an old lighthouse planted beside the green. I knew Doonbeg, Lahinch, and Ballyliffin were going to be great, but finding a dash of camera-worthy golf in Greencastle was a treat, and one that I would celebrate by stopping into the pub on my way back into town.

And there was Sean. Same seat, same glass, two sips from empty. I'd like to say I thought better of letting him drive me back to the B&B again, but he did such a good job the first time. Besides, there wasn't any sign on the place, and I figured I was far too sober to find it.

———————

The next morning, we woke bright-eyed and refreshed, the bath-tub having warmed life back into Brian's ankles. We were ready to say good-bye to Donegal and the Republic of Ireland, heading into Northern Ireland on the ferry across Lough Foyle. We showered and headed for the breakfast room where we found a few plastic tubs of corn flakes and a tall pitcher of OJ. I hadn't seen a more lovely table in weeks. I sat down, morning sun pouring through the window onto our simple breakfast spread, and both of us smiling. I felt moved to say grace. Until, from the kitchen, as if from a megaphone:

"How do you boys like your eggs?"

Brian and I bolted upright in our seats, eyes wide with fear.

Our hostess burst through the door in an apron, hair up in a net, two steaming plates in her hands. "I haven't done a breakfast in a while, but I didn't want you to head off hungry."

She dropped our first courses in front of us, two floppy cuts of ham that, when viewed through eyes that had been promised cereal, looked like the Odor-Eaters drying on the radiator in our room, the meat's gray pallor all the more pronounced next to a bursting roasted tomato.

"Oh, you didn't have to . . ." was all I could get out. Brian looked at his plate, speechless.

"Your eggs? Fried is okay?"

"No, really, this will be plenty for me . . ."

"They're already cooking." And she was off.

My fork—it weighed four tons, the silver welded to my napkin. And then she was back, sliding two sweaty egg Frisbees under our noses.

"Thank you."

And I was thankful. Thankful that she had gone through the effort, even when she was out of practice, thankful that she had gotten up early and made such an effort. And I was thankful for my paper napkin, as I proceeded to roll my eggs into my ham, and fold my ham into my napkin. Brian sat across from me silently watching me work, an incredulous look on his face.

I stood, placed my breakfast in my pocket, and headed for the bathroom, leaving Brian stunned and staring at his impossible full Irish. I could hear her from the bathroom, "Where did your friend go! He must have been hungry!" and I almost felt bad as I watched the yolk burp its way back up into the toilet (took three flushes to get it all down), but I did the best I could with the circumstance that presented itself—nobody got sick, nobody's feelings got hurt. Well, except for Brian. Twenty minutes later, he walked into our room, shame on his face.

"D'you eat it?"

He shook his head. "I tried. I couldn't."

"Where is it?"

He reached into his pocket and pulled out a floppy piece of pork.

The kid was learning.

I stood on the bridge of the ferry, wind in my face, looking ahead to the green mountains of Derry. A few nights before, back in Portsalon, Brian and I had become friendly with the bartender, a girl with hippy braids who was reading a book on Donegal folklore between pints. We talked about where we were headed next, and Brian asked her, "So you call it Derry. Then where's Londonderry? It says Londonderry on my map."

I looked down at my feet, coughed, fidgeted to say it was time to head for the pool table. Brian's intentions were innocent, but it was a no-no of a question, particularly after ten o'clock, and in the company of a dozen sotted Irishmen who might be too eager to give him their opinions on the matter. She saw it for what it was and smiled.

"Well, I'll explain it like this. There are some people who think it should be called Derry. And there are other people who think it should be called Londonderry."

Brian waited for the rest of the explanation. "But why?"

Someone wanted a Guinness, and she seemed pleased by the interruption.

"You'll figure it out."

ῂole 460

279 over par

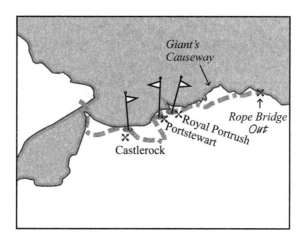

A LONG WITH MY GOLF CLUBS, A SAUSAGE ROLL, AND A HOB-
bling brother-in-law, I brought with me into Northern
Ireland the baggage most tourists carried with them, prejudices
born from regrettable headlines and a bare-knuckled history, pre-
conceptions that the north was at best a more guarded, at worst
a more dangerous place to travel. But in acknowledging those
stereotypes, I endeavored to overcome them, vowing not to be
swayed by the Irish elsewhere who told me I might find the folks
up there a bit cold, and not allowing myself to be influenced by
so many late-night college viewings of *In the Name of the Father*.
I set off on the ferry from Greencastle, prepared to take in Northern Ireland as an unbiased, open-minded, purposely naive traveler, ready to be surprised and delighted by a country that was no
longer living under those old headlines, but, like the rest of Ireland, getting on with it, and getting on well.

My intentions were quickly undermined by one of the guards
at the pier (and wait—why guards here and not the Donegal

side?) who informed me that I shouldn't leave my backpack outside if I needed to use the restroom in the ferry station, for fear that it might be stolen (by whom? A gang of seagulls?), which unfortunately, not five minutes into Derry, had me thinking about my father's old set of golf clubs.

He was traveling Northern Ireland with twelve buddies on one of those bus, golf, pub, bus, golf tours. On their second day of ten, they stepped out of their hotel, refreshed and ready to take on Royal Portrush, only to find that their bus had been broken into during the night, the cargo holds popped open, and ten of their twelve sets of golf clubs had vanished into the County Antrim air, seized by golf-mad paramilitaries, no doubt. Ten players were left renting clubs for the rest of their dream golf trip—Dad wasn't one of them, his old Wilson Ultras being passed over by thieves who were evidently club snobs, separating the wheat from the golfing chaff in the dark. The golf went on, and with their insurance loot, Dad's friends were all playing with shiny new sticks that spring while he was stuck with his old set. But that warning at the pier had me remembering that incident, and feeling very aware that I was carrying with me a pricey laptop and a set of clubs that, unlike Dad's sticks, would be worth a go.

I reminded myself that there were surely as many sticky fingers elsewhere in Ireland, and that I came from a city where my jack-o'-lantern had been nicked three Halloweens in a row. I asked Brian to watch my bag, and reemerged from the restroom ready to be impressed. We loaded up on energy blocks and mapped our beach route to Castlerock. Walking the strand around the coast would easily save us an hour, keeping us off a road that seemed to wind an impossibly long route to town.

I checked with the station guard that our route made sense, making sure that the beach wouldn't be cut off by inlets or sea cliffs. "Is it okay to walk the beach?" I asked her, and the look in her eyes said we'd better pay close attention.

"Oh, I wouldn't do that," she said. "Not at all. It's not safe— see those red flags? The army's doing maneuvers today."

There's an army?

Along with *grave illness* and *acts of God*, I added *unforeseen*

military maneuvers to my list of circumstances that justified vehicular transport, and I asked the station guard to call us a taxi.

During our cab ride to Castlerock, we learned why the road
to town took such an indirect route, winding us around a vast
British army and prison complex, one that I would later be told
housed IRA prisoners near the end of their sentences. The cab
cruised through streets lined with union flags, the lampposts all
draped in red and blue, a more proudly British display than I had
ever seen in my months living in London. Brian and I sat quietly
behind a cab driver with a shaved head and the first iron-pumped
physique I'd seen since leaving the States. He had the concrete
look of a Manhattan bouncer, and I accepted that we were indeed
not in Kansas anymore. Five minutes on the ferry had taken us a
very long way from the convivial backwoodsiness of Donegal,
where they might share a few cops between a half dozen towns,
let alone host an army. Nonetheless, no one in the North had yet
to offer an unkind word, the taxi had come quickly, and Tony the
cabbie rocked a blend of Bon Jovi and Def Leppard that had us
bobbing our heads all the way into town. There were differences
here, certainly, but it was the people that mattered, people who,
I was confident, would prove themselves as welcoming and curious as the rest of the quick friends I had made along the way.

And then we walked into the Castlerock Golf Club and
learned that sometimes the stereotype just sticks.

I was looking forward to playing Castlerock, a golf course that
Donegal golfers had described as being overshadowed by its
neighbors, but just as deserving a links as nearby Portstewart and
Portrush. Brian and I arrived in town and met up with a college
friend of mine, Sean, a casual golfer and a roaming business con-
sultant who had been given a pass from his wife for four days in
Ireland. I checked us in at the clubhouse reception desk, and after
some lunch, we headed into the pro shop to do some shopping.
We were met in the shop by someone who I assumed was an
assistant pro, perhaps the ranger, who eyed us with immediate

suspicion. Perhaps he was judging us by our four-day stubble or our accents, but as I went to purchase a yardage book, he snapped a quick, "Who are you with?" with a lilt of suspicion I hadn't experienced since the time I tried to sneak onto Merion.

"We're with us."

He shook his head, his face overcome with a condescending sort of confusion, as if we were speaking a foreign and inferior language. We explained that we'd been told we could play any time before 2:30, when an outing would have the first tee, and I figured the conversation, or lack thereof, had ended there.

We walked out of the pro shop with our souvenir golf balls, slightly put off, but ready to rip it on what looked like a fun up-hill par-four in front of the clubhouse. But our friend was quick on our heels, following us out of the pro shop like we'd pocketed something. I wasn't two steps to the tee box before he stopped me with a "Do you have golf shoes?"

"I play in these," I explained to him, referring to my pair of brown leather walking shoes that for the last two months had been my lifeblood, my shepherd, my friend. The golf shoes went home two months ago, I explained, tossed overboard to lighten my load. Having traversed twenty-plus golf courses to this point, this was the first time I'd heard my pair of Keens questioned, but that didn't particularly matter to my friend.

"You can't play in those shoes," he seemed somewhat pleased to inform me.

"I can't play?"

"No."

"I can't play?"

A shake of his head, long and slow.

"Seriously?"

"You can't even set foot in the clubhouse in those shoes."

He didn't know it, but this had now become personal. He was talking shit about the shoes that had just carried me 600 miles. I had siblings I felt less attached to.

"That seems strange to me," I politely protested. And he came quick with a, "Why does that seem strange?" that had a sort of *let's drop the gloves* ring to it. The episode proceeded in a similarly unpleasant manner for a few minutes, until he walked me into the office to further embarrass me by checking if we had paid, as if we'd come all the way from America to experience the rush of sneaking onto the Castlerock golf course in our sneakers. Things were put back together by a club secretary who interceded, only approving of my shoes when he got wind of my having jotted down a few opinions from time to time (a card I try to not play, but this was an occasion if ever there was one), and who defended our friend by explaining, "He was only doing his job."

And that was a fine explanation. I worked in a pro shop. I had seen power trips behind the counter turn duffers away from a golf course, tails between their legs. But there was a way to do your job like a pro, and a way to do your job like a . . . well, you know what I mean.

When I finally calmed down after having been taken for a fence-hopping freeloader in Buster Browns, I walked out to the first tee where the golf bouncer now turned golf buddy gave us his five cents of advice for the opening hole, a par-four that bent right and bottlenecked through the dunes. He stood there watching us, as if to prove his point that we didn't belong. I could hardly see the ball through the steam pouring from my eyes. I squeezed the grip of my three-wood as if trying to wring oil from the rubber. I didn't care if I never broke 100 anywhere else on that island, or if every ball hereafter died a hosel-rocket death, because I pounded that three-wood hot center hard, maybe the best opening shot I'd hit in years. Deep, and working its way up into the neck of the fairway, a gentle tail shaping it along the bend, dropping it dead center in the short cut.

"Nice shot," he said.

You're damn right it was.

I played angry for the rest of my round at Castlerock, which was a real shame, because Castlerock was a lovely golf course, and that unpleasantness in the pro shop was an anomaly—I had walked hundreds of miles, played twentysomething golf courses, many of them somewhat exclusive, stayed in fifty different hotels and B&Bs, and I didn't meet a disagreeable person until day fifty-four. I would have had a dozen tee-time snafus or table-service blowups in Florida by this point, I was sure. Castlerock didn't teach me that the folks in Ireland and Northern Ireland were unwelcoming—rather, it made me realize that, incredibly, 99 percent of them weren't.

If you were doing the Portrush and Portstewart swing, Castlerock was not to be missed, a quality course I'd put up there with the Enniscrones and the Murvaghs of the south. And their new nine-hole course—the Bann Course—was pure joy, with towering tee boxes and tucked greens spread over a craggy seascape. Wild and playable, it was a placement course that didn't require a driver, just an eye for playing banks and bounces and a good imagination. It gave Cruit Island a run for its money as the top nine-holer in Ireland, and if I found myself back in Castlerock, I'd play it twice before the big course. And no matter if they were giving away FootJoys in the parking lot, I'd be playing in my Keens.

As we made our way to Portstewart, there were plenty of clues to remind us that we had arrived in a country within a country. The biggest change was one unnoticed by most, but we the walkers sure noticed—the roads were wider, with comfortable shoulders and fresh pavement. Two lanes were the rule, not the rarest of exceptions. There was national rail service all along the coast—while Brian spent a chunk of his vacation on the bus from the airport to Donegal, Sean zipped into Castlerock on rails, making it from Belfast in an hour and a half. Infrastructure seemed superior in the North, these counties benefiting from the bells and whistles that come with being part of Great Britain. It was also hard not to notice a striking lack of pubs, at least in comparison to the counties we'd come from, where there was a tap for every man and woman in the town. In Donegal, a town the size of Castlerock would have four pubs per block, but we counted two in total, and neither felt warm enough to warrant a second pint.

So it was with a different kind of hangover that we arrived in Portstewart, egos still bruised as we checked into a place called the Strand House, a guesthouse that the tourist board owed a thank-you card because it took three bitter Americans who vowed to never change another dollar in this part of the world and turned us back into cheerleaders overnight.

The proximity to the golf course—two minutes, and that was with Brian's hobble—opened us up to the possibility of better days in Portstewart. It didn't matter if you had a van with a masseuse, a bus with a bar, a golden helicopter to take you back to your castle, there was something decadent about course-side accommodations that just made me want to keep playing until dark. The drying room for bags and shoes was the first I'd come across, and a much-appreciated touch. But the rooms—fresh and new, linens starched an immaculate seaside white, thick comforters and flatscreen TVs, Jacuzzi tubs and showers with enough pressure to knead the knots out of my back—absolutely stole our affections (as did the fact that they were priced at modest B&B rates). Our hosts, Tom and Ernestine, struck the perfect note, the one between accommodating and overbearing, that had us wanting to put them in our golf bags and take them with us.

During the incident of the shoes-of-ill-repute, we had been warned that our footwear wasn't going to pass muster anywhere else in the North. Portstewart and Royal Portrush? Not a chance. Step foot on the grounds of Royal County Down in those? Blasphemy, beyond the pale. (For the record, it wasn't like I was showing up to play in Air Jordans; my Keens could have passed for the pseudo-spikes being hawked in the catalogs). So I was a touch anxious as I reached for the door of the Portstewart pro shop, braced for another scolding. I told Sean and Brian to wait outside.

I stepped inside and walked down a long row of golf bags, where I found a blond woman and an older gentleman fretting over a full booking sheet.

"Hi. I'm Tom Coyne," I squeaked. "I think I have a tee time for three o'clock?" I sounded like a ninth-grader trying to buy beer.

"Yes, Mr. Coyne, welcome to Portstewart. We've been expecting you."

I waved Sean and Brian in, and Sean consumed with vigor, beating up his Visa card and small-talking with the woman behind the counter about the trip from Boston. The gentleman handed out course maps and gave us a quick tutorial on the layout, told us we were free to head to the tee whenever we liked. Their open arms might have had something to do with my opinion of Portstewart's opening holes—as I was soon explaining to my playing partners that we had just played the strongest opening stretch of holes I'd found anywhere in Ireland—but all credit there really went to the links.

I had decided that a links needed some time to warm up and work its way out to the water, but Portstewart kicked off with a *wow*, the tee box pointing us toward a deep valley and a fairway cradled by impossible sand hills, as if you didn't have to drive your golf ball so much as parachute it to safety. On the second hole, dubbed Devil's Hill, you glimpsed just a sliver of the green between two massive dunes jutting into the fairway like icebergs. At only 360 yards, it took two perfectly judged irons to climb the slope up to the green, perched a good club and a half beyond your first guess. The front nine went on snaking through the hills until we reached the back, where the course seemed to step away from the dunes and take a breather, working toward the River Bann and closing with a less stirring second act. The disparity of the two halves came as no surprise, considering that the front nine, thanks to a bold 1992 redesign, was a hundred years younger than the back.

Where the town of Castlerock seemed a few closed factories past its prime, Portstewart had a style about it, with upmarket eateries dotting a seaside promenade. It was a charming beach getaway that hadn't succumbed to the kitsch of arcades and amusement parks, which were the first thing Sean and I bumped into after leaving Brian at the train station and heading along the beach path to Portrush.

The only course on the Irish mainland to ever host the British Open (1951, won by Max Faulkner), Portrush was one of four courses in Ireland granted the Royal designation by the Crown, the others being Royal County Down, Royal Belfast, and the somewhat oxymoronic Royal Dublin, whose members decided to hold onto their moniker after independence. Ireland's first pro golf tournament was played at Portrush in 1895, the first Irish

Amateur Championship in 1892, and everyone from Harry Vardon to Jack Nicklaus to Phil Mickelson had teed it up on the Harry Colt redesign. But there was some doubt as to whether I was going to add my name to that list when Sean and I arrived at the first tee to find a rather official-looking gentleman standing on the tee box in jacket and tie, gray hair well-behaved in the wind, standing at attention with clipboard in hand.

We approached, treading gently, resisting the urge to bow or kneel or beg for his blessing. He was just the starter, but with so much history, and the fact that we weren't allowed in the club-house (closed to guests on Sunday, we were told, after Sean spent fifteen minutes walking circles around it, looking for an open door) and couldn't even get into the place to use the men's room (the starter pointed us to the bathroom in his hut), I was royally intimidated. I felt like I was back home, where the higher a course was ranked, the more nervous you were about deciding where to change your shoes. Not that I had shoes to change anyway, and not that the starter noticed that fact at all—he shook our hands and welcomed us to Portrush, wished us a good day and offered us the tee. I put a driver down the right side of a generous opening par-four, while Sean, eager to make Boston proud, stepped up to the first at Royal Portrush and grounded out to the pitcher, his ball not quite reaching the ladies' tees.

Since the age of nine, I had given the same directive to every golfer who'd failed to reach the reds—*drop 'em*—but at Royal Portrush, I bit my lip and walked a straight line to the fairway, happy that my shoes didn't squeak.

If you had told me that I was going to play one course in Ireland that had hosted the British Open but not told me which, I would have fingered Portrush by the fourth hole. The course had a major championship largeness to it, no tricks and few blind shots, mostly straight-ahead golf played over a vast, tumultuous stretch of seaside. Unlike its nineteenth-century peers, Portrush was a course where we indeed needed driver, and where the un-scratched greens looked like they'd been rolled out of the sod truck yesterday. We could hear the waves and feel the breezes as we searched the whiskers for our golf balls, but we rarely saw the water, the course sunken into the sand dunes. It wasn't a track that gave you a sore neck from trying to soak in the vistas, but there wasn't a single miscue or meek note anywhere on the golf course, just test after test, and most of them, sadly, a bit too much for the shots we'd brought with us. For purists and historians, and anyone who could figure out how to get into that clubhouse, Portrush was as good as it got. But Sean was in Ireland for four nights, and he went home with three times as many snapshots from Portstewart, for two-thirds the price.

We were on our way back to our B&B after a lasagna dinner that was as good as the trays served in South Philly (lasagna was an Irish menu mainstay—in pubs, at takeaways, in Chinese restaurants, and it ranged from acceptable to damn delicious) when we heard the sound of pipes and whistles coming toward us from down the street. A police car crept up the road, followed by a procession of cops in yellow jackets clearing the road for what sounded like the woodwind section of a grade-school orchestra. I expected to see kids coming up the street, tooting on recorders and kazoos, but what we saw was a marching band in royal blue, a few dozen pipers, and one young man pounding a big white drum. Behind the band were men in dark suits with orange sashes, all carrying umbrellas, some wearing bowler hats. Sean came to Ireland for just a few days, and Irish history buff that he was, he was treated in Portrush to his first Orange march.

For hundreds of years, Ulster Protestants had marched on July 12 to celebrate the victory of the Protestant King William over the Catholic King James at the Battle of the Boyne. It was a breakwater moment that forever shifted power within Ulster and Ireland, and reshaped political dynamics for all of Europe (had a battle on an Irish river gone differently in 1666, there might have been a Catholic Crown in England allied with the French, making for a very different Europe and New World). It was a day that Catholics would prefer remained in 1666, the history made current every summer when Protestant lodges and societies around Ulster donned purple and orange sashes (orange for William of Orange, purple for royalty) and banged their gongs, for some a celebration of heritage, for others, it seemed, a chance to remind their neighbors what the score was.

I had read of the marches as legendarily contentious affairs, rife with bottle-throwing and upturned cars and donnybrooks. And here I was in Portrush, watching my first parade that to me, like all parades, seemed a little bit silly. There were no protests, no religious slurs being bandied about, nary a Pope joke within earshot. In the paper that morning, we read about the closing of the British Army base in South Armagh. During the height of the Troubles in the 1970s, when soldiers had to be airlifted in and out of the base on a daily basis, it was the busiest airport in all of Europe. And now it was empty. As if that wasn't proof enough that tensions in Northern Ireland had indeed simmered down, we watched a sectarian march cut through the heart of Portrush that Sunday evening, and aside from two kids who used to share a dorm room in Indiana, nobody else seemed to even notice.

The next day, Sean's last, we parted ways after a visit to the Bushmills distillery, where an enthusiastic exploration of the history and methods behind Irish whiskey left us convinced that whiskey distilled in Ireland was the planet's purest libation, with the power to heal the sick, nourish the hungry, and opinionate the thirsty. Whiskey came from the Irish *uisce beatha*, meaning "water of life," an etymology that did little to dispel the stereotype of the ruddy-faced Irish drunkard. But who were we to talk—there weren't any ruddy Irishman in our tour group, where dozens of us endured an hour's explanation of the distilling process (Irish was distilled three times, while scotch cut the corner at two, and bourbon bubbled through the pots only once) for our one free mouthful of whiskey awaiting us at tour's end. They sold Bushmills in the snack bar, too, and I sent Sean home with a leftward lean and breath that might have gotten him booted off his 757.

At the Smuggler's Inn, I overpaid for a bed a few hundred yards from the entrance to the Giant's Causeway, perhaps the most stunning natural wonder in all of Ireland, and one that I had been lucky to visit on a day trip when I was studying abroad. Thousands of perfectly hexagonal stones jutted out into the sea, basalt columns forming a sort of staircase chipped out of the mountainside, steps that you stood upon and still didn't quite believe. It easily made my top three to-do list, along with the

Cliffs of Moher down in Clare, and the sight I headed out to that morning to visit for the first time, the Carrick-a-Rede rope bridge.

With Sean headed home, it was back to life on the road with the old companions. Passport in the zippered breast pocket, energy blocks on the left hip, wallet on the right. From over my shoulder came the steady crackle of forged blades wrapping against one another, a clicking cadence I heard in my sleep. And in my back pocket, my best mate, a tear-proof, waterproof map of Ireland. There was a photograph on the cover of the map, a fisherman in wellies looking unbothered as he strode across a rope bridge that appeared to be suspended miles above the sea. I grew to feel a kinship with this stranger, sitting at a breakfast table each morning as I worked out my day's route, just me and the map and that photo of a gray-haired tightroper, the guy who made my walk feel like the cake variety.

The Carrick-a-Rede bridge had been suspended over the waters of the Atlantic for hundreds of years, used by fishermen to cross from the mainland out to a promontory of rock where they could string their nets and trap the salmon swimming through the channel in between. It was a good hike from the coast road down to the tip of the headland, more than a mile up and down a few hundred stairs, during which it was impossible not to think of the fishermen hauling their gear and their catch—how they built that cottage on the promontory or hauled that rusted steel winch out to the island seemed as much of a miracle as the Causeway down the coast.

I stood at the entrance to the rope bridge, a towering cliff to my right, the granite made white by the thousands of gulls tucked into its cracks. Behind me was the expansive beauty of the Antrim coast, green hills rippling into the mist, and birds circling the blue waters, indifferent to the waves crashing on the rocks below. A dolphin swam in a still cove beneath an eroded rock face, and I was watching for it to break the surface again when I was told it was my turn to cross.

I stepped out onto a board that dipped under my weight, and looking down past my feet, I saw black rocks chewing up the turquoise water a few hundred feet below. I had always hated heights and I was an absolute sissy during takeoff, but the rope bridge didn't ruffle me a bit as I bounded my way across the swinging planks. I stopped in the middle of the bridge and swayed gently in the breeze, just to look down and to check—no, I really wasn't nervous. I'd come for golf, but somewhere along the way, I'd picked up a simpler sense of contentedness, maybe even a peace. I had food to eat and a bed in my future and enough tread left on my shoes to get me there. Good enough. In a busier life, I found ways to worry and reasons for the bridge to give out. It was vanity, really, to assume that a rope bridge had been waiting centuries for me to be the one to break it. Living as a dot on an endless road had begun to make the world feel larger and this walker feel smaller—not insignificant, but a bit less complicated, shedding worries with each mile until it was just me and my sticks and a view I hoped I would never forget.

I carried my clubs across the bridge and arrived upon a large stone tabletop covered with shaggy green grass, where I dropped my pack and walked down to the northernmost edge of the promontory. I found a rock jutting out over the water like a thumb. I sat my butt in the grass and slid myself out to the edge, wrapping my legs around the stone and leaning out over the water. That morning at breakfast as I studied my map, I calculated that after crossing the rope bridge, I would have traveled past my journey's halfway mark. I dangled my feet over the waves, this course feeling more possible than ever. It was all downhill from here.

IN

hole 532

314 over par

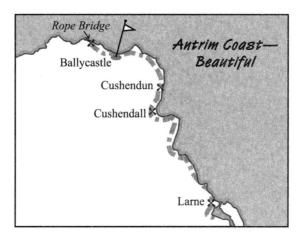

E XCEPT FOR WHEN IT WASN'T.

The charcoal church spires of Ballycastle had just broken onto my horizon when the afternoon headache started up, the one that had been warming in my shoulders before it leaked into my spine and burst into my skull from the top of my neck. It felt like my pack was bolted into my bones and had dropped its anchor back in Bushmills. At a crossroads, I found a sign pointing to the Ballycastle city center, and one to the town harbor—which way to the B&B, I couldn't tell, but after twenty minutes wincing my way toward my first guess, the spires hadn't grown larger by an inch.

I stopped. I hurled my bag to the side of the road, disappointed when it didn't disappear into the brush. I felt it beginning to inch its way free of my fingers—I had resisted it all the way around Ireland, but there seemed little use in fighting the perpendicular digit now. My feet had accomplished plenty, I figured. It was time to see what this thumb of mine could do.

It was a common misunderstanding among the Irish when I explained to them that I was traveling their country without a car at my disposal. "You're not taking lifts?" They seemed less surprised that I was hiking than that I wasn't hitching. Thumbing was a relatively common and safe pastime in Ireland, I was told—not as popular as it was just ten or twenty years ago, when it was considered an Irishman's duty to stop his car and offer a lift to a stranger on foot. (And they're called lifts in Ireland. Ask an Irish woman for a ride, and you might end up wearing her drink. Or her.) A good barometer of how similar Ireland had become to the rest of the busy world was the fact that in my eight weeks walking the roads, I had been offered a lift less than five times. I declined each of them, and frankly, they were more trouble than they were worth, a kind driver pulling over and rolling down his window and asking me to hop in. It was that same awkwardness of trying to explain to a hostess why you weren't interested in her breakfast sausages, pleading with a stranger that *no, no thank you, I'd really rather walk,* until they sped off, no doubt resentful of the fact that I'd taken them for a kidnapping lowlife and thus rebuffed their generosity (in Ireland, accepting hospitality is a must, no matter the inconvenience). But on my way to Ballycastle, I would have handed over my wallet and my passport for one of those munificent motorists. So as I went to start swinging my thumb . . .

I saw a young man off to my right, sitting in a wheelchair by the entrance to his housing development. His hair was like every other teenager in Ireland—tight on the sides, Beckham sloppy on top—and he wore a Manchester United jersey. He looked left and right, then wheeled himself out onto the shoulder and started down the road I had just quit a few minutes before. Ahead of me, I didn't see any convenience store he might be heading for, no nearby neighbors he might be visiting. He pushed himself along the road, hands turning his wheels at a decent clip, and the oncoming cars leaned over the center line, same way they did for me, drivers lifting a finger off the steering wheel to wave hello. I put my pack back on my shoulders, and I walked until I was sitting in a stain-glassed pub off the square in Ballycastle.

Ballycastle was circled on my map for its golf course, but it was well regarded for its *craic*. It had the nod-and-smile main street I missed in Castlerock, with the simple-life niceties that had been overshadowed by the wealth of Portstewart and the slot machines in Portrush. It was back to butchers and barbershops, pubs with hurleys on the wall and a Gaelic games sporting goods shop down the street. The town signs in both English and Irish translation had reappeared, and it felt like I'd hiked back into Donegal, the easy welcome we received at the golf club at the end of town only going to bolster that impression.

My other big sister, Tina, and my brother-in-law, Tim, had just arrived to join up with me for a few days along the County Antrim coast. When I arrived at Ballycastle, Tim was already sorted in the pro shop with his rental clubs and a hefty provision of golf balls, and after meeting the captain of the club, who asked that we tee off ahead of him (we politely declined), any anxiety I'd been feeling about this particular round evaporated quickly. The golf clubs I'd visited over the last week had been a bit differ-ent, and the same could be said for Tim's golf game. From time to time, it resembled altogether different pursuits—field hockey, lumberjacking, scuba—but he had arrived at the perfect course, one void of any raised brows or top-buttoned starters, a place where he wouldn't have to answer for the woman in jeans who was following him around with a camera—*Honey, you're sup-posed to hit it in the air, do it like him*—fighting a losing battle against her giggle fits all the way around their golf course.

Ballycastle was two golf courses in one. The opening five holes were plain parkland, tree-lined runways borrowed from your closest muni. The holes were made more interesting by the fact that they worked their way around the ruins of Bonamargy Abbey, circa 1500, resting place of Ballycastle's reclusive "Black Nun." Her name was Julia McQuillan, and during the seven-teenth century she spent her days making uncanny prophecies about everything from horseless carriages to boats made of iron. Ever penitent, she was laid to rest by the entrance of the church at her request, so that worshippers would forever tread on her grave. Locals claimed that she still haunted the ruins of the Abbey, but if she did, she must have had a soft spot for golfers. There was no other logical explanation for Tim's drive on number four, which went screaming into the bottom of the graveyard wall, only to be spit back out and sent bounding down the fairway. Tim in the short grass? Surely something supernatural was afoot.

Ireland had been tough on my brother-in-laws. I had gotten word that Brian had just now lost his limp back in New Jersey, and Tim, who had just turned forty with a resolution to reclaim a few notches on a tight belt, had been having Irish troubles of his own. He'd been battling the phone box of a shower in their guesthouse all week. *Electric shower* sounded like the world's deadliest home fixture—up there with submersible toaster, kiddie cutlery—but in Ireland, more often than not you needed to flip a switch to get the hot water flowing. Tim had been squeezing into the shower and torturing himself with a trickle of ice water until I got the word to him that he should look for a cord in the bathroom and pull it. I also heard of his trials in the streets of Ballycastle, where more than once he had left a shop and fought his way across a busy road, looking the wrong direction for traffic, dodging buses by a hair and hopping into the safety of the driver's seat, only to find that, once again, hooligans had gone and switched around the damn steering wheel on him. Tim surely deserved better on his vacation, so my hopes were raised for him as we crossed the street and headed for the sixth tee at Ballycastle, where the golf was sure to change. And change it did, from breezy country stroll to wind-battered mountaineering expedition. Eying the black sea cliffs of Ballycastle, it occurred to me that if Tim's day was on its way to better, it was going to have to first make a stop off at worse.

Stepping onto a tee box by the water's edge, the golf course looked like it had erupted out of the ocean, fairways and greens tossed to unlikely heights atop the rock face. After being lulled into a slumber by the opening holes, I looked out at what lay before us, distant dots of golfing colors roaming the grasses at an altogether different altitude, and I wondered, "How the hell do we get up there?"

Unbothered by the test at hand, Tim stepped up to the tee box on six, unsheathed his three-wood, and proceeded to throw to third base. I had seen plenty of perpendicular mis-hits from irons before, but this was my first encounter with a three-wood shank, and I learned that if you wanted to make your shank emphatic, the three-wood was the tool for the job. Tim's ball fired out right and struck the roof of a lovely white cottage that, in the 116 years of the golf club's existence, had probably never been touched by a golf ball. No matter what else he accomplished on that golf course, Tim could say he came to Ireland for the history, and made some of his own.

His game came together nicely on what was a toboggan ride of a back nine. Short and a little schizophrenic and not as tidy as its neighbors (for every hole with a flag in it, there were a good dozen of the rabbit variety), Ballycastle was good *craic*, especially for Tim, who flirted with a few pars on the second nine and carded a very respectable 49. In the clubhouse, the captain of the club introduced us around the bar, and each member took turns trying to buy the Yanks on holiday a pint. It was one "Welcome to Ireland" after another—the Ballycastle golfers would hardly let us leave. And after my doubts about the North, I had the same experience in the postcard village of Cushendun a few days later (picturesque as a postcard, and about as big as one, too), where I stepped out of a bone-soaking rain to dry myself in Mary McBride's pub. I ripped into a toasted ham and cheese sandwich in Ireland's smallest pub (an historically protected site, the original barroom was just big enough for a foursome), squeezed in at the bar next to a white-haired gentleman reading a newspaper and sampling the soup of the day: creamy stout in a tall glass. We struck up a conversation over the tennis on the television, and he inquired about my accent, and how it had landed in Cushendun.

"From the States," I confirmed. "I'm a golfer. I'm on a golf trip."

"A golfer? A golfer from America," he said, relaying the news to his pint. "Well let me tell you. Would you believe there's a golfer from America over here this summer who's playing every golf course in Ireland, and would you ever believe, he's walking his way between every one of them?"

I knew there had been stories in the papers in the South, but it was hard to believe that word had found its way up here, into literally the most miniscule pub on the island. I pointed to my backpack dripping in the corner and told him that I would believe it, because I was the guy. He insisted on buying me a bowl of the soup of the day, and bragged to the whole bar how he was sitting next to a celebrity. Which meant ourselves, plus a sleepy looking barmaid who wasn't quite impressed enough to take her eyes away from Rafael Nadal.

Belly fortified with brown walking fuel, it was back out into the downpour and off to the town of Cushendall. If I would have known how the skies were going to behave for the next thirty-eight days, I might have stayed there in McBride's, or maybe built an ark, but on that Thursday I convinced myself that every rain had its end, and humped it for the next town. I found a place called Johnny Joe's with an old coal-burning stove in the back room, where the bartender stoked the fire and passed me a Guinness. I stretched out legs turned pale blue beneath my waterproofs and dove into the evening paper.

I was halfway through the sports pages when the light grew dim and the newspaper type went murky. I looked up from the paper and found the whole room had gone dark and hazy, because over to my right the iron stove was pumping out black smoke like my mother's old station wagon. Guest that I was, and not wanting to offend the bartender, or his stove, I sat in the back room trying to read through a fog thick as jelly, hands fumbling around the table for my pint—*ah, there it is*—until the barman burst into the room with arms flailing, rushing from one window to the next. "Jaysus, are you alive in here? I can't hardly see you!"

The flue had been closed, but I sat there as if I hadn't noticed—*Smoke? What smoke?*—while clouds poured out the windows. The Italian restaurant upstairs evacuated out onto the sidewalk and the fire brigade was called, locals lining up outside as if ready to start passing buckets. Feeling too stupid to move, I waved my paper at the smoke and stuck it out until the air cleared. It eventually did, and before long the back room was the place to be, with an *eau de anthracite* and a furious game of hearts between me and a threesome of Canadians. The barman played guitar after his shift, and we shared a night of good conversation where

I was once again a minor celebrity, the blind American with a crap sense of smell.

During that week wandering the Antrim coast through the raindrops on my way down to Belfast, I felt particularly grateful for my good fortune, wishing I could send a note to the thousands of other travelers with Irish itineraries who had ignored these distant stretches of the country. Ireland's southwest was undeniable, the mountainsides and seascapes of the Ring of Kerry plucked from a photographer's portfolio. Sligo's mountains spewed poetry, and Donegal's landscape felt as unspoiled as the moon. But inch for inch, the Antrim coast was the most relentlessly beautiful corner of Ireland. The Giant's Causeway and the Carrick-a-Rede were obvious assets, but it was the coast road I loved so well, arched tunnels carved through sea cliffs with a walled roadway snaking its way along the water's edge, the waves splashing up onto the pavement. All along the road from Ballycastle down to Larne, as you rounded each turn you arrived at yet another of the nine Antrim glens tucked into a green mountain valley, patches of white walls and slate roofs gathered at the bottom of the hills like rain.

It was a landscape of dramatic peaks and dips, not unlike the experience of traveling Northern Ireland, which I had found to have its own sort of unevenness. The North was far less tourist-savvy than the southern counties, with fewer accommodations to choose from (though they seemed to be making a concerted effort to catch up) and fewer restaurants and music pubs to scribble about in your journal. There was also a curious shift in attitudes from town to town, conspicuous when you happened to be spending an evening in most of them, fishing for a few minutes of conversation. One night I was laughing and losing at hearts in Cushendall, the next I was in Carnlough, not a smile in the town, it seemed, bored back to my hotel room by seven o'clock. There were clubhouses where they wouldn't let you leave, and just up the road, a clubhouse where they wouldn't let you in. We found streets lined with British flags in villages that could have been on the Cornwall coast, next to towns with signs spelled in Irish, with a top-class pitch for the traditional Gaelic games. There were pubs we left without a penny in our pockets, not far from pubs we left with lager still in our pints.

When I could get the conversation, I inquired about the differences, and some folks described it as a matter of wealth. The stuffier towns were rich with doctors and lawyers, while the *craic* was to be found among the carpenters. Others told me it might be a matter of wealth, but it was first a matter of religion. There were Catholic towns, and Protestant towns, and if I couldn't tell which I was in, I could heed the explanation of one of my hostesses who, though Church of Ireland herself, decided to open her B&B in a predominantly Catholic village. It seemed a less buttoned-up place that might attract more tourists. Or, as she explained, "There's loads of pubs. And the people stay out later. It's a bit more relaxed here. I guess they're not all worried about getting up for mass in the morning."

I had read a small pile of history books, but her explanation of the dynamics of Northern Ireland was as fitting as any. There were the people who had more to lose, and the people who had less, and the former were praying damn hard they never would.

My walk through Antrim ended in Larne, a town from which I intended to take the train south into Belfast (at the top of my list of transportation allowances was a dispensation for travel into and out of major urban areas, particularly when headed for the heart of a centuries-old sectarian conflict). After having been thoroughly wooed by the rest of Antrim, I found Larne to be unremarkable in almost every way. The gray sky blanketing the buildings had a post-industrial permanence to it, and the place didn't offer the quaintness of a town nor the buzz of a big city, the rainy streets down to the seaport stuck somewhere in between. Larne did have some history—it was famous for an incident in 1914 when weapons were smuggled through its port to arm Loyalists opposed to the Home Rule movement. Celebrated in an exhibit in the city museum, I found the coverage of the Larne Gun Running to be careful and enlightening, while the treatment of the history of IRA gun-running felt far less thorough. (I know, I should have been over this by now, but it still struck me as funny how differently history sounded when told a few miles apart.)

I was wandering town looking for some sunshine and a pub where strangers weren't staring at me like I had come to Larne to steal their horse, when I came across a monument in a town park, a tall bronze sculpture depicting what might have been the happiest gang of emigrants Ireland ever shipped. Father standing proud in his waistcoat and brass buttons, mother draped in her Sunday best, junior with a smile on his face imagining a summer in Boston, dreaming of Fenway. The emigration monuments down in Mayo of those drab coffin ships with skeleton frames, the iron all wilted with death—what a downer. When you left from Larne, it was all smiles on board, and per the monument's inscription:

> ... *dedicated to the memory of those first Ulster emigrants who sailed from Larne in May 1717 upon the 'Friends Goodwill', bound for Boston. They were to be the first of many. There is no other race in the United States that can produce a roll of honour so long and so shining with distinction. And who shall deny our claim to have done more, much more, than any others to make the United States.*

Way to go, race, I thought. I wasn't sure if Scranton Irish via Connacht still counted, or if they were talking about that race that left Ireland before the place ran out of food. 1717? Darn, they probably were.

I made my way toward the edge of town where the mood quickly went from suspicious to surreal. In the space of a few blocks, I had wandered from a typical Victorian heyday British town, replete with ivory-pillared doorways and soot-stained storefronts, and stumbled upon a junkyard of the apocalypse. In an empty lot, I found a pile of scrap wood and old tires piled to the sky, four stories of busted pallets and discarded furniture.

Packs of young boys who looked like they'd just been pulled out of *Lord of the Flies* were scrambling all over the woodpile, tossing plywood and banging two-by-fours, climbing to the top to raise their arms and push aside the former king of the hill.

I had two explanations for what I was looking at. Either the Larne council had better get busy making concessions to its waste management union, or the children of Larne had seized control of the town and were going to burn the whole place down, one footstool and bald tire at a time. Before stopping to ask, I thought it best to turn around and head the other direction.

But there it was again, on the other side of town—another barricade from the set of *Les Mis*. This one was in the courtyard of a modest housing complex, right next to the swings and the bouncy horse a little girl rode while lads tossed sheets of cardboard onto the pile. There were faces in windows watching what was going on in front of their row homes, but they weren't looking at these hellions stomping box springs and sofas into scrap—they were looking at me. I thought it wise to leave, but I couldn't help but stare—not because I had never seen such a junk pile, but because this pile was surrounded by Union flags and banners for Ulster, and a half dozen orange flags emblazoned with the letters UVF. The Ulster Volunteer Force was an outlawed Protestant paramilitary group responsible for hundreds of murders during the Troubles. The little girl rocked back and forth on her horse, a UVF flag snapping in the breeze above her head. I dared myself to reach for the camera, but thought better. There was another sign as well, an official-looking notice put there by the city, presumably, at the edge of the courtyard. It asked residents to please not burn tires on this designated bonfire site.

We had a bonfire once in high school. We burnt pine boughs and an empty case of Busch Light. Whatever they were up to, it was going to be one hell of a party.

bole 550

327 over par

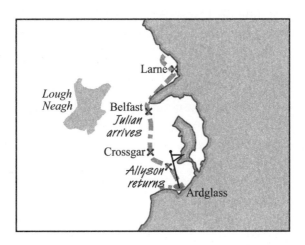

BEFORE SETTING OFF FROM PHILADELPHIA, ALLYSON ASKED ME which compatriot I was most looking forward to joining me on the links. Aside from herself, of course. I told her that it was my English friend Julian's visit I was most anticipating. Not only because Julian was a big-personality extrovert, the kind of guy who could make a best friend at an IRS audit, but because he had a great can-do, no-worries, it'll-get-sorted attitude. This was vacation, there was golf, he was a ferry ride from his hometown of Manchester, and they even used sterling—how tough could it be? Translation: Julian was going to do next to nothing to prepare for this trip, and thus brought with him the sort of potential travel disaster that would either buoy my spirit about how well I was doing, or finally push me onto that plane.

Among my friends back home, Julian was the one most likely to get the waitress's attention. He was tall with surprisingly good teeth and an unthreatening British build, and he wielded his deep Manchester drawl on unsuspecting Philadelphians with potency.

Want a better table? Want them to put the Phillies game on? Send the Englishman. He'd lived in the States for years now, but had maintained his British-man vanities—snappy scarves, those pricey sneakers unfit for sport, spending sixty bucks to have his hair tossed in a salon—so I wasn't surprised when he arrived with a backpack bursting at the zippers. While I'd whittled my load down to a T-shirt and sawed-off toothbrush, Julian seemed to be showing up for every meal in a new ensemble. He forgot to pack his toiletries, left the waterproof hat I gave him at home, and while he wouldn't give me a final tally, I counted at least a half dozen T-shirts, three pairs of shoes, two pairs of jeans, two sweaters, and a hoodie. Julian would eventually admit that he had packed for his two weeks on the road in slightly less than five minutes. It took me five months to carefully allot every square inch of my backpack, and I still felt unprepared. This was going to be horrible. I couldn't wait.

I was also looking forward to Julian's English perspective on this place in the world where his country had played such a significant role. *The* significant role, really. Julian didn't have a mean bone in his body—like any self-respecting limey, he could find one after eleven pints of Boddingtons if obliged, but I had the sense that he, as many proud Englishman might, thought of Ireland as that patch over there where they drank a lot and made bombs out of clock radios and turned out a good rock band once in a while. Not a bad spot for a guys' weekend, but essentially a cranky little brother—nay, more like a nephew—who wasn't quite ready for the grown-ups' table. And if he didn't view the Irish as such, that didn't mean that wasn't how some Irish viewed themselves. In *Links of Heaven*, Eddie Hackett explained, "We Irish had a terrible inferiority complex, with the English occupation and the way we were terrorized and savaged." Ireland had been pushed around to the point where it was hard to feel too good about anything Irish, so Eddie Hackett built golf courses to change that. And maybe that's why I was taking my friend from Manchester to go play them.

I started by showing Julian that Belfast, for all its baggage, was one fantastic city. We headed for the center of town where ivory sculpture seemed to drip from every corner of city hall, the copper-green dome dominating the city skyline. From the seat of Belfast government, the wide promenades of Donegall Place and Royal Avenue felt like Regent Street in London, the sidewalks crowded with upmarket boutiques and swanky restaurants. We found tucked away tapas places and authentic Thai cuisine, and the tour of historic Belfast pubs took us from a wonderfully filthy cottage to a cozy corner Victorian pub with portraits of Wilde, Beckett, and Heaney on the walls. The scene heading out toward Queen's College was brilliant, the streets lined with ethnic cuisines and bookshops and nightclubs we were too timid to sample. We loved Belfast and couldn't help feeling sorry for the place, a bustling college town smeared by decades of bad press, a modern-feeling city ripped up by problems that, in the shadow of chichi boutiques and a Tesco superstore the size of a city block, felt foreign and small. But shortly after an early pasta dinner (Gordon Ramsay be damned, Pizza Express was the UK's culinary benchmark), we were reminded that Belfast wasn't all sunshine and street fairs.

Through the center of town hummed steel-paneled police vans that looked tougher than the trucks our troops were wheeling around Iraq. Street cops bloated with bulletproof vests marched in a row, clearing the street where just minutes ago Asian tourists had been hunting for handbags, and here came the flutes again. This was my third run-in with one of these bowler hat parades, but this Belfast variety was different. Frankly, this one had balls.

It had marchers by the hundreds, dark suits draped in orange sashes, red-cheeked men with bass drums hoisted atop their potbellies boom-booming their way down the avenue. There were teenagers hoisting silk banners of a triumphant King William of Orange, and marching bands done up in regalia of a distinctly military flair. The parade stretched on for a mile, with boys that might have been six years old tossing batons along the way, girls in braids trying to push notes out of their flutes. We followed them around the corner, back toward our hotel, where one side of a row house was painted with a masked gunman pointing a machine gun, explaining that YOU ARE NOW ENTERING LOYALIST SANDY ROW. It was a welcome the tourist board probably wished the Sandy Row residents would reconsider, but it was just a taste of what we would find when we hopped into a black cab and asked for a tour of West Belfast.

I had misgivings about taking a tour of Ireland's most un-photogenic side, the infamous Shankill and Falls Road neighbor-hoods where fifty years of bad blood were still separated by a concrete and barbed-wire wall. But taxi tours of West Belfast seemed to be one of the city's main attractions—the tourist office advertised a wall full of competing tour companies—a sign that things had cooled off, it seemed, that the turmoil had become the stuff of leaflets and brochures. A conflict that had captured the Western world's attention since the 1960s, a crisis visited by pres-idents and senators, a problem that plagued so many prime min-isters, it was all going down in, per my map of Belfast, just a few city blocks. We couldn't come this far and not see what all the fuss was about, particularly since I had an Englishman in tow who had grown up to a soundtrack of IRA bomb scares, and whose hometown had a hole ripped in it in 1996 by a 3,000-pound explosive (no casualties thanks to advance warning from the bombers, from a time when there was honor among terror-ists). Julian wasn't particularly bitter about the devastation to Manchester's downtown—it was his opinion that the shopping district was much improved since the IRA forced the city to re-build it. Don't ever doubt that English resolve.

We jumped into our taxi and buckled up as our driver broad-cast himself via a headset into our speakers in the back. His name was John, and from the backseat we eyed a mullet that was too earnest for snickers—it demanded respect, his hair tight on the sides and spiked high on top, with straightened blond locks cas-cading down between his shoulders. If we were at all unsure about the kind of tour we had signed up for, John rolled into a well-rehearsed introduction:

"I'll be taking you on a tour of West Belfast today, an area of this city that has been devastated and dominated by a conflict be-tween Protestants and Catholics. You might know it as the Trou-bles. We'll be going down the Shankill Road, and then heading back up the Falls Road. What's the difference between the two? I live off the Falls Road. I'm Catholic. I have an Irish passport, I sup-port Glasgow Celtic, and I pray for the Pope in Rome. If I lived on the Shankill Road, I would have a British passport. I'd support Glasgow Rangers, I'd hate the Pope, and I'd love the Queen like she was me mother. That's the difference. That's it there."

For the next hour, we toured the Protestant and Catholic sides of the "peace line," Julian and I scratching our heads to see that there were indeed walls dissecting West Belfast, Cold War–style cement and barbed-wire barricades splitting neighborhoods right between a row house. They were intended as a temporary measure to quell violence in the neighborhoods, but new walls were still being built, and some of them had been in place for forty years. The barricades averaged a quarter-mile in length and grew to a height of forty feet in spots. Gates in the peace line remained open during the day but were closed at night, and if you didn't make it home before they shut, John explained, it was a right pain in the bollocks to drive all the way around. But it was a reasonable concession for the peace the walls had brought, he figured—denizens could get along well enough during the day, but at night, after a few hours in the pub, it was too easy for a kid to walk down someone else's street and find himself some trouble. And the wall made it that much more difficult for folks with more dire intentions to see them out and make an easy escape.

For a Catholic who offered his opinion of Orangemen thusly: "The difference between apples and oranges? There's no such thing as an apple bastard" (one of his many zingers, along with, "The *Titanic* was built in Belfast. Took a thousand Irishmen to get her afloat, and one Englishman to sink her"), we found it interesting that most of John's tour was spent on the Protestant side of the peace line, where we snapped pictures of murals immortalizing everyone from Queen Victoria to Oliver Cromwell to our own Andrew Jackson (an Ulster Scot, who knew?). It felt awkward enough hopping out of a cab to take pictures of a housing project where people were just going about their day, but we felt particularly uncomfortable when John pulled up next to a mural of Stevie "Top Gun" McKeag and handed us an umbrella. "Now go on, get out there and get your pictures, don't mind the rain." McKeag was a Protestant paramilitary who died in 2000 after a suspicious drug overdose (rumors pinned his death on rivals within the Loyalist cause). He was reportedly responsible for killing at least a dozen Catholics, and he was the perennial winner of the "Top Gun" award from the Ulster Defence Association (as *The Observer* described it, the Oscar for top assassin). John pointed to a van parked across the street with two serious-looking men in the front seat, and casually noted that they were here to touch-up the mural in preparation for the upcoming Loyalist festivities. We lowered the camera and stayed in the cab. The temperature felt a touch cooler farther down the street, where Julian got out of the cab and I took a picture of a befuddled Englishman in a Notre Dame Fighting Irish T-shirt, Julian shrugging in front of a brick wall that read ANYONE CAUGHT DEFACING LOYALIST MURALS WILL BE SEVERELY DEALT WITH.

On the Catholic side, the murals seemed to muddy the political waters a bit. The Shankill message was clear—British and Protestant, good, those who opposed that, bad. The Falls Road mural of Republican hunger striker Bobby Sands was reverent and well drawn, and the hands breaking free of British shackles made an obvious point, but the mural near the Sinn Fein office calling Palestine "the largest concentration camp in the world!" felt like a bit of a non sequitur, and while I understood the sentiment behind the Frederick Douglass painting, I was surprised to find a mural directed at me, extolling USA: TAKE HANDS OFF CUBA. The mural of George Bush sucking oil from a pile of rotting skeletons left me wondering if the IRA needed to get back to basics, perhaps bring in a branding firm to streamline the message. Keep it simple, I thought, stick to the broad themes, the way the last mural we visited did, a painted wall advertising taxi tours of West Belfast.

John took us back to the peace line and handed us a blue marker, and Julian and I got out of the cab and signed our names to the wall amid thousands of others from all over the world. On our way back to central Belfast, we drove past a small park on the Shankill side where it occurred to me that the garbagemen must be on strike in Belfast, too. It was another heap of old furniture and packing crates and again, more tires, this mess the size of a basketball court with unwieldy kindling piled three stories high.

"They're getting ready for the twelfth," John explained. "At the stroke of midnight, bonfires all over Ulster will go up. If you go up in the hills and look back down, it looks like the whole world's on fire. They're remembering the Battle of the Boyne, when King Billy defeated the Catholic King James. You'll see the marches in town. That's what they're celebrating. Though they'll march for just about anything. Somebody farts, they'll have a march about it."

There was nothing more tiresome than the American who, after a few jars in his local Bennigan's, started spouting about the glory of the cause, telling stories of how his granddad was an IRA man. History books and newspapers and the stories coming from the front of the cab, they might all have informed my observations, but that's all I felt entitled to—my observations, perhaps a modicum of opinion, but certainly not a stance. The tour and the murals had their effect; there was an undeniable rallying charisma about the whole thing—it made a kid from the 'burbs want to pound a fist on the bar, raise a flag, pen an ode to fallen heroes—but I reminded myself, I was here to play golf. And as a golfer, if someone was banging a bass drum in your backswing, you might notice. And as open-minded as you'd like to remain about why they were doing so, you might not be able to help yourself from pointing out that, first, burning tires en masse to commemorate anything is absurd. Abusing the environment in celebration of one's heritage? It might strike you as unnecessary. You might also come to understand the importance of celebrating British culture in Ulster, but you might further notice, particularly if you were traveling with an Englishman who was genuinely quite modest, as most Englishmen were, the garishness of the everywhere Royal colors, the ten-story bonfires, the paintings of a 400-year-old king, the overdone, in-your-face Britishness of it all. You might find it immodest in a way that doesn't feel very British at all. And banging one's drum in places where one knew that it inspired hatred and fear—more so than malevolent, you might just find it in bad taste. And you might ask yourself, isn't bad taste about as un-British as it gets?

You might, but not me. I was just here to golf.

On the walk from Belfast to Crossgar, Julian learned of the danger of wishing upon a roadside mileage ("Six more miles! The last bleeding sign said six more miles!"), but he made it to town in his high-style, low-comfort sneakers, through the orange blisters and the all-over shin pain that had become welcoming gifts to all my guests thus far. We checked into a B&B on the edge of town, and Julian collapsed atop his bed in our pink bedroom replete with faux bearskin rugs and posters of sparkling unicorns. Watching Julian hobble his way around a fourteen-year-old girl's bedroom, trying to keep his shredded thighs as far apart as possible—it warmed me with a small sense of accomplishment, aware that I could now do the miles and still cross my legs in the pub afterward. There was a time when that maneuver would have felt like a miracle, but I had lost fifteen pounds since then, lightening my load without sacrificing any more clubs, and it seemed as if my blisters had all but given up.

With the passing days and weeks, I was becoming aware that no quantity of half-cooked bacon, no amount of Irish rain running down my back, and no number on any scorecard could change the fact that my wife had gotten the crap end of this summer. For all their silent stretches, my hours were passing rather quickly, and between the speeding Nissans and the hungry thistle, there were plenty of surprises to hold my attention on this course. But Allyson was home where the only surprise was how long her husband had actually been away, and she was surrounded by reminders that our life built for two was down a man. The time difference didn't make things easier—we spoke almost every day, though I was asleep by the time she left her office, and when she did catch me in the afternoon, the conversations were quick and unfulfilling—*How are you? Good. Tired. I'm walking. Call me later. Love you.* Two months between visits felt too long for me, but for Allyson, it was a matter of her mental well-being—another night talking to the dog about reps and warranties insurance seemed an unhealthy possibility, so she found an assignment that needed attention in her company's London office, and on her way over, she made a detour to County Down.

Julian and I met up with Allyson on July 4 in the Downpatrick bus station, not far from where St. Patrick was supposedly buried in the graveyard of Down Cathedral (an understated grave for Ireland's patron saint; just a long slab of granite marking the spot—and in his own act of ecumenical goodwill, a saint so dear to Irish Catholics was buried outside a Protestant cathedral). When Allyson stepped off the bus from the airport, Ireland was instantly all-*craic* again; it wasn't a golf slog or a recon trip, it was a chance to collect things to tell her about, and now that she was here, I could stop mumbling imaginary conversations on the road, trying to remember all the details that were never going to make it into a forty-second phone call. Allyson standing in Ireland didn't seem as strange as it had in Sligo, and traveling as a threesome made things feel like home. Back in Philadelphia, Julian was our favorite third-wheel.

We made our way to the seaside town of Ardglass and settled down for two nights in a lovely wood-shingled cottage across the street from the Ardglass clubhouse. While some clubhouses felt like castles, in Ardglass, it actually was, the bar and locker room stuck inside a fifteenth-century castle set smack on the edge of the sea. Standing in the parking lot at Ardglass, our bedroom with golf-course views was to our back, and to our front, waves spit foam onto the first fairway. To our left, a pro shop situated in a gray stone castle, and a little farther to our left, the best restaurant in town serving Italian dishes that surpassed the standard Irish interpretation. And next to the restaurant was the Old Commercial Bar, the kind of dark, snug place where you'd want to sip your last pint, a pub we found it much harder to get out of then to get in.

The three of us toasted one another, and Ardglass. We sat comfortably cramped in the corner of the pub, chatting up locals who all welcomed us to their town. Our accents informed the room we were indeed here for the golf course, and we quickly learned that we happened to be sitting next to a proud Ardglass member named Gerry. Dressed in a blazer and golf shirt, he looked as if he had popped in from a business meeting for a pint or seven. Thin hair and a chip-lover's belly, he sidled up to our table and took us under his wing, the sort of Irishman who kept those Airbuses from JFK full. Ireland: crap weather, primeval roads, and an exchange rate that felt like a stickup, but such Irish pitfalls turned into Irish charms when you met lads like Gerry.

Gerry refilled our glasses and took us through each hole at Ardglass as if we were playing the course with him. "First hole is a magnificent hole, fantastic par-four up the hill. The mounding around the green is just exquisite, it's perfectly natural. Best opening hole you'll play in Ireland, the best."

The second hole was no slouch either, apparently. "Best par-three in Ireland, that's what I think, honestly, second to none. A hundred sixty yards off the side of an ocean cliff. Just beautiful." But not to be outdone by, "The third is just magnificent," and, "The fourth might just be the best hole on the course." By the time we got to eighteen, Julian and I were ready to blast through the door and play the damn thing in the dark.

The subject turned to the courses I'd played before arriving in Ardglass. "Is this your first course in Ireland? Where else have you played? I could give you a few ideas, there's great golf all around this area."

Allyson looked down at her bar mat and shook her head as I said, "Well, let me see," and then recited every links between Ardglass and the Shannon airport.

It was as quiet as Gerry had been all evening. He squinted as if he couldn't see me across the table, and then smiled.

"You're joking."

"I'm not."

"He's not," Allyson said.

"You played all those courses?"

I nodded.

"Jesus. I never even heard of some of them."

We discussed the remaining itinerary, and Gerry quizzed me on upcoming links: "Are you going to Portmarnock? Royal Dublin? Are you playing the European Club?" And then his eyes lit up a little, as Gerry lowered his chin and whispered as if he had a secret for me.

"Are you going to play the Old Head?"

In the few years since it opened for play, I knew the Old Head of Kinsale had already achieved legend status among the taking-the-private-jet-to-my-helicopter crowd, but I didn't know it was seen as a prize by the Irish themselves. For Gerry, it was his dream to play Old Head, but as it was perhaps the most distant course from Ardglass on the entire island, and the fact that the greens fees were as legendary as the course itself, Old Head had remained just that for Gerry, a dream. Until I gave him my cell-phone number.

"I'll be in Kinsale in a month," I boasted. "You get yourself down there, you're playing Old Head."

It might have been the pints that had inspired me, or Gerry's generous Irish spirit that had turned me magnanimous, but on week ten, I was officially an Irishman—I'd told someone that I could do the near impossible, with no idea how.

Gerry couldn't join us for golf the next morning, so Julian and I made up a foursome with the club's vice-captain and the greenskeeper, and we quickly learned that for all of Gerry's hyperbole, he was hardly off the mark. The opening four at Ardglass were wonderfully preposterous golf holes surging across a craggy coastline, our tee balls played over oil-colored cliffs capped with mossy fairway. I counted thirteen favorite holes for Gerry, but I narrowed mine down to the eleventh, a par-five reclaimed from the sea (one of the members built a two-hundred-yard stone wall, by hand, to protect the fairway) that looked like a fool's proposition from the tee box, the fairway squeezed between a wall of thistled death on the far side, and ocean boulders on the near one. Looking back from the fairway, you could see the landing area was actually quite generous as you worked your way toward a green nestled into a nook beside the water. It was a short course at 6,200 that could play a thousand yards shorter or longer, depending on the wind (downwind, I was able to drive a three-wood through the par-four eighteenth and into the parking lot, finishing with a scrambling bogey), and the sea was in view on almost every hole, uncommon even for a links.

The string of memorable holes at Ardglass was interrupted by a feature I found more fascinating than any vaulted green or hidden fairway—the course was dotted with white stone cottages, each modest shelter a few hundred years old. One-room homes that had long sat empty, they looked like lonely pieces on an endless landscape, ghostlike reminders of an Ireland that must have felt so cramped and yet so vast at the same time. One of the cottages came into play on the par-three seventh (Julian found himself on the wrong side of it, tempting him to play through the window) where a shallow impression was still visible in front of the cottage door. It looked like the remains of an old sandbox, and our host explained that it was the remnants of something called a famine garden, a tiny patch of vegetables grown for the family. Gerry said that on Captain's Day (the Irish equivalent of member-member, the biggest day on the club's calendar) they would open up the cottage and get a fire going and sell cans of beer inside, thus giving Ardglass not only the oldest clubhouse in Ireland, but the oldest halfway house as well. If you weren't playing well or if the rain was falling, he explained, the cottage on seven was usually where your round ended.

Following our eighteen, I was eager to get a look around the castle that Gerry had tried to convince us was haunted. After a recent refurbishment, the clubhouse was as elegant inside as it was ancient out, and our host forced us to try the Guinness and beef pie, a flaky pastry soaked in savory gravy and tender chunks of sirloin that recharged my appetite for Ireland's back nine. Gerry had told us we might be interested to meet the Ardglass chef, a talent of which the members were all very proud. Following our lunch, the chef came out from the kitchen to meet us, a young man who couldn't have been thirty years old named Gerard Sands. Sands, as in Bobby Sands, son of the man whose likeness we had just taken a half dozen pictures of on the Falls Road, the mural of his smile the most photographed painting in Ireland, or so our cabbie had claimed. Sands was a Republican prisoner who succumbed to a hunger strike in 1981 in protest of the treatment of Irish prisoners in British jails (he was actually elected to British Parliament on his deathbed). Gerard had an easy resemblance to his father, but we didn't ask about his dad or his surely unwished-for celebrity, all of that Belfast business feeling far away in Ardglass with a belly full of steak and a scorecard on the table. He told Julian they had something in common, that he'd grown up in England where he learned to love cooking, and that he hoped to open his own restaurant some day. Gerard shook his head at my mode of transport, and he spent a generous amount of time with us during a dinner rush, gregarious and genuine, and seeming pleased that Allyson wanted his recipe for Guinness pie.

There seemed plenty of superlatives to offer about Ardglass, but our opinion was best summarized by the fact that, after counting the minutes to the end of this summer-long Irish adventure, Allyson found herself poking around town the next morning, looking for houses for sale. (Turned out we couldn't afford an Ardglass rowboat. But still, she was looking.)

The next morning, I woke to Allyson sitting upright in bed, her face askew as if she'd just bitten into a bad peach.

"What's wrong?" I asked her.

"What's that smell?"

"What smell?"

"*What smell?*" she said. "You can't smell that?"

I sniffed at the air and looked around our small bedroom. "What are you talking about?"

"Is that," she paused, looking at my clothes piled atop a backpack in the corner, "your *shoes?*"

My nostrils had long been desensitized to the cloud of funk that hovered above my Keens every night, their waterproofness having been compromised by week three, but Allyson's nose was learning what seven hundred miles smelled like—an aroma reminiscent of the forgotten ham sandwich that spent a summer in my seventh-grade book bag. She had brought me Odor-Eaters on her last visit, but they'd been worn paper-thin and now seemed to soak up the stink rather than repel it. She put my shoes outside on the window ledge and shut the window, stuffing her face in her pillow as I rolled over and fell back asleep. Didn't smell so bad to me.

We took our time shuffling out of our beds and plotting our course for Newcastle, where we would be taking on a course some considered the finest links on the planet, the Royal County Down. Excited as I was to be headed for one of the top-ranked courses in the world, it wasn't all smiles in our threesome as we turned up the hill from Ardglass. It was a nineteen-mile stroll to our next tee, an improbable distance considering the state of Julian's backpack (I think he went shoe shopping when I wasn't looking), and the fact that Allyson's had firsthand knowledge of what twenty Irish miles felt like. It was imperative that I devise a better way. I studied the map and wagered that a few miles out of town, it would be possible to leave the main road and drop down onto a beach that looked uninterrupted all the way to Newcastle. A far more direct route, it would cut a good four miles out of our day. If we weren't careful, we'd be bumping into the golf course before we even had a chance to loosen up.

It wasn't my map that let me down; it was the map's key. The symbol for beach was evident enough, but there was nothing to denote an expanse of slippery, serrated rocks, and no map symbol could have warned me of a rainstorm that, even as the black sky poured down upon us, I was imagining reliving a few months into the future, hearing the details of the afternoon replayed to me in couples' therapy, or perhaps in a divorce court where I would be wise to plead no contest.

My initiative to cut miles began with promise as we left our footprints on a long stretch of dry beach, but the question marks started popping over our heads fast as we turned a corner and saw our beach had petrified into stone, and where it wasn't stone, it was ankle-deep with water. We waded through streams and tried to plot a path across long stretches of beach boulders slathered in seaweed. It wasn't a beach, it was a stress test for the human tibia—how many times could one slip on a moonscape of wet rocks with fifty pounds on his back before shattering an ankle? We were halfway to figuring out when the rain came, and too far gone to turn back.

I had never walked a beach in a rainstorm before, and it was a strange and powerful sensation, the vulnerability of exposure without any shelter in sight, not a shack or even a tree, just wind and water in all directions. It was a humbling feeling, to be so inexorably linked to the elements. It was liberating. And then it was very, very cold. Allyson and I stopped to pull on our rain gear, but the momentum of frustration kept Julian plowing ahead, as if he might push on past the black clouds that seemed to stretch on to Scotland. By the time I caught up to him to offer him my rain hat (far more valuable to a links golfer than any umbrella), he already looked like he'd been bobbing for apples for an hour. And by the shattered look on his dripping face, he hadn't gotten a damn one.

I implored my team to keep the faith, reminding them that

the best Irish sun came after the toughest Irish rain, that there was no chance of a rainbow if there wasn't a little water along the way. I thought all of that, but none of it quite left my lips, for fear that if I opened my mouth I might drowned.

My positive thinking was vindicated in the end when after three miles of rain, we did find some bright sky that turned into a sunny beach drenched in yellow. Soon our hair was dry from the breeze and we were slapping on the Coppertone.

For untold miles we walked a stretch of pristine sand, no sunbathers or fishermen, not a paw print in sight. There were no beach homes in the dunes above us, just long empty fields. It was as if Ireland had turned into our own private island, no doubt a reward for our perseverance. And before very long, in the distance, there they were, blocks of color at the water's edge, a palette of civilization that could only be Newcastle.

We dropped our bags in the dunes and drank from our bottles with vigor. Julian sprawled in the grass and peeled off his shoes. The skin on his heels was like the rind of a grapefruit, a pale layer peeled away from the pink meat underneath. He looked at what was left of his feet and laughed.

"That," he said, "was crap."

"We're almost there now."

"And thank god for that."

We toasted water bottles and lay back against the spiny grasses, faces soaking in the warmth. And then I sat up, quick.

"Shit."

"What's wrong?" said Allyson.

"Do you hear that?"

"What?"

"I didn't hear anything," Julian said.

But something wasn't right. It hadn't been right for the last hour. We'd walked too far without seeing a cottage or a footprint or a beach path, and I'd been in Ireland long enough to know better. In the back of my mind, I had been listening for something, so when I heard them, I had no doubt about what they were.

"Listen. There," I said, looking toward the dunes lying ahead of us. "Gunshots."

hole 568

341 over par

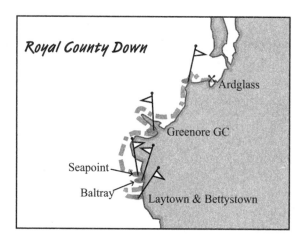

THEY TOLD ME I WAS HEARING THINGS. MY STORY ABOUT THE army base that Brian and I nearly infiltrated near Castlerock didn't impress them. Gunshots? Come on. All we were doing was walking along a quiet beach, a more benign offense impossible to imagine.

They had a point. We hadn't seen any signs or warnings, and it wasn't as if we'd hopped a fence or tunneled our way out onto the sand. And maybe my ears were playing tricks—I'd passed enough lager to fill a swimming pool, and I'd been having night terrors about breakfast sausages. My mind could be misled.

"There's Newcastle," Julian said, strapping up his pack and lowering his chin. "So let's go to Newcastle."

All was quiet as we continued down the beach, silent as we went, ears perked for danger on the breeze, but there was nothing. The *pop pop pop* I had heard could have been carried on the wind from a construction site behind the dunes; there were any number of explanations. But then we saw signs posted along the edge of the sand. Tall, red placards, too far away to read. We said nothing, hoping in our silence that the signs were posted there to warn swimmers about rough surf or dangerous undertow, which was optimism stretched to the extreme, seeing as the beach looked like it hadn't seen a swimmer this century, and the waves were bathtub size at best.

It was the tower that convinced us that something was officially awry. We approached it in the hope that it was some sort of lifeguard facility, only to find that the column was an eerie stack of bricks and steel all alone in the middle of the beach. We'd walked from our private paradise into an episode of *Lost*, and suddenly, as if we'd tripped a wire, the tower began blasting a metallic alarm. We stood there, hearts stopping with each beep, until the alarm paused and from the tower crackled a recording out of East Berlin: *YOU ARE IN A DANGER ZONE. YOU ARE IN A DANGER ZONE. YOU ARE IN A DANGER ZONE.*

We found the first mention of a danger zone convincing enough, but the recording played in a loop until our eyes were moist and our arms were flailing as we tried to surrender to an unmanned observation tower. Allyson was deep into a spree of profanity that had even Julian blushing when a camera atop the tower turned its eye to us. I stood there recalling my other failed shortcuts—tiptoeing through chilly streams, parading about a cow pasture—all holidays when compared to ending up on the wrong end of a British Army base.

Julian tossed his pack to the sand and dropped his ass on top of it. He lifted his arms to the camera as if to say, *Shoot or shut up.*

"Julian, we gotta get out of here."

"Go where?" he said. "Back that way? The last path onto the beach was an hour ago. I'm not going back. If they don't want to let us through, they can come down here and arrest us. At least then they'd have to give us a ride."

"To jail."

"Better than walking back. I am not walking back and undoing the miles we already did."

A disembodied voice came over the tower speakers, and a

garbled English accent told us that we were to collect our gear and return from whence we came. "Proceed no further on this beach," was unmistakable through the static. So on a beachhead near Newcastle, in the County of Down, two Americans and one boiling Englishman surrendered to the British Army. We turned around and headed back over our own footprints.

I wandered up the beach toward the dunes for a better look at those signs. MILITARY FIRING RANGE, they said, KEEP OUT. From the top of the beach, I could now see over the beach grass, to where twenty white targets were planted atop the dunes. And then came the rattle of gunfire, *crack crack crack, crack crack crack*, stopping and starting. You could feel the air breaking into pieces. We made our way back up the beach, double-time, all three of us white-faced and aware that we had been thirty paces from being the backstop for a kid from Bristol's machine gun.

It was hard to read the history books and not grow ambivalent about the "Brits Out" issue. There had been hundreds of years of hair-pulling about the British being allowed to hang around Ireland for so long, during which India, the Colonies, and half the African continent had figured out a way to send the empire packing. The truth of history was that the English army didn't bother with Ireland until invited to do so by one of Ireland's own, a dispossessed king from Leinster (more on him later). The English liked it so much, they stuck around. Could you blame them? Again, it was a question beyond my experience, I reminded myself, and not my argument either way.

But as for that length of beach between Ardglass and Newcastle, the one that had been officially designated an "area of outstanding natural beauty," a stretch of unspoiled strand that someone saw fit to lop off from the rest of County Down and turn into a firing range (I later found a nautical map warning fishing boats away from nearby waters), that beach was most definitely our experience, and an experience about which we all had earned our opinions by the end of that long day. Entirely by accident, we had glimpsed the predicament of playing host to a foreign army. The British Army didn't deny us our civil rights, they didn't burn down our homes. They just made us walk really, really, really far. By the time we had dragged ourselves off that beach and found the road to Newcastle, delirious with hunger, too tired to even lift our jaws—none of us said it, but I think even the Englishman had taken a side.

I found it interesting that the two most prestigious courses in the North, Portrush and County Down, were both situated in towns where the principal pursuits besides golf were bumper cars and bouncy castles. Newcastle had a lovely beach promenade that was crowded with places none of us wanted to visit, the streets busy with sandy weekenders and sun-ripened toddlers. In perfect contrast to the boardwalk feel of the rest of town, the Slieve Donard perched at the north end of Newcastle was one of Europe's most luxurious hotels, a red-brick palace with turrets and steeples set against the mountains of Mourne, with rooms that were only two decimal places out of our price range. One of the few remaining railway hotels in Northern Ireland, it had been visited by everyone from Charlie Chaplin to Tiger Woods, and was popular with Americans who came for what was on the other side of the hotel, the links of Royal County Down.

There was a story about Royal County Down and an infamous, perhaps mythical placard regarding its members. (Aside from the testimony of a fireside storyteller four pints into his evening, I could find no evidence of this sign's existence. But what Irishman ever let proof get in the way of a good story?) As it was told to me, a group of members from another well-to-do golf club had traveled to County Down to sample the links. Upon completing their rounds of golf for which they had all paid a healthy fee, they headed to the clubhouse for a friendly libation. Unlucky for them, the Royal County Down clubhouse was closed to nonmembers, and they were asked to leave. Unpleasantness ensued, the result of which was a sign being placed in the banished golfers' own clubhouse that read: ALL VISITORS WELCOME. EXCEPT FOR MEMBERS OF ROYAL COUNTY DOWN.

On the morning we arrived in the parking lot of RCD (that's what the cool kids called it), we were given a perfectly warm welcome. Granted, it was by the locker-room attendant, who handed us a scorecard through the window (all the doors were locked). But the first tee was empty and he told us to enjoy ourselves and have at it.

And have at it, we did. With no caddies (I would have splurged if the pro shop was open, but all the windows were dark at eight A.M.) and no yardage book, Julian and I walked out to the first tee in the morning mist, goose bumps like golf balls. We turned to each other, and Julian said exactly what I was thinking, a question we would be asking each other all morning long as we traversed the storied hills and valleys of Royal County Down:

"Where the hell are we going?"

Part of me was hoping that I wouldn't care for County Down, that I would be able to debunk the mythos, expose it as an overhyped pretender bolstered by tales of snobbery. The locker-room-window handoff struck me as strange, I couldn't begin to guess where Allyson might find a bathroom, and the ranger conspicuously stalked us for four holes before approaching to ask, "Excuse me sir, are you a member?" to which I probably shouldn't have responded, "Not yet!"

It turned out that the club had kindly accommodated my schedule and snuck me out on a members' day, thus the dark windows and curious ranger. So they weren't a bunch of snobs, and their course was nothing short of remarkable. Manicured perfection was blended seamlessly with punitive wilds in a way that I had only seen equaled at Pine Valley. A target course to the extreme, there seemed a mad genius to the place, mounding no reasonable designer would consider, a routing through the dunes that could have only been uncovered by luck or providence (it took Old Tom Morris two days to lay out eighteen holes at RCD for the sum of four pounds, though the dunes already held the bones of a golf course where locals had carved nine holes out of a rabbit warren). I had teed it up all over the globe, taken on more than half the links in Ireland, yet I went around Royal County Down counting nine, maybe ten holes where I thought to myself, *I have never played a golf hole like this before*. It had all those intangibles that made your spikes feel as if they weren't quite piercing the turf, one of those rare courses where you could feel a perfect handshake between the hand that created the land

and the hand that shaped it into a golf course. Royal County Down wasn't above the hype, and it certainly wasn't beneath it. It was over to the side of all the hyperbole, content to be what it was. Allyson rarely teed it up herself, and after chasing me around so many golf courses over the years, another fairway was as exciting as cereal for dinner. But she got it right as she stepped softly up to the first tee to snap a picture. "This is cool," she whispered. "It feels like we're about to play in the Masters."

Wrong course, but the emotion was spot-on. Our fondness for RCD was all the more meaningful considering the fact that Julian and I spent the day without the faintest clue where we were hitting. Next time, I would get a caddy or spring for the yardage book—if the pro shop was closed, I'd hunker down and wait. Because County Down won the award for most necessary local knowledge—it was a landslide, there were no runners-up. On its website, RCD defended its surplus of blind shots with a quote from Tommy Armour: "There is no such thing as a blind shot to a man with a memory," which seemed a convincing argument. But for Julian and I, our memories were full of pebbles on the roadside and footprints in the sand, sitcoms on the BBC and that stick of anti-chafing balm I told him he didn't have to return. It was a shame that we played the course with blinders on, making a mockery of such a fine links by not knowing if we should tee off with driver or a seven-iron. Precision course that it was, we came to the crest of so many hills to discover that we would have been better off with the latter. And on more than one occasion, we ascended a tee box and teed up in one direction, thought better of it, turned around and teed off in the other.

I wouldn't call it the most fun course in Ireland—it was the toughest links I'd found yet, and if I wasn't able to cling to bogey golf, I would struggle to justify the trip (at $300 for a weekday round, double bogeys felt especially dear). As Julian explained over a pint in the Slieve Donard afterward, "I believe you. I'm sure it is a great golf course. But all the holes look the same when you're staring down at the weeds."

For seventy-one days I had been living in an Ireland that was, literally, beyond the pale. Per my college Irish history professor, the expression referred to the palisades (ditches, really) surrounding Dublin, a territory of English influence from the fourteenth century onward. Within the pale, civilization; beyond it, chaos, at least in the Anglican worldview. In Newcastle, it was a less teary good-bye to Allyson, who would be back in nearly a month's time (her tears, not mine—I still had Julian to snuggle), and my friend and I headed back into the Republic via a passenger ferry from Warrenpoint to Omeath. Julian and I squeezed in eighteen holes at the Greenore Golf Club down the road (an enjoyable parkland course set on the edge of Carlingford Lough), and walked back into the old pale, into a town once considered the northernmost edge of civilization.

Dundalk was famous for its proximity to the birthplace of Cuchulain (koo-hullin), the warrior-hero of Irish legend (sort of the Irish Achilles, re-imagined in the poetry and drama of W.B. Yeats). But we weren't here for the history. As Julian walked down the main street in town, his head on a swivel, he muttered in reverent awe, "There are five thousand pubs in Dundalk."

It occurred to me that this was Julian's first night in the south of Ireland, where zoning guidelines jumped from .2 pubs per city block in the North to the Republic's requirement of 14. And not only were the streets jammed with candidates for a pub crawl, but as Julian noted, even the ordinary businesses in Ireland looked like pubs. With brightly painted storefronts of carved wood and stained glass, names like O'Callan's or Jimmy Murphy's stretched over the doorway, the old-timey placards dangling over an entranceway could lead you into a Laundromat looking for a pint.

"There, that's a dentist. A coffee shop. That's a butcher," Julian pointed out. "And they all look like they serve Guinness."

From our feast of temptations, we settled on McManus's pub, and wisely so. As if Cuchulain wasn't an impressive enough local product, Dundalk was hometown to the Corrs, an Irish pop group with infectious, hooky tunes, the band topped by three sable-haired sisters. Their pictures hung behind the bar in McManus's, where they bartended as young ladies and perfected their craft by jumping in on the pub's regular music sessions. Julian tapped his toes along to his first session that night, a proper offering of young locals playing flutes and fiddles for their beers. As I listened to the music and sipped my stout, I couldn't help but wish it were ten years ago in McManus's with the Corrs girls behind the bar. Julian excelled at making beautiful women smile, and it seemed a shame to have missed out on the vicarious giggle-fun I would have gotten out of watching him try to get phone numbers from three sisters. Instead he made a bartender with blond dreadlocks laugh about his obsession with *Big Brother* (okay, *our* obsession), and we slept well in a four-star B&B that served a legitimate gourmet breakfast. We left the next morning with bellies full and wallets empty, and headed for Termonfeckin (yup, you say it like it sounds).

On the twelfth of July, we found ourselves just a few miles from the Boyne battle site. A few days before, we had watched towns brace themselves for what looked like July 4 meets New Year's Eve meets a punch in the eye, but in the south, the Boyne commemoration didn't even make the news. Just an hour up the road, it was drums and parades and four-story fires. Down the road, it was Thursday. We were grateful for a few hours of sun—they'd become a rare treasure of late—as we chased our golf balls around the young links of Seapoint.

Opened in 1993, Seapoint was designed by Ryder Cupper Des Smyth on linkslands more famously inhabited by its neighbor, the County Louth Golf Club (Baltray), where Julian and I were booked to spend the night in the clubhouse. We guessed our beds at Baltray were a few miles away, but we'd do the extra walking to squeeze in Seapoint, a course I hadn't heard of until the afternoon before. But that was the nice thing about the places I'd never heard of—they were usually less of a sucker punch at the register, and they typically rolled out a redder carpet.

We were met in the pro shop by the club manager, Kevin, a big man who greeted us like old friends. He walked us around the facility and played parking-lot caddy, running through the holes and filling our heads with advice. He was intensely proud of the place, and you got a sense that they weren't sitting around at Seapoint waiting to be crowned a top Irish links, but were busy busting their backs to guarantee it. Not fifteen years old, the clubhouse was already in the midst of a major overhaul, and the original design had been reworked by the father-and-son team of Declan and Ronan Branigan. But as Kevin described his course to us, he might have been confused by our jolt of excitement when he told us, "The Baltray course backs right up to our fifteenth tee." After doing the feckin' miles to Termonfeckin, to hear that our bed for that evening was just over that hill, Julian and I just about jumped in his arms.

We enjoyed Seapoint on the first sunny afternoon in a month, an adolescent links with a few parkland touches (marshlands, for example) and a generous, almost American feel to the fairways, a welcome change after watching Julian weep his way around County Down. The last four holes came upon us like a rouge wave—after working hard to convince us that we'd been playing a resort layout on the Gulf Coast, Seapoint's closing stretch headed for the ocean's edge and played as a pure links, towering dunes and cradled greens that had us closing to a crescendo. It was certainly a favorite course of Julian's, seeing as it was the course where we devised a match that allowed him to shoot 119 and beat me 1-up for the first round of beers.

It was late afternoon when we set off to hike our way across two esteemed golf courses under the weight of bloated backpacks, his purple, mine blue. I'd buried vanity back in Clare, and Julian hadn't bothered with his hair since the beach soaker near Newcastle (nostalgic for his native fry-ups, Julian couldn't help himself at breakfast, and the sausages had regressed his complexion back to a spotty age sixteen). On the roads, in the pub, facing honking horns or pointing fingers, we couldn't be rattled. But on the golf course, it was evident that we still had our soft spots. We withered under the gaze of passing golfers who couldn't make out how the hell we had ended up in the middle of their golf course, two lost backpackers trying to stay out of their way, and doing a pretty poor job of it.

"Did you see the look on that guy's face?" Julian said as we passed a foursome of silent, tight-eyed members. "Utter contempt."

We swallowed our pride and kept our eyes on our feet and

headed for the Baltray clubhouse in the distance, an imposing gray country house, ivy-covered walls and a slate roof with a modern expansion branching off the back. The place was rocking when we arrived—I'd heard the drunk-driving laws play scapegoat for a lot of empty clubhouses, but at Baltray, golfers were tucking into full plates in the dining room, spouses showing up at the bar for a proper Thursday outing. We ordered lasagna and asked them to put *Big Brother* on the flat screen, and all was good. (About *Big Brother*—while the American version might have been the basement-standard in television, in Ireland and the UK it was nothing less than a phenomenon, with its own section in the daily papers and twenty-four-hour Orwellian coverage down the dial.) Our room was just up the stairs, around the corner from the lounge. Our digs were spartan, two beds and a sink, but we would actually be sleeping in the clubhouse—it felt like the coolest sleepover ever, like we were locked in a golf fun park after close—roll out of bed and fall right onto the first tee outside our window. That was the plan, and it would have been a fine one, but the next morning we woke up and found that we couldn't quite see through that window, as it was coated with a rippling sheet of water.

As we fought our way around Baltray for five hours in a steady sideways downpour, I began to wonder if my hubris had brought on this summer's conditions, if my attempt to conquer Ireland on foot had brought on some cosmic stormy juju. To that point, it had rained for thirty-two straight days and, sadly, the worst of those thirty-two was my day in Baltray. The rain paused just long enough that morning to trick Julian into trying the course in a pair of khaki shorts. By the second hole, my rain suit had given up, and my shoes were piles of cold pulp. I had felt drier in a swimming pool, and Julian looked a special sort of miserable with water cascading off his chin and drip-dropping from the hem of his wrinkle-free Dockers. On number nine, he dropped his clubs in the middle of the fairway and stomped off the course, headed inside to change into waterproofs that had been doing a bang-up job keeping a hanger dry in our room. When Julian hadn't reemerged by the tenth green, I headed back to the clubhouse in search of my partner. Not in the pro shop, not in the lounge, and he wasn't in the bar—I found him up in our room, curled beneath the covers. Fingers clenching his blanket, he eyed me with disdain.

"Dude," I said in a tone of obvious disappointment.

"Dude yourself."

"You can't just leave your clubs out there."

"You get them," he said, rolling toward the wall.

"Get up. We didn't walk all the way out here not to finish."

Not a word from the bed.

"So you're a quitter?"

He thought about it. "A dry quitter."

I threw a towel at him and in ten minutes Julian was crossing the fairway, chin lowered into the rain, no doubt mumbling something inhospitable about my heritage.

I had heard Baltray described as Ireland's great hidden gem (with so many hidden gems, could they really all be hidden? Or really be gems?), and crossing it under my backpack the day before, trying to find our way through wild sand hills, I couldn't wait to trade the pack for my Mizunos and get back out there. But as we sloshed our way around the course, just us and a busload of Japanese golfers who would eventually give up themselves, I wished I had decided to spoon Julian instead of cajole him out of bed. By the end of the day, we were rain-drunk and slappy from our predicament and we laughed our way in. Julian was rewarded for his perseverance, playing the last three holes one over par, and we spent the rest of the afternoon boiling our skin pink and moaning like adult film stars in the steamy Baltray showers.

Drogheda—the name brought me back to an Irish history final and pages of my own scribble about a grumpy guy called Cromwell. The name Oliver Cromwell was stamped into the DNA of Irish Catholics, and nowhere more so than in Drogheda where, on September 11, 1649, his army of British parliamentary forces laid siege to the town. It was another episode from its history where Ireland played boxing ring for other people's problems,

England's Civil War between Royalists and Parliamentarians exploding upon Irish soil. Cromwell's army burned the churches of Drogheda, murdered priests, slaughtered women, and used kids for shields in a massacre that saw more than three thousand killed. The town was emptied and the handful of survivors were sold into slavery (estimates claimed that up to 20 percent of the native population of Ireland was killed or exiled as a result of Cromwell's conquest, and Catholic land ownership declined from 60 percent to less than 10). But today Drogheda was a happening river town and a natural base for exploring the most ancient sites in Ireland. Newgrange, an enormous and ancient tomb site that predated Egypt's pyramids was just up the road, and the tenth-century high crosses and perfectly preserved round tower at nearby Monasterboice were must-sees for history hunters. Drogheda got credit for its history, but it got love for its golf. The town was split by the River Boyne—on one side of the river's mouth, Seapoint and Baltray shared the same dunes, while just across the water, the links at Bettystown beckoned to come give them a try. So I did.

Julian ended his trip in Drogheda, catching a bus back to Belfast and a plane over to Manchester to catch up with Mum, but he was being replaced on the road that morning by an almost perfect stranger. A friend of a friend, I had met Chip on a total of one occasion. But he wanted to see Ireland, and too much time alone on the road was bad for the spirit and a bit dangerous, so I opened up my invitation to all comers, and shortly thereafter received an e-mail from a golfer who said he would meet me in Bettystown. I knew Chip was a nice guy, assured by our mutual friend that he was, indeed, "a good dude," but I was somewhat leery about traveling a week and sharing close and mediocre accommodations with a guy whose last name I didn't know. I think it started with an F, with a pocketful of syllables. And when I heard of his plans for getting his clubs around Ireland, frankly, I was a little scared.

hole 640

401 over par

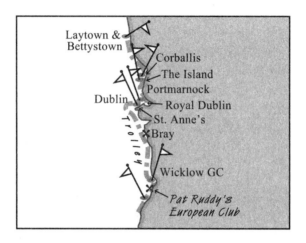

WHEN I FOUND A NITTANY LION STARING AT ME OUTSIDE the pro shop at Bettystown, a big blue cat stitched across the front of a Penn State golf bag, I had an idea who I would meet inside. Chip was mid-chat with the club manager, who had come by on his day off to ensure that we were welcomed properly to the Laytown & Bettystown links. Chip was goateed and bald with an olive complexion, skinny with a soccer player's build, and he was bright with expectation that morning as we hustled to the first tee at Bettystown. If this was a trip of me versus Ireland, I had been on a losing streak of late, the puddles and the rain eroding my resolve. I'd spent the last week daydreaming about how close I was about to come to Dublin airport, and how a quick side-trip home would fill me with new life. Chip arrived just in time. He had never traveled outside the United States before, so his enthusiasm for the next ten days couldn't help but rub off on me. And we had reached a spot on the calendar where we were about to play nine courses in as many days. If I was going to quit Ireland, it wasn't going to happen when there was golf tomorrow.

No matter where I looked or how far I wandered, Ireland was looking like more of the same bumpy field, the same half-empty pub, the same breakfast room at the bottom of the stairs with plaques on the wall and portraits of pale teenagers wrapped in graduation robes. But Chip's fresh eyes brought light back to the peccadilloes of Irish living that my months had me taking for granted, and his perspective on Ireland's curiosities reminded me that, indeed, they were curious, and in a few short weeks I would probably miss them. Chip was right to wonder—what was up with the two-button toilet? And had he been pressing the right one? (If there was any doubt, best to press both.) Red sauce? (Ketchup.) Brown sauce? (Delicious, and a panacea for all of Ireland's gastro-shortcomings—throw it in the fryer, and smother it in brown.) A döner kebab, that's something you eat? (Do you ever.) And why did every bathroom sink in Ireland have two faucets? (This was a question that proved Chip wise beyond his few days of washing his hands in Ireland. The separation of hot and cold faucets was a pervasive problem all over the island—a national bathroom catastrophe, really. How Ireland got wind power and Wi-Fi before it got lukewarm water remained a mystery to me, but maybe the Irish liked it that way, having their hands scalded raw on one side of the sink, before icing them down on the other.) I couldn't wipe the smile from my face the night Chip asked a waitress what kind of dressing came with his salad. (Her reply: "Salad dressing.") But my favorite Chip-leaves-the-mainland moment came outside a Laundromat in Bray after negotiating a price for our load of laundry. Chip stopped me in the street with a worried look on his face, and he whispered under his breath, "Dude. What's a jumper?"

Chip was the first golfer to arrive thus far with a full set of fourteen golf clubs. He'd fit all his clothes into one of his kids' schoolbags, but when it came to golf gear, he didn't skimp. He'd even brought with him his own pull-cart (called a trolley in Ireland), a banged up aluminum model circa 1972, held together by a bungee cord. I had weighed in against the pull-cart idea in an e-mail months before, aware that the roads were barely wide enough for two feet in a tight line, let alone a rickety conveyance, but my protests had little impact. Chip's full set was coming, and if that meant he had to bear stares and jeers as he wheeled his clubs through the heart of Dublin, risking his life along the back roads to Brittas Bay, so be it. You see, what I didn't know about Chip, but would fast figure out, was that my new friend from Philadelphia was an absolute golf addict.

Chip, I would later learn, had a putting green in his front yard (the *front* yard, not even trying to hide his golf dependency in the back), and for something of a quiet guy, he could spout Tour stats and Open history like an R&A librarian. He was here to play, and play he did: in seven days, he played nine rounds of golf (Bettystown, The Island, Donabate, Corballis, Portmarnock, Royal Dublin, St. Anne's, Wicklow, and the European Club). Not a record-setting tally, but pretty damn impressive when you're golf tripping without a car. With Chip's addiction to feed, my weeks of pedestrian penance quickly turned into a mad dash to gorge ourselves on golf courses.

Laytown & Bettystown (one course, two towns) was a find, a traditional nine-out, nine-in links packed with variety and vistas, short enough to leave the woods at home, but still hard and fast links fun set against the ocean. Corballis was a positively schizophrenic layout—we played the front nine wondering how we'd never heard of the place, the holes winding through rolling dunelands, tee boxes with towering sea views, undulations to make you queasy, as good as links golf got. And then the back nine took us across the street to four holes squeezed onto a soccer field, the course going from a natural masterpiece to a pitch 'n' putt. I guessed that the course was once a nine-holer, and it was a shame they hadn't let it be.

Sharing the same dunes with Corballis was a historic Irish treasure that flew just under the radar for most American golfers, the Island Golf Club. The Island was one of Ireland's original dozen courses and was one of the only nonmilitary private clubs in the country when it was founded in 1890. Up until 1973, the club was accessed by boat, a ferryman transporting golfers to and from the town of Malahide, and the course felt like it was still stuck in that past—wonderfully so—as the Island played like more of a landscape than a layout. It possessed the welcome quirks of golf holes from a time gone by, the course being home to Ireland's narrowest fairway on the 330-yard fourteenth, where the short grass was just slightly wider than an escalator, with an estuary to your right and death by heather on your left.

The club captain and secretary came out to the putting green to greet us, helping to give Chip the impression that I was somebody I wasn't, and we challenged a few Irish newspaper friends to a Ryder Cup rematch. I strapped my saddle to Chip's twelve handicap, which was being openly questioned by the back nine, and we secured the right result this time, American pride restored with a 4 and 3 victory. Not a long hitter with a bit of a jerky, slap-shot move, Chip played well in Ireland, regularly besting his handicap, a feat I had only accomplished a half dozen times in the last ten weeks. On the course, Chip had the intensity and focus of a golf-head, a guy I used to be, and he was a reminder to not just get through these holes, but to get into them.

We challenged ourselves to play Portmarnock and Royal Dublin on the same day, and found them both as good as advertised, and neither as stuffy as I'd been warned. Built on the remains of the old Jameson family golf course, Portmarnock had played host to the British Am, the Walker Cup, and twelve Irish Opens. It was an all-male course, one of Ireland's old-school clubs for the Dublin to-dos, where I was a little anxious about how Chip's trolley was going to be eyed by the starter.

We were a few miles from the clubhouse when a car pulled over, lads looking to belittle Chip's trolley, I presumed. But instead, a gentleman in a golf sweater had pegged us for golfing brethren, and he offered us a lift. I would have usually declined, but we were late for a tee time at a course that I didn't think was going to be impressed by our excuses, or my shoes.

"You playing Portmarnock?" he asked us, and we told him we were.

"Good course?" Chip asked.

"The best," the man explained. "Won't find a more beautiful old links in Ireland. Classic. And entirely playable. Doesn't beat

you up like some of the other courses you've probably been playing."

I looked at the logo on his sweater. "You're a member?"
"Me? No. I'm the pro."

Not only did we arrive at the tee under escort of the head golf
professional, the club manager welcomed us into the sprawling
white clubhouse and toured us around a building built for goose
bumps, a museum of Irish golf history lined with photographs
and the names of bygone champions, the gold and silver of old
trophies twinkling in the corners of dark mahogany hallways.
Aside from Chip being asked to change his black socks for white
ones (not so much a snobby request as a weird one), we were
generously received at Portmarnock, and sent off the tee early so
that we might enjoy the course before the tour groups arrived
and clogged the fairways. The pro was spot-on—the terrain was
a bit more tame, not the roller coaster of some of the western
links, but it was subdued in the noble sense of the word, a links
without gimmicks and without blemish, and not a single mediocre hole. And the pro was right again about it being playable:
Chip and I both broke 80 in a light breeze off the Irish Sea.

Nearby Royal Dublin was surely the only course in the world
built by the survivor of a maritime mutiny. Captain William Bligh
of *Bounty* fame didn't design the links, but he was responsible for
engineering a seawall that led to the formation of Bull Island in
Dublin Harbour, the island upon which Royal Dublin was situated. We reached the island by crossing a long wooden bridge
just wide enough for one car at a time. After being battered as an
artillery range during WWI, Bligh's island was given a golf course
by celebrated designer Harry Colt (Rosapenna, County Down,
and a few hundred more courses of note). Christy O'Connor
served as the club's head pro starting in 1959, and in the 1966
Carroll's Irish Championship at Royal Dublin, knowing he
needed to close with three birdies to tie for the lead, he finished
2, 3, 3 (eagle, birdie, eagle) to win. Royal Dublin felt more compact than Portmarnock, but was a course of the same high standard, making the most of its flattish harbor topography with
formidable bunkering and subtle humps and hollows lurking
around the property. They were impressed in the clubhouse to

hear that we'd played Portmarnock that morning, and the Captain bought us cheeseburgers and pints until Chip and I agreed that Royal Dublin was the superior of the two.

After a night spent wishing we had splurged for the Clontarf Castle Hotel next door (a rehabbed modern four-star hidden behind battlements and turrets, and far superior to our mold-scented B&B where the lady of the house was nineteen, Russian, and making out with her boyfriend in the sitting room when we arrived), we struggled at St. Anne's, a slightly younger links that covered the other half of Bull Island, backing up onto Royal Dublin. Royal Dublin's ninth hole bumped up against the south end of the St. Anne's links, and the old St. Anne's clubhouse served as an improvised halfway house for golfers playing the course across the street—if your husband went missing in action on the Royal Dublin links, the seasoned golf widow knew to try the bar at St. Anne's. The old clubhouse had been replaced by a modern compound where Chip and I both got lost looking for the locker room. It looked like a giant mushroom cap planted in the middle of the golf course—in its effort to blend in with the rest of Bull Island, its organic design made it stick out all the more. The course felt ordinary after Royal Dublin and Portmarnock, and the holes were either unfairly narrow, or Chip and I had slammed into a golfing wall, both of us losing balls as if trying to jettison cargo in a storm.

Chip and I put the clubs down for a few days and headed for Bray, and then for Wicklow. At the end of Wicklow town we came upon the first tee of a seaside track where it was a special treat to tee it up with members on a course unknown to Americans, no tour buses crowding the parking lot. We surveyed the packed Wicklow Golf Club from the third tee, and I asked our Irish playing partner if there was a tournament on at the club today, to which he replied, "Yeah, you're in it!" It was a modified Stableford tournament, Stableford scoring being the ubiquitous Irish standard—if you asked how someone fared in a tournament, they didn't say ten over or 92, they always answered in points: 27, 36, two points for a net par, one for bogey, etc. Four natural birdies for Chip and me left us just short of the prize table, but we were pleased enough with our round. While we'd heard of more storms up in Dublin, Chip and I soaked up the sun all afternoon, long shadows following us around one of my favorite finds in weeks.

Now Wicklow was not a great golf course. Short at 5,900 yards, and in need of a few more lawnmowers or more people to push them, I wouldn't recommend dropping your tee time at the European Club to give it a go. But considering that we happened to actually stumble upon it en route to the European Club in Brittas Bay, it felt like I'd uncovered another Irish secret—Greencastle, Ballycastle, Cruit Island, Bettystown, Mulranny, and now Wicklow, something of a semi-links perched upon cliffs above the Irish Sea, ruins of the Black Castle hanging off the rocks at the end of the first hole, hefty cannons still pointed at the waves.

Rather than focus on the fine points of course architecture and design, I had come to judge the golf courses of Ireland by a more essential set of criteria—number of balls lost, sandwich selection in the bar, proximity of the clubhouse to a B&B with a working shower, locker size (can the lockers fit, say, an overstuffed backpack?), and most importantly, number of times I reached for the camera. Wicklow scored above average in most categories, but it was among the Irish leaders in the last. You needed a pair of mountain boots and a few carabiners to repel your way around the mountainous back nine, but on a day where I was just trying to squeeze in an extra round for Chip, who was coming to the end of his first golfing trip abroad, we looked at the sea and rock and sky all around us that afternoon, and, sage course critics that we were, muttered to one another, "Man, this is pretty cool."

There was another important criteria by which I was judging courses—the sum of slobber-toothed canines residing along the route to the golf course. The Irish loved their dogs, and they loved to let them be dogs, meaning they didn't take them to puppy kindergarten or put disagreeable dogs into therapy. They let their dogs run free, to frolic and mate and chew on American tourists. There was no rabies in Ireland, so I had the sense that people got a dog, put some scraps by the door at night, and hoped Buddy didn't eat all the chickens. I never figured out the breed or mix thereof, but there was one particular type of mutt in Ireland, a terrier-sized devil with a tight blond coat and an angry little mug that had infested the island like locusts. They were everywhere, and there wasn't a widow in Ireland who wasn't harboring a gang of these little yippers, dogs who, somewhere in their history, had been bred to hunt redheads. (Dogs must have been a similar nuisance in England, because at first sight of a roadside puppy, Julian darted across the street before I could turn around to warn him.)

Dog lover that I was, I went into each dog encounter—and there were many, one hundred would not be an exaggeration—with the best of intentions, hoping I'd found a pup like that Lab at the Beach Bar who would take a treat or let me pet him, a dog to make me miss my friend back home. But what I usually encountered was a half dozen shrieking terriers whipping around the corner of their house, and me nearly jumping into traffic as they snapped and bounced like furry little racquetballs, trying to get at me over their front wall. And that's when there was a wall. We were five miles from the European Club outside Brittas Bay, clubs on my back, Chip still wheeling his, when I was reminded that that wasn't always the case.

"Did you see that dog?"

I hadn't. We were on an empty, tree-lined road, no homes or farms or traffic to distract us, and I'd retreated into a state of ambling zombiness for I didn't know how long. I turned around, and a quarter mile behind us, I saw a brown dog with his head low, loping along the side of the road.

"Is he following us?"

"I don't know," I said. "Where'd he come from?"

"We passed him like ten minutes ago. Way back there."

"Just keep moving," I assured Chip. "He'll get tired and head home."

We kept moving, an unspoken spring in our step. Every minute or so, I would look over my shoulder and see that the dog was still there—he hardly looked like he was moving, but he was somehow drawing closer. Then every thirty seconds, I'd twist around my pack to see that he was still coming, until I could make out the breed—a very sick Saint Bernard (of course, it had to be a Saint Bernard), its coat hardened with filth, a mangy armor of crap and mud protecting what I could tell was a malnourished frame, no doubt all skin and bones under the shag. His eye sockets hung open and looked heavy with fever, his eyeballs just two black dots swimming in red. It was all the more frightening that the dog wasn't barking but stalking us silently, as if he didn't want to alert anyone to an impending event.

"Let's go, move it, move it," I told Chip, lungs tight with panic. We both went to full hustle, me jogging beneath a backpack, Chip's trolley wheels rattling as loud as they could go. I looked back. The dog was ten feet away.

"Shit. Shit. Shit."

Looked back again, and he was five. And then Chip, "Tom, he's right here, he's right here," and I turned around to see that he was, his nose just about touching Chip's Nittany Lion.

There was no way we could outrun it. Choices were simple: grab the nine-iron and give him a whack; grab the nine-iron and give Chip a whack, leaving him for bait as I ran for my life; or pray for a farm, like the one we discovered off to our left. We hopped a cattle fence and watched the dog sit down beside Chip's bag and lick his lips. We headed up a tractor path to meet a very confused farmer who eventually understood why he was speaking with two American trespassers in the middle of a Wednesday morning. We were right to leave the road when we did, he told us, because there were plenty of sick dogs in the area that needed to be put down. He let us wait until the dog retreated out of sight. We hopped the fence and hit the road, turning around at two-second intervals—*Still gone? Yeah, still gone*—all the way to Brittas Bay.

I had called ahead to the European Club, hoping that I might cross paths with golf writer turned course designer, and one of the seminal names in Irish golf, Pat Ruddy, the man behind designs like Portsalon, Rosapenna, Ballyliffin, Druids Glen, and his baby, the European Club. I called a number that I guessed was the pro shop, and after two rings found myself fumbling, speaking to the man himself.

"Mr. Ruddy, if it might be possible, I would really appreciate the chance to speak with you in person. I'm going to be at the European Club next week. What I'm doing, actually, is I'm playing all the links in Ireland, and I'm walking . . ."

"I know all about it, Mr. Coyne. We've been waiting for you. We'll see you Saturday, then. I want to get a look at those shoes for myself."

Over the last few years, I had received hundreds of e-mails from readers who wanted to know what they had to do in this life to come back as me in their next. My uncle regularly inquired if I was going to perhaps be disappointed when I got to heaven. I'd spent two years chasing a golfer's dream around the globe, living life on the far fringes of professional golf, and for my encore, I'd gotten spousal clearance to go golfing in Ireland for four months. The former adventure wasn't the paradise it may have sounded like, and the latter had proven to be anything but a vacation. But in Brittas Bay, I decided that those readers were sending their e-mails to the wrong address, that they should have looked up Pat Ruddy, the golf writer I wanted to come back as, a man who twenty years ago found a stretch of untouched dunes south of Dublin, convinced a bank he had a good idea, and built himself his own golfing Mecca.

Like Hackett before him, Ruddy wasn't trained in course architecture, didn't apprentice at a big design firm or hold a degree in agronomy. As he explained to us over a meal of lovely beef stew and homemade apple tart in a simple clubhouse built for functionality, he came from a different era of golf in Ireland. In his sixties, Ruddy was a large man, bulked up by that stew, his mouth curled in a perpetual grin and, behind yellow-tinted glasses, a glint in his eye that gave him a look like he had another joke at the ready. He recalled a time when, growing up in Sligo, golf balls in a leaner Ireland were such a commodity that you wore the cover off them, then repainted the balls by hand—he remembered golf balls hanging from strings as the paint dried. And when your ball went missing in the high stuff, you got shoulder to shoulder with your foursome and shuffled your feet through the grass until the ball was unearthed. I had to imagine this sort of golf upbringing made him a straight hitter and informed his philosophy of course design, making him less sympathetic to bashers who considered fairways more of a nicety than a necessity.

There was plenty of evidence around the European Club that the place was the result of one man's uncompromised vision—the modest clubhouse, the twenty-hole layout, the quirky logo that looked like a scoop of ice cream on a footstool (it was a giant golf ball on top of a dolmen, a prehistoric stone tomb), touches that would have brought a board of directors to a stalemate but could just go ahead and happen when the place was all yours. Pat Ruddy's European Club philosophy was explained at length in a handout provided to all visitors, and Ruddy's writing made it clear that you weren't just going out to play a golf course, but were set to go take part in an idea. And that idea was that golf should be golf, and played for golf's sake. As Ruddy writes, "Our approach to golf is fundamentalist. Accordingly, you will not find any fussy furniture on our links. You might take it to be spartan while we think it is akin to the way the game was in the beginning and it should be now. Take your clubs, card, and pencil, and go out and do battle with a golfscape that requires no artificial adornment."

For a man who held onto golf balls until they needed a new coat of white, it was no surprise to read Ruddy's opinion that, "Golf is a game of skill." And in a disclaimer that would never make it past your greens committee, "We make no apology that the thoughtless and inept player may suffer on our links." With four different tee boxes to choose from, the course was intended to be playable for golfers of any skill level. But if your ego should have you playing from the wrong teeing ground, Ruddy asked one thing: "Please call it suicide rather than murder!"

Speaking to the man, you came to understand what it might take to step out on your own and contend that you could build a great golf course, that you were capable of creating one of the world's few true links courses, and the first genuine links built on Ireland's east coast in a hundred years. You had to be big—which he was, a broad man in his cardigan sweater and striped blue tie—but more important, you had to possess a sort of unsteady brilliance. You had to be a touch mad to look at a spread of bumpy grass from a helicopter and decide to bet your life on it. Ruddy seemed to have that sort of eccentric wisdom, and he certainly possessed the carefree confidence for the job. Our conversation ranged from the usage of railroad ties in his bunkers (apparently a common feature on links that well predated famed American architect Pete Dye), to the constitution of a truly sublime apple tart, to the possibilities of telepathic communication. His club was being born around the time Ireland was becoming part of Europe, and he wasn't afraid to stick his stake in the soil and announce to the world that his course deserved the title, that *the* European Club was down here in an unknown patch of a country formerly considered Europe's little brother.

Ruddy built his club as a place where "golf is played for its own sake rather than as a mere adornment of modern and social business life." In the one-story clubhouse, there was a simple pro shop, an unfussy restaurant with tables and chairs, a utilitarian locker room, and a kitchen. Not a sniff of pretension, the brick and mortar kept plain to let the golf course speak. There were no preferred tee times or engraved lockers or members' lounge—the only mention of status at the European Club were plaques posted around the course to let you know when you were about to play holes ranked among the top in the world (7, 13, and 14). "Golf has always been a welcoming game in Ireland," Ruddy wrote, "with no need to network socially to gain access to a game." A game. I had traveled 888 miles to that day to meet an Irishman in yellow glasses who explained what it was about golf in Ireland, why I wanted to do this in the first place, and why I hadn't stopped yet. The guy who repainted his golf balls as a kid filled our arms with Titleists and sent us out to put the swings to his idea.

The east coast Irish links had proved to be a tad sedate, high in quality but less histrionic, with fewer preposterous holes that Yanks like us had come to sample. But the precipitous and tousled terrain of the European Club showcased a variety of holes and shots that a more timid designer might not have attempted on his boss's property. Make the green on twelve 127 feet long? Why not? Stretch thirteen to 596? Might be fun. There was nothing haphazard about what Ruddy had made, but there was a playfulness to it—he admitted that he was trying to catch up to the ancient links of Ireland in a very short amount of time. That's why each nine was actually a ten, the extra hole allowing him to shut one down and tinker at will.

It was easy to sense Ruddy's pride in his golf course and his tenderness for the place—he could tell you if the foursome of guests that morning had been replacing their divots or not. I didn't know if it was the greatest course in Ireland, but it was certainly one of the best cared for, and I couldn't say I'd ever played a more entertaining eighteen (make that twenty—they were all open the day we played them). For a links that was still in flux, ever liable to Ruddy's imagination, it felt like there wasn't a blade of grass on the property leaning the wrong way. The variety of golf holes was relentless, but the place still hung together. He might end up reworking every hole on the course, but there was no doubt it would still work. It would still be Pat Ruddy.

It was Chip's last round in Ireland, and for his first time golfing outside the States, it was a hell of a finish. After watching Chip navigate the roads with his bag and pack strapped to the easy-rolling trolley I had once doubted, I began to long for a pull-cart of my own. And as we relaxed back in the clubhouse in front of that sweetest pint, the one enjoyed in feet just freed from golf shoes, he summed up his week with a, "Perfect trip. This was a perfect trip." Lashing rain, aching backs, more lost balls than either of us would like to admit. And Chip, who thought to bring his trolley, was right once again.

This trip wasn't merely a study in golf courses. In inviting ex-roommates, groomsmen, and strangers alike, these four months would be an education in the various species of golf buddy. I had spent long days with a number of types thus far. Joe had proven to be the non-complaining type, a tad insecure about his own golf acumen, too timid to ever take more than the three-iron, and ultimately succumbing to the reality that links golf is hard, balls are expensive, and if there was soccer on in the pub, that's where he was better off. Steve came to understand golf as a four-letter word, the bitter golf buddy who found the game boring to watch and impossible to play, and was not shy about sharing his feelings on the subject, content to spend whole afternoons calling you a douchebag as punishment for turning his summer's vacation into a wandering golf purgatory. Brian was the silently frustrated golf buddy who internalized his gorse rage until it ultimately burst his Achilles tendon to pieces. Sean was the uncommitted golf buddy, popping in for a quick three days before getting the hook back to his toddler, and Tim was the magical golf buddy who could send his golf ball to places you would have never dreamed possible.

The longest stretch had been spent with Julian, the buddy-first golf buddy, who was along for the *craic*, happy to head wherever the road might lead us, whether it was to a golf course, a pub, or a hotel room with a TV with *Big Brother* on it. He was also the golf buddy most likely to get me in trouble, as he did in Belfast, nearly earning us a night sleeping in the bushes at Queen's College. Our hotel's doors had been locked after ten, and we returned late from the pub looking for a way in. After five minutes of knocking, Julian informed me that I shouldn't bother calling reception, that he'd gotten the night doorman's attention, and that "Baldy-head is going to let us in." The only problem was that Baldy-head had already done so, and he was standing there in the open door eyeing Julian with disgust.

"What did you just say?"

We stood there, two blushing statues, frozen by embarrassment and beer. I was ready to interject with a number of misheard possibilities—*He said, Buddy here is going to let us in*, or *Come on, Baldy-head, this guy's going to let us in*. Not that I was bald, but it would have been better than what Julian decided to go with:

"I said, 'We're staying in room twenty-nine.'"

A dozen apologies later, we were giggling like fourth-graders back in our room. We didn't order the five A.M. wake-up call that came the next morning, but we certainly deserved it.

This was precisely the sort of situation Chip wouldn't have gotten me into, for better or worse, as Chip had proven himself to be the golfer's golf buddy, indifferent about accommodations or dinner plans, and unconcerned about a particular course's pedigree—as long as he was following his Titleist, he was happy. It was the next buddy up on the itinerary that had me a bit unsure. My second Tim of the trip was something of the anti-Chip. He was a seasoned traveler and a man who liked to steer the ship. Among our friends, Tim was the organizer of our golf and travel, and he lived by one mantra: There was always a better way. Buy those wood floors at Home Depot? Tim could half that price on Craigslist. Pay full price for those tires? Tim had worked a deal for his with a guy called Sal, using Phillies tickets as wampum. Get a good deal on your flight on Expedia? He could beat it, just give him a few hours on timsbetterway.com. Turning over the reins to me was going to be tough for him, this much I knew. But I was surprised that on his first night in Ireland, I was already making the disclaimer, "You're on your own, Tim. If you die tonight, it is not my fault."

ḣoLe 784

500 over par

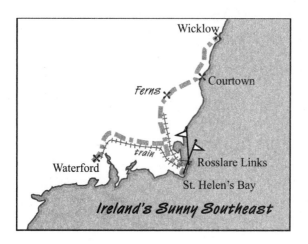

IT WAS NO SECRET THAT I LIKED A LITTLE ACTION ONCE IN A WHILE. Whether it was blackjack or a block pool or an automatic press, you didn't have to ask me twice if I was in. So there was something of a fat-kid-in-a-candy-store effect when I arrived in Ireland to find a bookmaker's shingle hanging on every corner, a woman behind the glass ready to take action on everything from Gaelic football to the ending of the Harry Potter book (seriously—death by Voldemort was 3-1). I couldn't help but show off to fresh Americans joining me on the road, walking into a Ladbrokes and scribbling down a wager on Tiger Woods—*hey, look what I just did*—as if I'd snuck off with a dirty magazine, giggly with the forbidden joy of placing a legal sports wager in a town the size of a tennis court. (Try to explain to a European that we can't gamble on sports, and you'll just be giving them one more thing to shake their heads at us about.)

I was at first captivated by the convenience of so much gambling vice, horse races running every five minutes on every TV in every pub. But after not placing a single winning wager in six weeks, a feat worthy of some long odds in itself, the Irish book-keeper started to lose his shine. I passed the Ladbrokes and the Paddy Powers with indifference. That is, until British Open time, where, unlike the Cork vs. Tipperary hurling match, I had a clue about what the hell I was betting on.

I headed into Ladbrokes in Bray and took three players to win. An inside tip from a golf journalist friend had me putting a fiver on Niclas Fasth. Retief Goosen seemed a sound value at 50-1, and in a moment of near-treasonous stupidity, I actually wrote down "Colin Montgomerie to win," surely the most absurd bit of fiction I had ever penned.

Chip was not only wise in the way of the traveling trolley, but he was a genius to put ten euro on Padraig Harrington at 20-1. Disgusted by Sergio Garcia's insurmountable lead, Chip handed me his worthless ticket on Saturday and headed for the airport, benefiting from one final Act of Uncommon Irish Hospitality when Pat Ruddy's son offered him a ride up to the airport, a mere two hours away. Chip was in the air when Harrington lifted the Claret Jug, and I'm still telling myself that he never found out about it.

Harrington had been the golf headline all month long, pundits debating whether their countryman would ever break through that confidence barrier separating a top-forty player from the top four. It was considerate of him to wait for 2007 to ascend the golf pyramid, the summer I would be there to enjoy an Irishman winning the British Open in a packed pub in Arklow. Tim had just arrived from the airport, where he experienced an act of Irish hospitality that surprised even me. He had struck up a conversation with the woman sitting next to him on the plane who happened to live in Dublin, and as they were disembarking, Tim asked her the way to the train station. With no innuendo whatsoever (they'd spent the flight talking about their spouses), she told him her car was parked at the airport, and it was just easier if she gave him a lift. He was going to Arklow, he explained—*no worries, hop in*—it was like flying into JFK and meeting a New Yorker who offered you a lift to Syracuse. Thanks to his friend, Tim arrived in time to protest Padraig double-bogeying the final hole of a major and still winning. Objections aside, we got wrapped up in the cheers and the roars of the locals who, in a move that shook the Irish sport establishment to its foundation, even turned off the horse racing for the playoff.

Spending a Sunday watching golf instead of chewing up miles was going to muddy our itinerary during a week when I was already trying to squeeze in a detour down to the southeast corner of Ireland, an unplanned visit to the links at Rosslare—but it was the Open, and an Irishman was leading. Hell, even Yahweh kicked up his feet on Sunday. So we stayed glued to the action as four million Irishmen sent up the loudest collective F in their country's history as Padraig butchered the last hole at Carnoustie. The playoff put us well off our schedule, and though it had only been for emergencies or scheduling snafus that I had taken a lift, I informed Tim that we would be taking a taxi to our next town, seeing as he'd just arrived from America, and seeing as I refused to walk in the dark.

Tim was a few years my senior, a reporter from my hometown paper who once looked me up for a golf story, and our shared interest in the game made us quick friends. He was exceptionally bright with a knowledge of politics that trumped all our friends (his dad ran for the Senate), but he had an overactive silly bone, and though his temples were going gray, he still had a tendency to dress like a kindergartner who'd been left to his own devices.

Now Tim wasn't cheap—quick to pick up a tab or throw around Phillies tickets, he didn't covet money as much as he adored a good deal. Something of an eBay tycoon, he'd sold cars and XXXL Allen Iverson jerseys on the Internet, and made a killing in Pope coins in the wake of the Pontiff's passing (Ronald Reagan posters and a Hunter S. Thompson first edition made similar postmortem profits for Tim). So I wasn't surprised to get his text from the airport: *SHOULD I INVEST IN DUTY FREE SMOKES AS CURRENCY?* Neither of us smoked, but with cigarettes going for $10 a pack over here, it was a business opportunity Tim couldn't pass up. What he was adamant to pass up, however, was the taxi I had arranged to take us to our next town.

"I'm hitching," Tim insisted. Considering this was Tim's first day in Ireland, that he had no phone and no idea where we were headed, if it was north, south, or sideways, I told him hitching alone at dusk was basically the worst idea ever. Predictably, my protests only strengthened his resolve, and soon I was watching Tim head off down the road, waving duty-free cigarettes at passing cars as I waited for my cab.

It wasn't the cost of a cab that bothered Tim, it was paying for a service that you could get for free just by sticking out your thumb. Sort of that disappointment I felt when I paid for water or wireless Internet (little old ladies were still charging me fivers for the signals in their B&B's). I arrived safely in Courtown, thirty euros lighter, with Tim nowhere to be found. I waited in the hotel, then headed out to scour the town for the neon green windbreaker he'd scored in an Internet closeout, but there was no such green in sight. As I contemplated an unpleasant phone call to his wife ("Yeah, hi, I lost your husband") and yearned for the erstwhile days of Chip and Brian, travelmates who stuck to the itinerary, I did what one does in such moments in Ireland. I went to a pub, a place called the 19th Hole, and toasted my friend-turned-roadkill with a lonely pint of lager.

On some subconscious level, I must have known that if there was any place on this planet where I was going to be reunited with Tim, it was in a pub called the 19th Hole. Drawn to it like a moth to flame, I wasn't three sips into my pint when a miraculous splash of chartreuse walked through the door, a familiar voice calling out, "You think any of these people smoke Marlboro Lights?"

An aside for the tax man: Tim had almost no success in funding his travels with duty-free tobacco. I lectured him a bit about it being a real downer to my story if one of my friends got abducted along the way, and he almost agreed, and the next day we did enough road walking to break his will. After twenty miles on the N30, the next time I suggested a taxi, Tim would be only too happy to pay.

We had arrived at a long golf-less stretch of the Irish golf course, the southeast corner that was like one of those pauses built into Florida golf courses, where you spent a half hour taxiing yourself through neighborhoods with names like *Twinkle*

Meadow and *Pelican Whisper* looking for the fifteenth tee. It started with a healthy walk to Ferns, a little town with history beyond its size. Once the capital of the kingdom of Leinster, the few blocks that made up the town were home to a restored thatch cottage of St. Mogue, an early Irish bishop who died in Ferns in 632, as well as the ruins of Ferns castle and a cathedral surrounded with weathered high crosses. One of the crosses marked the resting spot of a reviled king of Leinster, Dermot MacMurrough, the Irishman who, in 1166, invited King Henry and his army into Ireland to help him conquer his rival kings. Henry obliged, sending knights and nobles to fight for MacMurrough, Strongbow among them. MacMurrough was restored to power, but died two years later in Ferns, the same year King Henry declared himself Lord of Ireland, kicking off eight centuries of unneighborly relations.

With two pubs and a stylish eatery to refuel on another tub of lasagna, Ferns was an abundant surprise, well-stocked for a town of such tiny map font. The only thing Ferns lacked was the Ferns B&B where I had booked our room. Tim got an early introduction into the frustration of rural Irish addresses—*Ferns? How is this still Ferns?*—when we arrived at our lodging, four more miles up the road.

The Nowhere Near Ferns Bed-and-Breakfast was an old farmhouse where we were put into an orange room full of antique furniture and a television with rabbit ears—clean, and more than we needed, seeing as we could do little more than pop off our shoes and stare at the ceiling.

We'd suffered a major casualty during this leg of the course. The last remaining bit of padding in the heel of my left Keen had torn away, leaving my skin to rub against a sharp plastic edge for two hours. An amateur documentarian, Tim couldn't help himself when he saw the state of my foot. He grabbed his camera and snapped away at a blister the size of a fried egg, the skin having split somewhere along the road to Ferns, soaking my quick-wicking socks with blood, and leaving my heel looking like I had used it to put out cigars.

"You've got to e-mail these to that shoe company," Tim said as he clicked his camera, making exhibits for the lawsuit. I stuffed the heels with Band-Aids and medical tape. Tim offered his extra pair of shoes; we wore the same size, but I gratefully declined. I had made it this far with my Keens—906 miles—and I wasn't giving up on them now.

We drifted off to the sound of British game shows, only to be awoken in the middle of the night by the sensation that we were not alone. My eyes popped open and I stared at the ceiling above me, still glowing pink in the light from my reading lamp. Without my contacts, the wallpaper looked mottled and patched, as if the walls had turned moldy while we slept. But I looked harder, and I saw it wasn't mold. It was moving.

It was difficult to sleep the rest of the night with the sheets pulled tight over our heads, and with all the lights on the opposite side of the room turned on full glow, so as to lure the millions of tiny fruit flies to the other end of the room, where they coated the walls and bumped fatally into the hot bulbs. My strategy to leave the bathroom lights on was effective in luring bugs away from our beds and into the loo, where they fried themselves on the fluorescent tube, but in the light of morning we found a bathroom sink covered with thousands of murdered specks, like we had spilled a jar of pepper down the drain. Once we picked all the carcasses out of our toothbrushes—really should have put those away earlier—and survived breakfast, where Tim put his own unrequested poached egg in his napkin and sent it off to the septic tank, we were away from the Bug & Breakfast and down the road to Enniscorthy.

Sleeping under a steady rain of kamikaze fruit flies was one more scene from the film I had been watching, the one starring a traveling golfer who looked a lot like me, a ginger stepping from one awkward situation to the next, and me telling myself as I watched, *Nah, that can't be me. No way.* Hanging damp underwear from my backpack to dry as I hiked down a crowded main street; covering a twin bed with a protective layer of bath towels to facilitate a takeout kebab feast (I watched this scene almost every night); trying to remove a wine stain from a white golf shirt with warm water and Winterfresh toothpaste; struggling to open a condiment packet with my teeth and squirting the vinegar for my chips into my right eyeball, necessitating an emergency cold water dousing in the back of a greasy chipper; walking into a pub in rain pants, rain jacket, and not a stitch underneath (when you found a Laundromat, you made hay). But all such travel anomalies would feel like everyday joys of the road when considered next to an evening spent in a town that shall remain nameless, in a B&B that shall go without identification, with travelmates who were promised a heavy cloak of anonymity. Think of the worst guest experience you've ever endured, and know that in a short while, you won't feel very bad about it at all. The Bug & Breakfast didn't even register as unpleasant, not when measured against the terror and anguish of The Incident.

Once upon a time, there were three little bears: Papa Bear, Brother Bear, and Baby Bear. The bears went for a walk one day in Ireland, and after many hours on the road, they arrived at a cottage in the countryside overlooking a babbling brook. They knocked on the door and met a young lady with curly red locks and lovely green eyes, who welcomed the three bears into her home and showed them their room up the stairs. It was a small house, the hallway barely wide enough for the bears, and Papa Bear banged his head on the doorway as he stepped inside. They were tight but cozy quarters, three beds in a row with lace ruffles and wool blankets. There was no television, she told the bears, because it was an old home and her family all lived there too, and the noise through the walls would keep everyone up at night. The bears took note, and reminded one another not to snore.

The bears were hungry after their walk, so they walked to the pub next door and gobbled down a spread of meat and potatoes. They were thirsty, too, so they went to the bar with their bellies full, and drank a creamy Guinness for dessert. Baby Bear looked at a pretty bottle behind the bar, then turned and asked Papa Bear, "Paddy whiskey? Have you ever tried that before?"

"Do I shit in the woods?" the bear replied. "We've had some run-ins, Paddy and me."

Baby Bear asked the girl behind the bar for three Paddy whiskeys. Baby Bear gulped down his glass in one swig. Papa Bear shook his head at him.

"It's not a shot. You're supposed to sip it. Savor it."

So the little bear asked for another Paddy whiskey, this one for savoring. And he asked for one more, to wash the last one down. The three bears bumbled their way up the stairs to their room that night, and flopped into their beds, curled up under wool blankets, ready for a summer's nap.

Papa Bear had a hard time hibernating with a bladder full of beer, so in a few hours he found himself wandering around their small room, hunting for the bathroom. He'd been in Ireland for a long time, sleeping in an unfamiliar bed every night, and sometimes he forgot which way the bathroom was, or if he even had one—was it down the hall, or out in the backyard? He opened the closet—no bathroom in there. Opened the door, peered down the dark hallway—no bathroom there. Looked under his bed— no bathroom there. He finally turned on a lamp, and found a bathroom door at the foot of his bed. The other bears stirred and grumbled in the light.

"Sorry, fellas," Papa Bear said, sitting on the edge of his bed. "I was looking for the bathroom." But as he went to turn off the bedside lamp, he noticed something strange about his paw.

"Wake up, hey, wake up," Papa Bear said, shaking Brother Bear who was asleep in the middle bed.

"Huh?" Brother Bear stirred, eyes shut tight.

"Listen to me. We've got a problem," Papa Bear said, more afraid than a bear should ever sound. "There's poop in here."

Brother Bear opened his eyes. "Poop?" he said, as if he'd never heard of it before.

"Poop," Papa Bear said. "Shit. There is shit in this room."

"Where?"

"Here," Papa Bear said, lifting his paw off the floor. "What the hell is this?"

"Poop," Brother Bear said. "What happened?"

The two bears looked at the carpet in the middle of the room, and saw Papa's footprint stamped into something very, very bad.

"Did you do that?" Papa Bear asked.

"No!" Brother Bear answered. "Did you?"

"No way."

"Then who?"

They put their heads together and tried to figure it out. Maybe it was a bird! But the window was closed, and to make that mess it would have taken on ostrich, maybe a pterodactyl. Did the family have a dog? They didn't hear one, and they hadn't noticed one earlier. Were there wombats in Ireland? They didn't think so. Or did the family downstairs really hate bears? They couldn't think why, and it was their own carpet, anyway.

"So where did it come from?"

They turned and looked to the bed against the wall, where Baby Bear was snoring with his face under the covers. "Hey, get up," Brother Bear said, shaking him by the shoulders.

"What?"

"What the hell is this?" Papa Bear said, lifting his paw into the light, his toes jammed with bear mud.

Baby Bear's eyes flickered to life. He sat up in bed and looked at the carpet.

"Oh, shit."

Baby Bear never fully explained to the other bears how it happened, just told them that he'd gone into the bathroom and, in an understatement to end all others, admitted that he "didn't do a very good job." He hurried to grab a towel and began scrubbing the floor, while Papa Bear ran to the bathroom, cranked on an electric shower that roared like an old lawnmower, rattling every rafter in the house. He lifted his leg as high as he could, forcing his toes into the way of the tinkling water. But as he stood in the bathroom doing upright splits in front of the mirror (Papa Bear caught a glimpse of himself, and it wasn't pretty), there came a pounding on the room door. He shut off the water and listened.

"What is going on in there? It's four o'clock in the morning." It was the mother from downstairs and she sounded none too happy.

"Nothing, everything's fine," Baby Bear called through the door.

"Why is the shower on? I can hear someone scrubbing through the ceiling. What's going on?"

"I spilled something," Baby Bear said. Back in the bathroom, Papa Bear shook his head. *Did you ever.*

"We've had enough of this," she said. "Go to bed right now."

They did. Papa Bear with dirty feet, Baby Bear with tears in his eyes, and Brother Bear with a smile too big for his pillow.

The next morning, Baby Bear was on his knees early with hand soap and a towel, scrubbing his knuckles raw. He had done the best he could, but the stain was ground into the fibers. The other bears packed their things and pretended not to know him, as if they were checking out of a hostel where they'd been forced to room with a stranger.

In the light of day, the bears saw the extent of the mess, confirming that their room had indeed been visited by the crap fairy, and that she had arrived angry, and possibly drunk. Their dirty paws had spread smears and dobs of unpleasantness from one end of the room to the other—on the lacy bed skirt, the woolly blankets. Baby Bear did the best he could, rang the towels as tight as he might, then followed the bears downstairs to pay Ruddy-locks, whose eyes had gone from soft green to a simmering shade of I hate you.

"We don't take credit cards," she told them. "And the nearest cash machine is twenty minutes away."

They opened their wallets and counted out their cash. Of all the mornings for the bears to not be ten euros short, this was the one.

"This is totally unacceptable," she explained. "You kept us up all night, running the shower and carrying on, and now you don't have the money to pay us? I don't understand what you were thinking. What's wrong with you?" she said. She was probably five years younger than any of them, but she made them all feel like little cubs cowering in her doorway, tails stuffed between their legs. The bears scraped together six euros in change, then offered an extra twenty dollars American. She looked at the coinage and the greenback in her hands with disgust.

"Totally unacceptable."

The trio grabbed their things and hustled down the road. None of them said it, but they each knew that getting stiffed by three Americans was going to be the highlight of her day.

This was an incident not well-handled. We made our way quietly to our next town, finally admitting over lunch that we had done something terrible. But we also realized that it was a situation that we were in no way equipped to handle—this was a first for all of us, and while better men might have confessed to their mistake or left a gob of money, this was perhaps the most embarrassing experience of our lives, and we learned that when you confront that moment of ultimate shame, particularly shame of the bathroom variety, you shut down. (By the way, don't bother trying to match names with bears—though often unmentioned, overlapping visitors saw me traveling in a threesome on a dozen different occasions.) So we wimped out and pretended it didn't happen, told ourselves that they might not notice, that the room didn't really smell that bad (it stunk like a rainy day in a stockyard). Judge us if you will, but I don't care if you are Gandhi, Mandela, or Abraham Lincoln—there is no way to be a stand-up guy when it comes to poop on the floor.

The thought of that girl's face when she opened the door—it haunted me all the way around our next golf course. But by day's end we had put it behind us, toasted in the clubhouse, vowing to take the incident—rather, the names and places to which it could be matched by spouses and/or significant others—to our graves. The lads headed back to our B&B to make phone calls home while I lingered around the pro shop before heading back up the road, the late Irish sun still high at eight o'clock. I took my time, grateful for the solitude. The mayhem was miles away and Ireland's peace had returned. Until I rounded the corner and saw my buddies standing in front of our B&B, talking with two women. And when I realized who they were, those red curls, those pale cheeks flushed crimson, I actually felt myself stop breathing.

They had no idea where we'd come from, where we were headed, had no credit card details, no contact number, just, "Tom Coyne" in a reservations book, which was an even less helpful clue considering my first name is actually Robert. But I had arrived with golf clubs, so the mother and daughter from the scene of the Shitcident had been driving around the countryside all day, hunting for us in every B&B in a twenty-mile radius, honing in on golf towns, and finally pinning us down. They had called the

Garda. They had called the tourist board. They had Googled me and started a file—they had pictures and my bio, my reviews from Amazon.com (for the record, I believe that all my poor Amazon reviews have been submitted by these women under various aliases). They made a few things very clear to us—their disdain for even having to look at us, which I didn't hold against them, and the strict Irish health code that could have a B&B quarantined for a dirty carpet. Coming from a country where soiling a hotel carpet meant you did your best with a bath towel and left twenty bucks for the maid (come on, what did you do that time you threw up in the Hyatt in San Diego, call the fire department?), the extent of our malfeasance was becoming clear, and we couldn't get the apologies out fast enough. Whatever they needed, it was theirs, we told them. No price was too high. But when they came back the next day and told us that a postcard-sized stain on their carpet was going to cost us $3,000, we thought about calling the cops ourselves.

Stymied by daily ATM withdrawal limits, it took us three days to scrape together the cash to purchase five discarded bath towels, two sets of sheets, two bed skirts, one bath mat, two duvet covers, two irreplaceable artisan wool blankets, rent one steam cleaner that didn't work, pay for the entire carpet to be torn up and replaced, cover the cost of all the canceled reservations in the meantime, and throw in some cash for labor at a healthy hourly rate. Truth was, they could have asked for $100K and we probably would have paid it. There was no room for bargaining with their estimates—twenty-two dollars felt steep for a shabby bath towel, but we were on the road and in their country. And when you've crapped on a carpet, you pretty much lose all leverage.

We learned much from The Incident—some obvious lessons about Paddy whiskey and B&B etiquette, but some insights that wouldn't be fully formed in my mind until weeks later. Ireland was a place you could count on, where there were no strangers, and that's what brought us there from a country where you don't know your neighbor's name. Threatened by modernity and supermarkets and suburban sprawl, at its heart, in its living room, Ireland was still the old Ireland. You still knew if your neighbor was well or ill, if they were on holiday, or if they were staying out later then they used to. There was something priceless about a life that was, above all else, about people. It was a bond I envied, but one that I also came to wonder about, and one that would make me realize how very far away from home I'd been, and for how long.

It wasn't the money that troubled me (I wrote my share off—giving my accountant a receipt for "excrement damage" was a chance to relive the shame all over). It wasn't having to explain the hole in our checking account to my wife that had me wondering if my welcome had been officially overstayed—as long as I promised I wasn't the depositor, Allyson seemed to sympathize with my predicament. I explained to her that I couldn't confirm if it was me or wasn't, the three bears having sworn a pact of mutual deniability (it really wasn't me). The lingering problem seemed to be that no matter how far I walked away from that place, as long as I was still in Ireland, I wouldn't be able to truly leave it behind. I was from the country of get-away, start-over, founded by and filled with history's greatest escapists. But our friends from that unnamed place had found us in a haystack without even knowing my real name. They had the police hunting down our addresses a few days later, the tourist board calling me weeks afterward, and they told us that friends of friends had been listening to us in the pub the evening before The Incident, and overheard us joking about our lack of cash (not only creepy, but entirely untrue). In Ireland, your business was public property, and I was confident that if years from now I showed my face in that town, or in any village up or down that road, folks would know me, or know what I'd paid for, and apologies and stacks of cash aside, I'd still be a son of a bitch for sure. And if I met the wrong sort of smile in a pub (there were two kinds of pub smiles in Ireland, one that said, "What can I get you, friend?" and the other, "I'm going to punch you in the eye now"), someone might give Tom Coyne a shot, no matter that I'd plead with them that my name was really Robert.

Memories were long in Ireland—handy if you were looking for long lost cousins, and no doubt comforting to come home to that kind of consistency. Less comforting if you were from far away and the Garda had your name. And a little bit scary if you weren't proud of yesterday and couldn't walk very fast.

I knew Rosslare was there, but I pretended not to see it down at the bottom of my map as I charted my route. It wasn't a big player on the links scene, skipped over in some of the Irish golf literature, and at mile 925 it seemed like an unlikely detour as we made our way from Brittas Bay to Kinsale. On a map scaled for a walker's pace, it would be like taking off for Chicago from New York, but deciding to swing by Atlanta first for a quick eighteen. But over the weeks, the links-informed at the Island and Baltray had been asking if I planned on visiting Rosslare, and I was having a harder and harder time fumbling for an excuse as to why I would play every true links in Ireland but one. So Tim and I shook off the bugs as we walked our way into Enniscorthy, where I made another executive decision according to the provisions for vehicular transport: more golf was more important than more walking, so in the case of unforeseen courses, rides would be permitted. The train from Enniscorthy turned a week's detour into an eighteen-hour excursion to Ireland's sunny southeast.

The papers called it the wettest summer in Irish history, forty-nine consecutive days of precipitation in Dublin, but as I worked my way south, I found that folks were tired of the whiners up in the capital city. In Ireland, there were the Dubs and there was everybody else, one big city and a whole lot of country. But just because the Dubs were getting drenched, we were told, didn't mean they spoke for the rest of Ireland.

"We've had a lovely summer down here," our host in Rosslare informed us. Granted, Larry was invested in the St. Helen's Bay resort in Rosslare Harbour, but he had some science to back up his marketing. From the St. Helen's clubhouse that sat atop a cliff overlooking the beach, you could actually see where the waters of the Atlantic and the Irish Sea came together, two slightly different blues spilling into each other, creating unusually windy conditions where the clouds just didn't gather for very long (while it sounded like brochure-speak, later research showed that Rosslare logged three hundred more hours of sunshine a year than the average town in Ireland). It was dry backs and light breezes as Tim and I made our way around the St. Helen's Bay links, a family-friendly layout with little definition, its most interesting feature being an old famine wall dissecting the golf course (the construction of stone walls gave employment to desperate tenants). It was a good place to take your kids and not worry about losing too many golf balls—there were tennis courts and a golf academy and a village of cottages for Dublin renters.

The first fifteen at St. Helen's played like ordinary parkland, big fairways with holes of a vagueness typical for a young layout (the course dated to 1993), but on the final three holes, we were suddenly thrust into Lahinch. We spent the last half hour overlooking a beach hundreds of feet below, battling those winds through a winding tunnel of dunes vaulted high atop a sea cliff. And steak dinner and a visit to Culleton's pub afterward, a top-five drinking establishment where you still felt like you might have been imbibing in a working grocery (a role that yester pubs used to serve) was a chance to talk hurling and Wexford pride with Larry. He was a former all-Ireland hurler, and his home team of Wexford had just found themselves in the All-Ireland quarter-finals. In the GAA system, you played hurling or Gaelic football for your local club teams, but your sporting life's biggest honor was to play for your county. To take your senior (over 18) team to the All-Ireland championship against the other thirty-two counties, and to win it all at Croke Park in front of 100,000 fans was the Irish Super Bowl, and the Gaelic games seemed to be the most rabidly supported amateur sporting event in the world. Larry didn't give Wexford much of a chance against Tipperary, but he'd be watching—and good thing. They upset the heavily favored Tips, fifteen to seven.

The golf professional was not the fixture at Irish courses that he or she would have been in the States. Tee times were handled by the office, and matters of club importance would be settled by the captain. Most courses didn't have a range or a teaching facility, and the pro was often just the guy who sold shirts, if they had a professional on staff at all. That was the notable exception at the Rosslare Links on the other end of town from St. Helen's, where Johnny Young ran a proper pro shop and was a golden-haired throwback to golf pros who didn't sell clubs, but sold the game. He assured us we were in for something special, stuffed our pockets full of granola bars, and walked us out to the first tee to show us our way.

This was the links for which I'd justified our train ride, and for its part, Rosslare lived up to the fare. A bit untidy around the edges and haunted by the meanest wind I'd ever experienced on a golf course, Rosslare was as authentic a links as you could play, nine holes heading down the coastline, and nine battling their way back in. The rugged course felt as if it had changed very little from 1905, aside from whatever the wind had done to it. But even in the unreasonable breezes and a healthy dose of gorse, Rosslare was playable—Tim went around the back with one golf ball, a John Daly Super Distance ball he was beside himself about finding on the front. A 43 on his last nine in Ireland, he was pleased with Rosslare as we rushed for the Waterford train where I would resume my route to Kinsale, and he would head for the airport in Shannon. Though I'd encouraged Tim and offered him access to my Wi-Fi, he hadn't booked a room for that evening before his morning flight, sure he'd find something cheap in Limerick when he got there.

I explained to him that he should really consider calling ahead—*here, use my phone*—informing him that Limerick was a busy city likely to be packed for the weekend, not a place to be wandering the streets alone at night in a lime green jacket (it was ugly enough to start a scuffle). But Tim was back at the steering wheel now. He was going to do it his way.

"I don't know where I'm going to stay," he explained, climbing onto his bus. "I'll figure it out when I get there."

Did Tim spend a free night sleeping in the Shannon airport, carton of Marlboro Lights for a pillow? It was too bad I couldn't find a Ladbrokes. It would have been a lock.

hole 820

515 over par

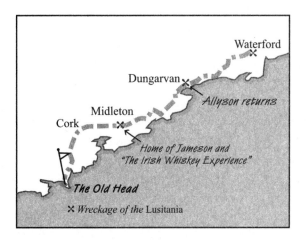

THE THREE-MONTH PASS STAMPED INTO MY PASSPORT BACK AT
the Shannon airport was nearing its expiration, so I would
need to hang around Waterford for an extra afternoon—the immigration officer I had been tracking since Drogheda was going
to be in town on Thursday, my only chance for a new stamp.

The customs officer in Shannon stuck me on a bench for a
time-out when I told her I planned on staying in Ireland for four
months. "For what purpose?" she asked.

"For golf."

She lifted her eyes from her paperwork, squinting at me for a
better look. "And your address while in Ireland?"

"Actually, there's probably a hundred of them," an answer
that got me pulled out of line and sent to the bench where, after
showing off my itinerary, I was told I'd have to catch up with an
immigration officer somewhere along the way for an extension of
my landing permit, and that it wouldn't be guaranteed. So in
Waterford, I left my every possession with a Polish woman at a

laundry around the corner, and headed to the police station with my passport and a news clipping in hand. A story from the *Irish Tribune* that testified to my purpose in Ireland and included a photograph of me smiling in front of a donkey with a golf bag over my shoulder, my case for an extra month in Ireland built upon the fact that the donkeys seemed to be on board.

I expected to knock on the door, sit down for a chat, a cup of tea, and be on my way—I'd called into a dozen police stations to discuss my impending expiration, and the local Garda station was typically a pretty sleepy environ, where the cops seemed surprised to find a visitor ringing the bell. But the line to get into the immigration office in Waterford stretched down the hallway. It was an hour before I finally got into the important room, squeezing up against the window for a seat on the radiator, where for another thirty minutes I watched a Chinese couple plead with a woman in a police sweater, confused as to why their pile of papers was not the right pile of papers. An African woman with a tall tangle of hair had brought her friend to translate for her— there was a fee associated with her new visa that she wasn't able to pay. An Aussie waited with his Irish girlfriend, and a Russian in work boots was in a hurry to get back to a jobsite. They were young and from all over the world, lining up for all that Ireland had going for it—health care, a stout minimum wage (8.65 euro, or $13), low unemployment (4 percent), and a demand for unskilled labor. Who was going to stock the shelves in all the new superstores, clean the new hotels, pull the pints now that Irish kids had better things to do? If you could handle yourself behind a cash register, Ireland needed you. In those ninety minutes cramped in a government office, I came shoulder to shoulder with the Irish prosperity I'd been reading about. I'd seen that the Irish had holiday homes and Land Rovers and the expendable cash for Sunday sprees, but more impressive was the fact that we internationals were all waiting here in a crowded, sweaty office on a sunny afternoon, hopeful for a chance to hang around the place for just a little longer.

My interview lasted all of nine seconds, and I didn't even get the chance to show off my news clipping. Once they heard the words, "No, I'm not working," they scribbled an extra thirty days into my passport and sent me on my way.

I struck out for Kilmacthomas as I worked my way along the bottom end of Ireland, the Copper Coast it was called, a stretch of the country that was light on golf and overshadowed by the well-worn tourist path west of Cork, but a pocket of Ireland that was full of finds for travelers willing to get away from the guidebook. Revisiting a favorite theme, the B&B with a Kilmacthomas address was nowhere near Kilmacthomas—the lady of the house had to chuckle when I rang and told her I was hunting around the town, looking for her street. But she was kind to drive to town and pick me up that evening, and on the way back to her home, she stopped off at her favorite beach near Bunmahon. It was a perfect cove at low tide, a mile of glassy sand cupped between dark sea cliffs, a crumbled outcropping of rock dividing the waves. The water glistened in the last bit of light, and we walked the strand and she talked about her late mother—they came to walk here every evening—as if she'd known me for years. She pointed to the cliffs surrounding us and explained that in the 1800s, there were more than a thousand miners camping in every nook and cranny of these hills, that at night this cove would be lit up like a city with men come to Waterford for the copper. The place was empty now, ours the only footprints in the sand, the ruins of an engine house atop a hill in the distance the only reminder of a former purpose.

It was near dark when we arrived at her home in the countryside, where I learned that running a B&B was only one of my host Carrie's ambitions—she operated a small farm in the backyard, and like most country farmers, she was a dedicated haberdasher as well. It was creepy at first, as if I'd walked into a slasher movie—*all alone in the Irish countryside, an unsuspecting hiker wanders into the house of hats*—but on closer inspection, it was really quite charming that every inch of Carrie's front room was covered with hats to make a pimp blush, flowers and feathers dangling from pizza-sized affairs. The renting of elaborate headwear for the horse races was big business in Ireland, Carrie explained. She'd emptied the room for the Grand National, and with the Galway races coming up, she'd be just as busy. How the hell anyone knew she was there, that a few miles from the coast there was a house full of peacock feathers—it seemed a miracle, and another reminder of the power of word of mouth in a culture so skilled in the art of the chat.

I ate a breakfast of the brightest scrambled eggs—they were orange, neon almost—while the eggs' provider clucked at me from the other side of the kitchen window. Full-bellied, I worked my way down the coast through lovely Stradbally, where the town square was bursting with roses and where I found the most perfect thatched cottage on earth, tidy green hedges with colors spilling out of flower boxes, a graying brow of thatch hanging over walls as white as wedding cake. Thomas Kinkade would have wept. I half expected a hobbit to step through the arched green doorway and bid me on my way.

Allyson arrived in Dungarvan at ten o'clock on a Saturday evening, frazzled from a day of missed trains and bouncing buses and a hundred-dollar cab ride. We hadn't picked Dungarvan because it was easy to get to from Dublin airport, but because four days from Dungarvan we would be dropping out for a decadent three-night stint (three nights! I'd feel like I was moving in), in what I considered Ireland's perfect town.

Our room in Dungarvan was clean and comfortable enough to shake off Allyson's cobwebs, and dinner at the four-star bistro in the heart of town was a worthwhile splurge for a peppercorn tenderloin that was my summer's top meal, yet it was but a tease when I imagined the eats for which we were headed. Youghal's harbor was lovely in the late afternoon, and Midleton shouldn't be skipped by whiskey drinkers (similar to the Bushmills bit, this one a Jameson-centric tour called "The Irish Whiskey Experience," where you learned that whiskey that evaporated during the distillation process was called "the angel's share," and where your ticket stub secured you enough whiskey to get you buying Jameson magnets and rugby shirts in the gift shop). Cork was huge but brilliant, its pedestrian-only promenades of shops and restaurants maintaining an Irish-town feel to a bustling European city. The wooded grounds of University College Cork were worth a morning stroll, its gothic quads and stone corridors making scholars out of passersby. But lovely as it all was, it was all just in our way on the road to Kinsale.

As we bandied plans and possibilities on our back patio the summer before, Allyson's only nonnegotiable request was that she be there when I passed through Kinsale at the southern tip of County Cork. I had been talking about the town since I spent a few hours there in 2004, our bus leaving us off for a pint in the idyllic harbor town, where the tide brought the water right into the central square. Kinsale had a wandering, medieval design, or a lack thereof—haphazard and snug streets in a town dating to the Romans and expanding outward with each occupier, giving it the feel of a town within a town within a town. As Ireland's reputed gourmet capital, a municipality with thirty-nine pubs (enough for every citizen of Kinsale to get thirsty at the same time and still have a spot at the bar), Allyson had chosen wisely. Not to mention that it was home to the golf course I'd been seeing in my sleep.

WELCOME2CORK! NEED A LIFT? SAY HELLO TO THE BRIDE. PADDY

Back in Philadelphia, Patrick had been a steamfitter and a rising star in his union. Not quite six feet, but a meaty, square-jawed kid from a working-class Irish neighborhood, he'd played college football and been blessed with the confidence and sense of humor essential for survival as the youngest of seven, meaning he was a ballbuster, with no less than a million friends. His stories were performances, full-body affairs told with wide eyes, "Dude, listen to this," that you wouldn't dare not. He had an uncanny memory for names and conversations—introduce him to a hermit and within ten minutes Patrick would have figured out their friends in common. But a few years earlier, when his wife's career skyrocketed, he was left with a decision: Quit his job and move to Ireland, or don't. On its face, it wasn't a decision, it was a dream, but it would be no easy transition for Pat, who went from steamfitter to Mr. Mom, from America's buddy to the stranger down the road. With his daughters off to school, Patrick had more downtime than he knew how to juggle, and after a few tough months, after checking off everyone of those thirty-nine pubs (he showed me the list, and it was impressive), Patrick decided it was time to go back to work. Shy as he was, Patrick—Paddy by now—drove out to the golf course he'd been hearing about, this Old Head of Kinsale, and asked the caddy master for a loop.

I hadn't seen Patrick since a long-ago round in Doonbeg, but when we met in a pub at the top of Kinsale's main street, it was as if we'd just teed it up the day before, both of us brandishing a fresh bevy of wisecracks. We met his wife, Teresa, who I insisted calling by her proper name, St. Teresa, and who had a sense of humor well suited to her husband. Paddy introduced us to his two daughters, Maura and Neve, who were busy with summer camps and learning the Gaelic games (Patrick broke down Gaelic football for them: "It's like soccer, but you can pick the ball up. That's awesome!"), but they had still taken the time to make a banner for us with tall red letters that read WELCOME TO CORK!

Allyson and I checked into our guesthouse, then headed for the eatery whose reputation seemed to hover above all the other esteemed restaurants in Kinsale. At Fishy Fishy, we felt like we were in a Martha's Vineyard seafood spot, the queue wrapped around the corner but nobody complaining. The chowder stuck to my spoon with golden cream hugging chunks of local catch. Soaking up the sun on the front patio, our lobsters came from the waters over Allyson's shoulder. We were in Kinsale for three days, and somehow wound up in Fishy Fishy on each of them.

When we weren't studying menus, we were filling up on the abundant history of the fishing town. Kinsale's location at the southern tip of Ireland, along with its uniquely angled harbor (the inlet had a sort of hook to it) made Kinsale a highly defensible port, and a particular threat to the empire to the east. A prevailing southwesterly wind made for a one way street from Kinsale to England's west coast—if England's enemies got a foothold in Kinsale, they'd have a free run on London. So a small town at the bottom of Ireland became an outlet for centuries of British anxiety. The forts overlooking Kinsale Harbour were among the most advanced of their time, built to defend against the Spanish threat to England, and later the French; Charles Fort

looked down upon the town and was the world's best preserved
example of a star-shaped British fort. The Battle of Kinsale in
1601 saw Spanish-Irish forces succumbing to the English, solidi-
fying English control of Ireland and ending the old Gaelic order,
leading to the Flight of the Earls and the Ulster Plantation. Catholic king James landed in Kinsale in 1689 before being defeated
by King William of Orange, who would seize Charles Fort by at-
tacking it from land the following year. And so as not to be ex-
cluded from Kinsale history by her imperial rivals, Germany got
in on the act in 1915, sinking the *Lusitania* eight miles off Kinsale's Old Head.

While England, Spain, and France were inexorably linked to
the fate and fortune of Ireland, Germany's role was not to be over-
looked, particularly when it came to the Ireland of today. Many
an Irish public-works project owed Berlin—the deep-pocketed
sugar daddy of the European Union—a hearty round of *danke
schöns*. And while dollars were the driving force behind the Irish
golf boom, Germans seemed the next most links-addicted; I'd
met dozens of Germans on holiday in Ireland, both north and
south. Deserved or not, German *golfspielers* had a reputation for
being a bit serious, a tad high-maintenance—if the caddy master
came calling with a German couple, let's just say no one would be
injured in the rush to grab their bags. I'd hit into a German
woman in Killarney when I was nineteen, and my butt still cinches
up when I recall that incomprehensible tongue-lashing. I waited
a good ten minutes before she was out of view on the next hole
before accidentally blasting the biggest drive of my life.

"Where are they? Did I hit into them? Where are they?" I
begged my caddy.

He shielded his eyes, looking far up the fairway, and with a
big smile said, "Ah, don't you worry. She should be getting up
any minute now."

It was a run-in that made me particularly fond of a story I
heard on my first visit to the Old Head of Kinsale—like all good
caddy stories, it was probably thirty tellings removed from its
truthful state, but that was irrelevant in the pursuit of laughs.
Our looper explained to us how he'd recently been out with a
German husband and wife who worked him like a Clydesdale.

Their bags were heavier then Guinness barrels, and they'd been barking orders like he was hard of hearing. At seventeen they stopped to snap some pictures, and the husband pointed out to the sea and asked the caddy, "*Lusitania*? Where? Which way?"

"Why are you asking me?" the caddy replied, dropping their bags on the tee box. "Ye are the fuckers that sunk it."

Patrick hung up the caddy bib to join me as a player at Old Head, along with the director of golf, Danny Brassil, with Allyson on camera—at Old Head, framing snapshots was almost more fun than the golf. So three golfers, and room for one more.

The texts had started rolling in a few weeks after leaving Ardglass, messages from a Gerry who I vaguely recalled as a gin-and-tonic man, remembering little else about him. He was curious if I was still headed to the Old Head and still looking for some company. I kept the messages in my unread box and hoped my phone might soon be out of range. Where I was from, promises made after eleven P.M. that had anything to do with tee times, business and/or travel plans, loans of personal property, etc., were to be considered null and void until reaffirmed in the sober light of day. I thought my offer had vanished with that evening's lager. But this was Ireland, and I had learned by now that when an Irishman told you he was going to do something, no matter if he was announcing his intentions to a table of fourteen empty pints, he was still going to do it.

I was essentially golfing these courses at the charity of the clubs. I couldn't say who I could or could not ask to join me, really, but I knew I couldn't say no to Gerry. If there were any Irish traits that I hoped rubbed off on me when I returned home, it was their relentless hospitality, and their commitment to the irrational—this wasn't a country of "I can't," this was the land of "I'll get it sorted." So that Thursday morning, Gerry started out from Ardglass, about as far away as you could get from Kinsale without a boat, driving eight hours through holiday weekend traffic. In the end, Old Head couldn't have been more accommodating—I didn't need to beg or fax the clipping of me and the donkey. They assured me we had a foursome set, with a spot booked for one Gerry Ryan (didn't know his last name, Ryan sounded safe enough). He had traversed the country alone, no place to stay on a weekend when the town was booked solid, driven by an aging barroom promise. And that's how special Old Head was. Gerry wasn't the fittest man I met in Ireland, but I think he would have walked there with me if he'd had to.

I was familiar with the mixed feelings surrounding one of the most ambitious golf courses ever built. The miracle that is Old Head began when a few brothers from Kerry bought what was essentially an island at the end of Kinsale, spent years covering it with soil and fairway, and built a golf course on a piece of property that you'd be afraid to traverse as a goat, let alone a golfer. (Lore about the purchase of Old Head says the farmer sold because he was tired of losing sheep off the cliffs.) Looking at an aerial of Old Head, a giant rock draped with fairways and set against an endless blue Atlantic, it almost looked impossible— not to play, just to imagine.

Along with glowing reviews from golfers turned speechless by Old Head, I'd also heard protests about its price (at €295, or $425 a man, it wasn't for the disinterested), and heard complaints from purists about the manufactured quality of the place. Too American, too expensive, and it was wrong for a golf course to cover up this historic rock, cutting short a traditional lighthouse walk (the "Free the Old Head of Kinsale" campaign held an annual "people's picnic" beside the club's gates in protest of the headland being closed to the public). And while I would typically sympathize with a number of these points, particularly the last one (I couldn't see why locals on a stroll out to the Kinsale lighthouse needed to be turned back at the gates), I granted myself dispensation from giving a damn. I wasn't terribly concerned if the place was for millionaires, or if it was indeed overrun by Yanks (membership was more than 80 percent American). Hell, I was American. And if Old Head was for millionaires, then I was going to have to devise a better plan to become one. Because I left the place once again convinced that the Old Head of Kinsale was simply the most spectacular golf course in the world.

Spectacular. Not the most classic, not the most historic, not the most challenging, not the best in Ireland, even (Carne was still top of the pops for me), and though dubbed a links, there was nothing truly linksland about the place. But as we crested the hill on the road to Old Head, and we all glimpsed our green playground floating in that big blue pond, $425 felt like a fair deal.

There was value at Old Head beyond its vistas—this was a place with a customer service Ph.D. From the reception we received at the gate (always a warm one, provided you weren't waving a FREE THE HEAD banner), to the Old Head's Fifth Avenue pro shop, where Patrick made the director of golf rue his offer of "Go ahead, pick out anything you'd like," to the ten minutes of Old Head history imparted to us by the reverent and well-practiced starter, we had the sense that we were not only about to do something very special, but that everyone was excited for us to be doing so. By the putting green, we shook hands with one another through the Stone of Accord—it was the Old Head logo, a stone like a tall tombstone with a hole cut into its center through which the Celts would shake hands to finalize a contract or a marriage. The course was peppered with ruins and relics—some reproductions, but some entirely authentic, like the crumbling walls of the original lighthouse, where monks had kept a warning fire alight, or the remains of stone huts dating to the Iron Age. The headland had once been inhabited by the Eireann clan, a Celtic tribe that lived in Kinsale since times B.C. and was said to have kept a navigational fire burning on the Old Head for hundreds of years. With the aid of a zoom lens, you could make out steps carved into the rocks below the second fairway, the stairs cut there in 1601 for an arriving Spanish Armada on its way to the Battle of Kinsale, and on the par-five tenth, you played over a Druid burial ground (no ball-retrieving allowed, the small graveyard was strictly off-limits). But the history was just seasoning for the meal we were about to tuck into, and the truth behind all the Old Head hype hit us like a stiff wind as we walked off the first green and eyed numbers two, three, and four, a stretch of cliffside holes that picked us up out of a golf course and dropped us into a dream (if you had a fear of heights, it would have been more like getting tossed into a nightmare). Just a few paces from the fairway, we leaned out and watched as the waves washed into the oily crags far below our feet, a fisherman in a small boat pulling his traps out of the water. When we remembered our morning's purpose—*oh yeah, golf*—we threw our drives out over the ocean and trusted the wind to bring them back. It turned out that those opening views were just setting us up for number twelve, which Paddy introduced as we made our way up a hill to the tee box: "You are about to play the best golf hole in Ireland."

"World" wouldn't have been an exaggeration, really, a par-five where we confronted a cascading wall of black stone that seemed to pour itself into the ocean, gulls ducking in and out of sea tunnels far below the fairway. I was told to knock driver over a crown of stone where I was guaranteed a generous fairway, from which I might have a go down into the bowling alley of short grass that led to a green chiseled out of the headland, a wall of granite for my backstop. The fifteenth, dubbed Haulie's Leap, was another hole to sit by and soak in. It was named after Haulie O'Shea, the course builder who, one afternoon in 1994, was excavating the hillside tee box with his digger. The brakes gave out and Haulie starting rolling toward the ocean, forcing him to leap from the driver's seat as his digger tumbled off the cliff and crashed into the sea. It's still in the water today, along with Haulie's cell phone, about which it's said he was much more distraught than he was about the digger.

Our weather turned less than ideal—the rain blasting off the ocean, slightly less pleasant than getting hosed down in prison intake—but a little wet couldn't spoil the day, no matter that the clubs were coming out of our hands, or that I hit three hosel-rockets on the back nine and barely broke 90. Gerry smiled his way around the course in a dripping purple sweater (it was a recurring irony that Irish golfers always seemed the least prepared for the rain), none of us in any rush to finish eighteen. On that final hole, we each grabbed an old golf ball and made the long walk to the black tee, a tee box four paces deep, with a lighthouse wall to your back and a drop-off to your front that wasn't for the acrophobic, or the slippery-fingered. I wouldn't let Allyson leave the tee without taking a swing from one of the most fantastic teeing grounds in golf. It was only a 250-yard carry to dry land, and she'd taken lessons six years ago. She finally relented, grabbed the driver, and I readied the camera. And as she stood there trying to remember how to grip it, fingers shriveled from hours stuffed in pockets full of water, I envisioned my Mizuno 460 outdistancing the Titleist I'd given her, spinning slow motion on the breeze as we watched it fall to the whitecaps below. Not that it would matter much—the rest of my bag had a date with the surf in three weeks time. But Allyson held on tight and even made contact, then took the camera back and erased the picture.

So Gerry got his souvenir scorecard from Old Head, along with a half dozen brochures for disbelieving friends up north. That night at dinner, over steaks and spuds that Gerry was only too happy to splurge for, he explained, "That was the most amazing golf course I have ever seen. I mean, Tom, how do you even begin to write about a place like that?"

I toasted my friend and told him, "Easy, Gerry. I write about you."

ḃoLє 838

532 over par

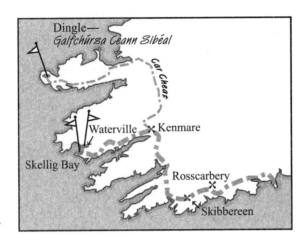

S HE HAD TIGHT BLACK CURLS, HER HAIR ALL KNOTTED UP INTO
a ball and the loose strands just touching her shoulders.
Brown eyes and fair skin, she was a country sort of thin, spindly
as she made her way to the middle of the room where a dozen of
Rosscarbery's drunkest sat like stumps around a table of empty
glasses. It was Monday afternoon, and the men mumbled orders
for the next round, draining the last drops out of their holiday
weekend. Unbothered, she smiled and collected their glasses,
"Another one, Kenny?" calling them by name, no matter that
their eyes were too soggy to unstick themselves from her blouse.

She was wearing too-tight sweatpants, the kind with something like *crazy* emblazoned across the backside, and a tube top
that would have been illegal in Ireland twenty years ago, at least
for a nineteen-year-old (all of us Americans carried a debt on
our souls for the fashion horrors we had inflicted on the rest
of the globe—in towns that weren't big enough for a butcher's
shop, I would see thirteen-year-old girls splashed with blush and

dressed up in half their clothes, doing their best Britney impression). She brought me another pint and inquired about my accent. I sat up in my seat, half blushing at the attention, and I boasted of my homeland—*America, yeah, that's me.* I explained that I was hiking my way around Ireland, that I'd walked in from Timoleague and would be headed out to Skibbereen in the morning.

She turned to the white-haired man next to me who was as thick as a refrigerator. "You hear that, Dad? He's walking to Skib."

Dad? I shrunk up on my stool, and with ne'er-wandering eyes, burned holes into my newspaper. The man turned from where he'd been speaking in low, serious tones to his neighbor, brow wrinkled with suspicion.

"Walking? There's a bus to Skib, you know."

"Bus is gone," his daughter reminded him.

"It is. But there's a taxi."

"I don't mind the walking," I explained. "I've been walking all summer, actually. I started in Shannon, and I've been . . ."

"You started in *Shannon?*" she said, as if she'd only heard of the place in fairy tales.

"You're the American? The one from the *Examiner?*" he said, referring to the daily paper in which my tales from the road were appearing. And just then, someone screamed for help—we turned to the table where a toothpick of a man in a collared shirt with sleeves rolled up past his tattoos was leaning sideways as if into a breeze, yelling over the voices in the pub, "I close my eyes, and I picture, the emerald of the sea—come on, help me out, come on now," and the rest of the table mumbled along, the stool-sitters stirring back and forth until they looked like Weebles in a full-on sway.

"I miss the River Shannon, and them folks at Skibbereen. Those moorlands, and the meadows," and with a raised pint, "and their forty shades of green."

He sang with eyes closed and forgot the words more than once, and as labored a rendition as it was, everyone ceased their conversation to listen, and applauded when he was done.

"Four o'clock," the girl said, looking at the Guinness clock on the wall. "Songs are starting early."

Around the table the songs went—a more melodious "Fields of Athenry," and a second rendition of "Forty Shades of Green"—before an old man in a Hawaiian shirt interrupted a cup of tea to give us his best "Spancil Hill." The bartender's mother arrived, short black hair and a decade younger than her husband sitting next to me. She kissed his cheek and looked over to the singers, rolling her eyes. Their son was with her, a twelve-year-old who ran for a tube of Pringles from behind the bar and showed up his sister by pouring his dad a near-perfect pint of Guinness, all while one singer handed off to the next, like a slow fuse sizzling its way down the bar toward me.

I didn't sing. But a tattooed forearm came over the shoulder of the mom now sitting next to me. "Come on, Mary, give us a song now."

She turned her face away from his breath and smiled at her husband. "Go on," he told her. And she started in with "My Old Man," as sentimental a song as I had ever heard. The room went quiet as she stared into a spot on the bar mat in front of her, and in a smooth falsetto made me wonder if it was okay for an American to cry at four o'clock in a pub in Rosscarbery. I used to think sappy folks who got emotional over sunsets and paperbacks and Daniel O'Donnell ditties were suckers; I was from a jaded country of the relentlessly sarcastic, a place where legends were for debunking, romance for exposing, the sentimental to be proven silly. But as I watched the mother sing, and then her daughter taking her turn, reluctantly giving the room a song about lost love for a young Teddy O'Neill, eyes cast downward as she leaned against a row of bottles and sang, "*I see the old cabin beyond the wee boreen, I see the old crossroads where we used to dance. I ramble the lane where he called me his stoirin, and my girlish heart was so full of romance . . . ,*" and I understood what I really loved about this country. The place had imagination, unchecked. It was sentimental and a sucker in the best sort of way. It was a place you could sing sappy songs in the afternoon, and rather than have to elbow your buddy and make a joke about the singer, you could just listen and let the hairs on your neck tingle, and then applaud.

Not wanting big sister to steal the spotlight, the boy got in on the act as well, singing a song about Rosslare Harbour—these were old songs these kids were performing, older than pop music, probably older than my country. It befuddled me that they knew all the words, and I wondered how kids with Game Boys and satellite television could still sing lullabies for soft-eyed old men. It was nice, my afternoon in Rosscarbery. Maybe Britney's hot pants hadn't ruined the world.

Availing myself of neither bus nor taxi, I left a hotel overlooking Rosscarbery Bay and humped the fourteen miles to a town famous for its rally cry, "Revenge for Skibbereen," sort of the Irish "Remember the Alamo." It came from a sad song you were likely to hear coming from the corner somewhere in Ireland. Skib was hit especially hard by the famine (running out of coffins in 1846, they resorted to bottom-hinged caskets that could be reused indefinitely), and in "Dear Old Skibbereen," a father recounted to his son how the English burned him out of his home, the boy's mother dying from the stress, and the son vowing, "I'll be the man to lead the band beneath the flag of green, and loud and clear we'll raise the cheer, revenge for Skibbereen." It wasn't a tune for the politically ambivalent. Today Skibbereen was a quaint town in west Cork, busy with pubs and tourist shops and a heritage center with touch-screen exhibits, a hub for anyone looking into Famine history. I was interested to find the hotel where Michael Collins spent his last evening before being assassinated (and not surprised to see it was packed with a wedding on a Tuesday afternoon). And eavesdropping in a candy shop—no simple task; west Cork should come with those UN headphones, the accent was a bear—I learned that Skib was facing new challenges from an old story.

The Irish had a voracious sweet tooth, and a collective ice cream craving seemed to have gripped the country. I once remembered the circular Guinness and Harp signs hanging like streetlamps over so many sidewalks; I was now struck by the omnipresent, oversize plastic ice cream cone, and the sidewalk placard steering me toward the nearest freezer of HB fruit pops. It could be raining ice cubes, and you'd still find kids, adults, old ladies walking out of the convenience shop with a torch of twirled up soft-serve. I had my own weakness for sweets of the gummy variety, and in Ireland, there wasn't a village anywhere without a few shelves to keep me fixed. *Pizza? Sorry, next town over. Gummy tarantulas? Which flavor?*

I stopped into a small shop in Skibbereen to grab an *Irish Sun* and a sack of fizzy strawberries. It was a narrow shop lit by the afternoon sun, with an old man sitting low on a box behind a register that didn't need an outlet. You could flip through a hundred different papers, pick through shelves of kitsch, or buy a soccer ball or a model airplane or a Cork flag for your car. You got your newspaper, and then you got the real news from this man with deep lines in his face and fingers trembling for a cigarette. Collared shirt and wool pants, he was the town newsagent, and along with the butcher and the sole-proprietor chemist (pharmacist), the Irish newsagent sadly had no equivalent back home (the newspaper guy behind bulletproof glass and a stack of *Hustlers* just wasn't the same). As I searched out my treats from the shelves of plastic bins, I listened as a young boy with spiked black hair counted out euros into the man's open hand, his friend in a Cork jersey carrying a soccer ball and looking over his shoulder intently.

"One forty," the boy said. "Is that enough?"

The man looked into their white paper bag, raising a gray eyebrow. On his stool he was eye level with the boys. "One forty? Now you know that's not enough, Michael. Your mother's taught you better than that."

The boys hung their heads and returned to the candy wall to lighten their load. The bell on the door rattled, and a man in denim and a long beard walked into the shop. He had a heavy bag over his shoulder, and he handed a stack of postcards over to the man behind the register.

"They're hand-painted, I do them myself. Do you think you might be able to use them?" he asked.

"I'm sorry, I've got too much inventory as it is," he said, handing back the cards without looking at them. "I'll be closing up here at the end of the month. Can't compete with the Tescos and the Supervalus. Maybe you'd have luck with them," he said, and the man said thank you and closed the door behind him.

The boys had overheard him. They looked like they were going to cry.

"You can't close!" the boy with the soccer ball complained. "All the other sweets shops are gone! You're the last one!"

"Sorry, boys."

"That's not fair," his friend protested. "Where are we going to buy our sweets?"

"I'm sure you'll find your sweets somewhere. Now let's have a look in that bag," he said, his finger pulling the bag open. "Come on, now. You didn't take out a thing."

"We did! We took out the Coke bottles, and some of the fish."

The man picked up his head and crossed his arms, letting out a heavy sigh. He took their coins off the table, sliding them into his open hand.

"Now you be on your way."

The boys hustled out the door, two guilty grins running down the street with their bag. I dropped my newspaper and a small bag of candy on the counter, but the newsagent was still looking out the window, half a smile on his face. "With customers like that, it's no wonder I'm going out of business."

In the Rosslare Best Western, when I asked the young Polish girl at reception the way to St. Helen's Bay, she pulled out a map of the town and started drawing up a path that didn't interest us at all, showing us the indirect route along the main roads, turning away from the golf course before heading back toward it.

"But we're here," I explained, pointing to our spot along the beach, "and the course is here. We can't we take the beach?"

Her English had been perfect to this point, but something about beach didn't translate.

"We don't have a car."

"You don't have a car?"

"We'd like to walk there. It looks like we could walk along the beach . . ."

"No no no," she laughed. "I call you taxi. You cannot walk. It is three miles, maybe more."

"But if we were going to walk, would we be able to . . . ?"

"I call you taxi."

We eventually gave up and headed for the beach, and the looks from strangers as I crossed the sand in hiking shoes and golf bag were a small price for an hour in the sun, whacking driver off sand tees until we'd knocked our golf balls all the way down to the cliffs of Helen's Bay. I had faced the incredulity of strangers for three months now, but it never ceased to leave me wondering how damn lazy our planet had become. In Waterford, the receptionist at my hotel nearly begged me to take a taxi to the movie theater: "You can't walk there. It will take you at least twenty minutes."

I had met old men in pubs who heard of the distances I was doing, and told me of their own days when they'd made the walk from Killybegs to Narin, the time they hiked twenty miles to Dungarvan, and these weren't very old men. And if you wanted evidence that Ireland was a more ambulatory culture not long ago, it was out there on the back roads that weren't engineered for oncoming traffic, paths designed for moving sheep and cattle between fields, or pushing the cart into town. I could throw no stones at the mobilized Ireland as I hailed from the birthplace of combustion dependency, and from the first day I ever hit the Go pedal on a golf cart, I believed deeply that my walking days were done. It wasn't the fact that no one else was walking the roads that struck me (I'd come across less than a dozen other foot travelers along the way, and one of them was in that wheelchair), it was that using your feet to traverse any meaningful distance had been struck from the conversation, an option that somewhere along the way was swept off the table. Walking had gone the way of bloodletting, hickory shafts, my Jams swim trunks, passing from the essential to the unfashionable to the absurd.

While the Irish weren't obese like so much of America (I

couldn't imagine what Europeans thought when they visited and witnessed our mass in person—they must have thought we were trying to democratize the world by digesting it), they were indeed a bit doughy. What chance did Irish bellies, American hearts, everybody's ozone have if someone walking twenty minutes was stuff to laugh about over lunch with your mates? I had gone into this trip with dangerously high blood pressure and twenty pounds too many. I found a health-monitoring machine in a chemist in Midleton, and after three months of eating like a jerk and drinking like, well, like a redhead in Ireland, I had lost twenty-three pounds, and my blood pressure had gone from deadly to ideal without a single pill popped. Say what you will for diets and weight-loss gizmos, Ireland had proven that that good health wasn't any more complicated than right, and then left.

I crossed the thousand-mile mark near the town of Ballydehob. And in a perfectly Irish bit of fortune, my pedometer clicked a fourth digit as I crossed a small stone bridge on a bright August afternoon. I was perfectly alone, no farms or cottages. A few straggly sheep sat on their knees by a stream, and in front of me, a simple stone and slate church by the side of the road.

I dropped my pack and sat on the bridge, and I called Allyson back home to tell her where I was. I guessed she was asleep so I left a message on her voice mail, "Just crossed the thousand-mile mark. Feeling good. Almost home." I opened a heavy oak door and stepped into a church that felt smaller from the inside, sun shining through the stained glass across a dozen empty pews. I sat in the last row with plenty to be thankful for, the caddy who didn't want to go get the mail having hauled his clubs this improbable distance, nearly coming kneecap to headlight with thousands of cars along the way, and arriving here safe. But I don't remember really thinking anything like that, or thinking about anything at all in that church. I was tired and I had a seat. And it was good.

They called Cork the Rebel County, and as I made my way through Bantry and Kenmare, I watched the roads turn red with rebel spirit—there were Cork flags in every front yard, and the towns bustled with boys in red jerseys. Cork was in the All-Ireland football semifinals, and in case you couldn't decipher the accent, "Up the rebels," seemed a safe response to just about any utterance, usually good for a pat on the back. It was a much wiser choice than "Up Kerry," the place where I was headed and home of the Gaelic football juggernaut still looming large on Cork's horizon, a county commonly referred to simply as "The Kingdom."

The expression "Kingdom of Kerry" originated variously from a famous slight in the Irish House of Commons (Kerry magistrates apparently liked to do their own thing, thus gaining them the derisive Kingdom label) to much earlier roots in the first century A.D., when a king named Ciar won control of the southwest of the island and Chiarraí was anglicized into Kerry. But ask a Kerryman where the expression came from, and he might have told you it was called the Kingdom because it was the most stunning county in Ireland, the land blessed with an abundant natural beauty. History might not have agreed with him, but the landscape certainly did.

One of Ireland's largest counties, with hundreds of miles of coastline ringing its dozen peninsulas, Kerry earned its Kingdom status today for keeping Ireland's coffers full of tourist dollars—with the Ring of Kerry coastal drive, the lakes of Killarney, the fishing and the golf and a perfected blend of old Ireland with tourist ease, Kerry deserved to be one of Ireland's most visited destinations. Though it was off the course on this particular trip, if you were playing the southwest, no doubt you'd be putting your head down in Killarney, and you'd be lucky for it. Crowded with Americans but ready for them, Killarney boasted legitimate four-star hotels and a restaurant scene to rival Kinsale. There were pubs to keep you stinking for a week, even a few nightclubs for the foursomes of restless degenerates.

Killarney was the hub for touring the Ring of Kerry, the town a starting point for the procession of buses that ushered tourists and their cameras around a cliff-hanging coastline. The Ring was one long postcard of green valleys pocked with sheep and mossy boulders, the road winding along a jagged shoreline, salty waves washing over the rocks below. It was inspiring despite the crowds pulled over at designated vantage points and the inevitable traffic snafus (the narrow road forced buses to do the Ring in a counter-clockwise direction, embarking via Killorglin—if you were driving and didn't want to be sandwiched between coaches, best to go clockwise via Kenmare). The Ring was a loop for most people, a continuous circuit that left them back at their Killarney hotel. But for the truly fortunate, the Ring was a one-way street that ended at its apex, dropping you by the sea in the most aptly named town in Ireland, a place called Waterville.

In a less gloriously named town on the south side of the Ring of Kerry—Sneam—I met up with my cousin-in-law Jody, and his golf buddy Rich, who brought my tally of glossy-scalped, shaven-head road mates to three. Jody was a handsome, strong-shouldered portrait of health, sporting a Mediterranean complexion and a dense lawn of black hair that Rich and I quietly coveted. Jody was a few years behind me at Notre Dame, which won him quick acceptance from my Irish cousins, bypassing the vetting that would have been in store for a fiancé who was of Italian descent and named after a girl. He was a hopeful bogey golfer, and Rich was so golf-dedicated that he'd built a protracting PVC club protector to cradle his sticks in the cargo hold. But more impressive than such gadgetry was the fact that Rich had rented a car. It was the size of a Skittle, but it gave them the chance to do something so many of my travelmates had dreamt of as they slept next to me in pink beds the size of birthday cakes, unicorns and ballet certificates on the walls—tell my itinerary to go to hell, and go see Ireland as they pleased.

Hauling just my golf clubs (I stuffed my pack into Rich's trunk), I made quick miles to Waterville while they motored ahead to play Dooks and Tralee. They finally arrived in town to find that they were going to score a bonus day of golf. On previous trips, I'd heard rumors of a new Waterville track being laid down across the bay, and at the edge of town we found eighteen holes overlooking the renowned Waterville links on the other side of the water. The Skellig Bay course wasn't quite a year old, a Ron Kirby design (of Nicklaus and Trent Jones design pedigree), and a course that very nearly never happened. Remember that digger that plunged into the Atlantic at Old Head? The Haulie O'Shea of Haulie's leap fame brushed off his dungarees, replaced that phone, and bought a stretch of seaside to build the Skellig Bay Golf Club.

The course was in its infant stages with young fairways that felt loose from a night of rain. Skellig Bay had links features—sea vistas, scarce trees, vigorous breezes—but it wasn't built on true linksland, the kind of rollicking landscape we saw waiting for us across the bay. The mounding was sparse and felt artificial in spots, but what Skellig Bay had going for it was its setting, the holes perched upon an oceanside tabletop. Time would bring the grasses up and give the holes some needed definition, and once the clubhouse was completed (we were shuttled over from a neighboring hotel), Skellig Bay would be a worthy complement to the Waterville Links. Even in its unfinished state, we took an hour to play and snap shots on 13, 14, and 15, which played along the edge of a sea cliff, sun warming the Skellig beaches far below (it seemed that Old Head's drop-offs had stuck with Haulie). And eighteen, a sidewinding par-five split by a stream that worked its way toward a lofted green, was a classic finish that had me remembering an afternoon at Baltusrol.

In a painfully dear golf landscape, 50 euros for Skellig Bay was a bargain (wrap your head around 180 euros for its neighbor). And as we waited in the parking lot for our lift back to the clubhouse, Jody and Rich licking their wounds from a wind that had taken a hungry bite out of their ball supply, the greens crew treated us to a Haulie's leap reenactment. I looked up from my scorecard to see a riding mower bigger than Rich's rental car rolling backward down the slope from the starter's shed, picking up speed as it headed for an eight-foot drop over a retaining wall. Before I could even get out a "Hey!," the Toro was upside down, the driver's seat smashed into the gravel of the parking lot. Three Irishman stood atop the wall, scratching their heads at the underworkings of an industrial lawnmower, and Jody and Rich couldn't help but feel better about their golf, lost balls a small matter when someone had to convince his boss he didn't forget the emergency brake.

Golf in Waterville dated to the late 1800s, not a particularly rare vintage in Ireland, but it was unusual for a golf course of such an age to not be built as recreation for the British Army. Golf in Waterville began as a by-product of the transatlantic cable, nine holes set on a promontory into Ballinskelligs Bay as a distraction for cable workers (Charles Lindbergh flew low past Waterville's cable station, showing his wing numbers to let the world know he had arrived). It wasn't until much later, however, when an Irish-American named Mulcahy came to Waterville and enlisted the help of none other than Eddie Hackett and Claude Harmon (Masters champ and father of Butch) to do justice to the exceptional duneland.

An admitted curmudgeon when it came to the subject of gussying up a links course (a links' true beauty was found in its most un-gussied bits), I was disappointed to hear that Tom Fazio had been brought into update the layout, but the reviews of his changes were ever-glowing, any semblance of a yawn having been ripped from the Waterville dunes. I was interested to see what was new at Waterville, and I was thrilled to be bunking in a tidy yellow guesthouse within walking distance of the clubhouse, with a four-star seafood restaurant downstairs. But what had me most excited about our afternoon in Waterville was the text I'd received the day before:

NEED 4TH 4 H2O VILLE? PADDY

His whole face was a smile as he strolled up to the driving range in Waterville, and why not? I wondered if he'd ever had a bad day, or one he couldn't at least make you laugh about, and this was a particularly good morning for Paddy from Kinsale. It was warm enough for shorts (not really, but he wore shorts anyway), the sun was shining, and he was wearing the Old Head windshirt he'd snuck into my gift pile and scored for free. There was a driving range with glistening pyramids of complimentary golf balls, and in a half hour we'd be teeing off Waterville's first in a light westerly breeze, the hole cheekily called "Last Easy." Any of the above would have been enough to make the lads back in the caddy room in Kinsale jealous, but what was really lurking behind the grin walking toward us was the means by which Paddy had traveled to Waterville. As the crow flew, it wasn't a long trip (the reason you saw more and more helicopters parked beside the putting greens in the southwest—five minutes up and down in a chopper versus three hours winding around the cliffsides, coughing down your breakfast). Paddy hadn't talked his way into a helicopter, but he'd nonetheless managed a chauffeur.

The evening before, Patrick happened to mention to his friend Brendan that he was playing Waterville the next morning, and that, aside from the drive, he could not have been more excited. No way Paddy could have known he was setting up one of the summer's most impressive Acts of Uncommon Irish Hospitality. Brendan thought for a minute, then remembered he had a friend in Waterville with whom he would like to have tea. So he offered Patrick a lift to Waterville—he'd call on his friend while Paddy played, and drive Paddy home when the golf and the pints were finished.

Back home, if someone offered to drive me three hours over hills and hairpins, wait for me to play golf and skull pints, then drive me back home when there was nothing in it for him but a potential cup of tea with an old friend that may or may not be alive, I would have probably slipped out the back door. If I wasn't being made an accomplice in some criminal rouse, I'd at least suspect a stalker, and Googling someone's backstory would certainly be in order. But in Kinsale, it was a perfectly reasonable offer—your friend could use a ride, why not give him one? It was my favorite Irish refrain, one that you heard at every breakfast table, as banal as *you're welcome*, but still full of meaning—need a lift, Paddy? I'll take you. *Not a bother.*

"When I first got here, I'd be like, 'No way, I can't let you do that,'" Paddy explained as he loosened up on the driving range. "But you figure it out. They're not offering just to offer. If the Irish say they want to do something for you, they want to do it. So I was like, 'Hell yes, Brendan, I'll see you at nine.'"

We set off down the first hole, and I didn't know if it was that I had been around Waterville a few times before, but in a country where the holes could look the same—lovely but similar, a regular rhythm of dune, gorse, dune, pub—the holes in Waterville made memories. The second was a bold bully of a par-four running down and away from you with an approach shot into a backdrop of estuary waters and Kerry mountains. The par-threes were each unforgettable, the most stunning being the Mass Hole, where we hit five-irons over a yawning crater, a deep hollow in the dunes where Catholic mass was held in secret during penal times. Original plans asked for the twelfth green to be placed within the hollow, but laborers refused to break the ground where mass had been celebrated. Mr. Hackett was happy to push the green back and upward into the hillside, adding a few yards and a half stroke of difficulty (so if you doubled the Mass Hole, you could vociferously blame it on Jesus Christ without sinning). And the view from the tee box on the 194-yard Mulcahy's Peak must have been the most popular photo stop in Ireland. The tee sat at the peak of Waterville's tallest dune, every hole on the course in plain view, ocean rolling up onto the beach behind the green. My favorite hole was one of Waterville's most modest, the par-four sixteenth that stretched only 350 yards. Called Liam's Ace for the head pro who played it in one stroke on his way to setting the course record of 65, its fairway bent around the estuary to where the inlet met the ocean, with a tiered, elevated green protected by dune swells and a backstop of hungry beach grass. None of us hit more than three-iron off the tee, none of us had more than eight-iron in, and my double bogey was the best number in our foursome. No matter that the six kept me from breaking 80—any hole that reminded you why golf wasn't called bash was a hole dear to my heart.

With faces pink and pints topped to the brim, we replayed our round in my favorite clubhouse bar in Ireland—simple, old enough to feel classic, but not so old that you feel like you're sticking to something. It was the perfect size to feel cozy but not crowded, always a free bench for the next foursome coming off the eighteenth, with windows in every direction bringing the mountains and golden surf into the room. My taste buds for malt and barley had been sleeping one off since June, but the pints in Waterville were wonderful again.

The place had its ghosts—Payne Stewart died shortly after accepting the captaincy at Waterville, and he was immortalized in a bronze statue by the putting green. The ashes of the late Mulcahy who envisioned Waterville were buried on that tee box on seventeen—and its characters, the round and red-cheeked manager Noel who welcomed us so well, and Irish golf legend, long-ball Liam Higgins of hole-in-one fame, who had won on both the regular and senior European tours and today could be spotted around the Waterville pro shop. The faces and the links, the conversations and the souvenirs—there was a cumulative effect to the whole Waterville thing, all the ingredients in balance to concoct an uncommon golf experience. Paddy took his time before calling Brendan. It was one of those afternoons.

As with most courses in the southwest, we were surrounded by tables full of American foursomes. As we all sat in that room with sunburned smiles, I couldn't help but feel a little sad, even a little stupid. Out in the parking lot, there was a helicopter and a half dozen luxury buses. Rich and Jody had a Ford back at the Smugglers Inn, and Paddy's lift was on its way. Who was the genius here? Was I the lucky bastard I'd been accused of being for the last year, or was I the jackass? I had seen more than any traveler come to golf Ireland would ever see, but in the end, wasn't a low sun over links like these, a half-full Guinness next to a scribbled scorecard—isn't that really all anyone needed to see?

In the pro shop after our round, Paddy introduced me to Liam Higgins (Paddy had only known him for three minutes longer than I had, but as always with Paddy, they were already old friends), and he told me he'd been hearing about my trip and following the stories in the paper. I noticed a picture pinned on the wall behind him, a place I recognized. I asked him what it was.

He took it off the wall and showed it to me. "You know where this is?"

"I do," I told him. And in almost a whisper, he leaned in and said, "Eddie Hackett was here one day and he told me, 'Sorry Liam, but I think I've built a course better than this one, on the greatest piece of property I've ever seen.' That's the place he was talking about."

I was looking at a picture of the links at Carne, the links I had fallen in love with in what felt like a different lifetime, a course I had walked to via the same roadway on which my great-great-grandfather delivered the mail on horseback. It was a shame that I would never get the chance to meet Mr. Hackett, but I thought he would have liked what I was doing, would have thought it important that I'd taken the longer road and given his country its due. The rest of the room might be off to the bigger-name courses tomorrow, might be jetting off to Scotland for the weekend. But the guy on foot was on the same page as Mr. Hackett, and that felt good enough to me.

There was one links in Ireland that I had, months before, made a calculated decision to avoid: the Dingle links known as Ceann Sibeal (kee-yawn sha-beel), not because I wasn't curious to check out another Hackett course, but because those eighteen holes would take me on a week's long one-way hike out the Dingle Peninsula, at a time when I knew my tank would be empty—from the start of the peninsula, I was a three-day walk from Ballybunion. I could either be home in five days, or in two weeks. I didn't even bother flipping a coin, and went with choice A.

Fast forward to August—Rich and Jody with their cramped but useful automobile, and me having decided it was reasonable to use modern transport if it meant crossing the final links off my list. So I mashed myself into the back of their car and took a Rosslare-like detour out to Dingle at the bequest of the owner of the Dingle links, John, who had been following my itinerary and recognized an unacceptable omission on my schedule. The gall of the American who thought he could play every links in Ireland without teeing it up at the end of Dingle—it was the scuttlebutt around the town, particularly in Danno's Restaurant where John had been getting an earful from Danno (*So he's going to play every course but yours?*), a chef who whipped up my summer's best burger when I walked into his place to prove that I'd taken no shortcuts (except for when I did).

John confirmed one of my reasons for loving the seasides of Ireland. It seemed the farther you ventured out onto Ireland's edges—and the town of Ballyferriter was Ireland's most westerly village, sort of the tip of the island's big toenail—the more lively the characters, and the richer the *craic*. In his fifties with teenage mischief in his eyes, John was full of jokes and stories, but of all the corkers he would tell us that afternoon, his pronouncement on the first tee was his most hilarious. We stood there, the four of us, our wind suits so full of air that we looked like Thanksgiving parade balloons. In front of us, a long expanse of linksland was cradled between the rocky promontory of Sybil Head and the Brandon Mountains. Somewhere out in the mist was Blasket Island, not that we were looking for it, our backs turned to the wall of water blowing off the ocean. It wasn't wind so much as it was the hand of God pushing us over, trying to mash our noses into the turf. Four hours of misery stared us in our tear-strewn eyes, and John shrugged and announced, "Bit of a breeze today."

Ceann Sibeal meant "Sybil Head," the course taking its name from young Sybil Lynch of Galway who long ago schemed to elope with a Ferriter boy, a son of the first family of nearby Ballyferriter (Home of Ferriter). When Sybil's father got wind of her plan, he headed for Dingle and laid siege to the Ferriter castle. Sybil hid in a sea cave during the battle, but by the time the fighting ended, it was discovered that the waters had risen and swept Sybil out to sea.

I wouldn't compare Sybil's fate to our windy afternoon, but as I stood there hunched on the second tee on the links of Ceann Sibeal, our foursome teetering back and forth like four flagsticks, the place just seemed unlucky. And with each blast off the Atlantic, I became more aware that it wasn't just the golf pros and the pint-tippers that had been following my journey. God had been keeping tabs, too, and as a karmic kick in the teeth for getting in that car, He had unleashed upon us weather to make me do that which I swore I wouldn't: I quit.

But only for an afternoon. After a few dozen slashes into the breeze, none of us being able to find the fairway, or a single one of Jody's golf balls, we vowed to come back tomorrow and give Dingle another go. It was worth the extra night—Dingle town was alive with *craic*, that burger with Danno's homemade red sauce brought smiles to windburned faces, and the course ended up being a fine surprise. Even with John's proud assertions about the quality of his links, I was skeptical about Dingle, a course that you could see in its entirety from the parking lot, leading one to make a knee-jerk cow-pasture assumption. From the clubhouse, we looked out upon a big bumpy field that seemed to hold little mystery, but once we got our feet out into those bumps, the links began to grumble, the hills taller and pits far deeper than they appeared from the car park. The unmanufactured quality of Ceann Sibeal made you feel as if you weren't golfing the Dingle links, but Dingle itself, shaking your head at what a skillful designer that Atlantic breeze could be.

John invited us back to the club for the festivities that evening. Even though that day's tournament had been washed out (there was a prize on, as they called it), the post-tournament festivities were weatherproof and would go on, full swing. There was a strong singing contingent among the membership, he explained, and the guests would take their turns throughout the evening singing songs they might have been working on for weeks. The crooning would go on until well past midnight, when the party would move to a neighbor's, or possibly to his house, he admitted, where it wasn't unheard of to keep the *craic* flowing until five o'clock in the morning.

We politely declined on behalf of our livers, and on the ride from Dingle we all marveled at the Irish fortitude, rock stars at age sixty, putting in hours that made the college boys in us cower. But it reminded me of one of my first impressions about the Irish, one made during a non-golfing trip to Ireland's southwest when I was fourteen. For some authentic culture, a host pointed us toward a dance in the village hall, where I remembered sitting and wondering how the octogenarians in Ireland did it. Was it the water? That black stuff in their glasses? All evening long, old men spun around the room, twirling young ladies and making passes like they were on spring break. I told my mother I wanted to retire to Ireland, because it seemed that white-haired people here didn't just curl up and expire. They danced. They laughed at bad jokes. They smiled, no matter that their smiles looked like they had divvied up a single set of teeth. Old men flirted with young women, old ladies sipped whiskey and giggled over the day's gossip. Farmers who looked like skeletons in their boots, people we'd put in a home, or maybe a box, spent their days working cattle. I walked the roads with them as they slowly made their way from field to field, herding dogs at their heels.

Their secret? Fresh air and fewer worries were my guess—maybe not fewer worries, necessarily, but the Irish didn't seem to possess the same sense of entitlement I was used to back home, the one that gave us the right to sit around all day and fret about our plight. Where I was from, the line between life and death seemed a negotiable one, so many of us spending most of our living hours trying to put off our dying ones. The Irish, they just got on with it, too busy to try to reorder the inevitable. You lived, worked, died, and laughed as much as possible along the way—sounded like greeting-card philosophy, I know, but it was hard to dismiss. They had been around a lot longer and been through a load more shit, so it was worth taking notes. After three-plus months living a simpler life, I'd learned something I missed on that trip in the back of the tour bus, the one where we all smiled at the countryside and said, "How quaint," but thought, "How boring." Truth was, a simple life and a rich one were not exclusive ideas. And when it got too heavy, as it felt it was now, remember the most important part of the Irish formula, the laughing. We coughed out a few weeks' worth of laughs at John's tales of the queen, the parish priest, and the unforeseen consequences of cleavage, then backtracked to where the path had left off, and where I'd start walking from tomorrow.

Jody and Rich left for the airport and I made my way for the links at Dooks, a course just off the northern stretch of the Ring of Kerry. The first day alone was always a tough one, the quiet a little more blaring, but this was the home stretch, the last week, and I wanted to do the final holes on my own. I'd planned it that way, at least, until I heard a chime from my phone and saw another message:

TRALEE? PADDY

hole 874

578 over par

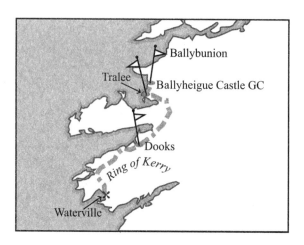

THE ONLY THING THAT STUCK WITH ME ABOUT DOOKS WAS THE toad. I had played the links in Glenbeigh on a previous trip with Dad, and sandwiched on our tour between Waterville, Tralee, and Ballybunion, perhaps we didn't pay very close attention to Dooks. I remember rain and gorse, and I bought a sweater in the pro shop because one thing Dooks did have—and still does— was Ireland's best golf logo, a bumpy, brown toad called a Natterjack, a protected species that burrows into the sands around the links.

Dooks was one of the oldest courses in Ireland, dating to 1889, when it was opened as a nine-holer for officers from the Royal Horse Artillery stationed at the Glenbeigh Artillery Range. Expanded to eighteen holes in 1970, its most interesting feature was that it was built on three sets of sand dunes, meaning the links was surrounded by Dingle Bay on three sides, with a new view at every turn—from the hefty McGillicuddy Mountains across the water and the gentle hills of Glenbeigh, to the Inch Peninsula in clear view across the harbor, the fishing village of Cromane within sight along the beach. Those officers had dropped their links into a divine crossroads of Irish vistas and waterlocked linksland. But none of this occurred to me until I arrived at Dooks for the second time, 108 years after the place had been born. I had collected and shipped home nearly fifty logo balls to this point. I was just excited about the toad.

I arrived at Dooks not only with memories of being underwhelmed, but with a prejudice regarding a recent major redesign. Redesign smacked of committees in city offices pushing lines around a blueprint, while the courses closest to my heart felt like they had been discovered more than built. Cut a hole within a valley, stick a tee box atop a sandhill, and where the sheep had burrowed into the dunes, put the sand traps there, same as golf's original bunkers. If there was redesigning to do, let wind and water do the job—give God a century, he would rework a links' topography a half dozen times. So I wasn't as excited as the captain, Donal, might have thought I would be when he boasted of Dooks' major overhaul, no less than sixteen holes reimagined by Martin Hawtree, who had touched-up Lahinch and Royal Dublin and had been tapped by Donald Trump to give his Scottish links a crack. He hadn't messed with the Natterjack, I was relieved to find, and I wasn't halfway down the first fairway when I had to admit to Donal that something was different about Dooks. Something good.

How a course could remain something of a secret when it sat a mile off the Ring of Kerry and happened to be the steal of the southwest at 80 euros was something of a mystery, but not for very long, I figured. The word was going to get out. What the redesign had done was essentially lift up the Dooks golf course to take advantage of its locale, showcasing the scenery that I hardly noticed twelve years ago. Unsightly hedges were uprooted and holes where extended to their natural conclusion by the water's edge. The greens and tees were elevated, and the mounding was reshaped to draw your eye into the surrounding mountainside. What was once a fun but forgettable links lost in pine trees and dense pockets of gorse was now a course built for your camera, which I sadly never got to use as I found myself locked in the midst of the President's Prize. The biggest days at any club in Ireland were the weekends when the captain and president hosted their tournaments (the captain was cock of the walk, while the president was typically a former club captain and more of an honorary position). It was an honor to be included in the president's event, even if my 29 points (84 strokes in American) didn't win me a pair of socks. Dooks had retained what I recalled liking about it, a relatively short quirkiness you'd expect from a century-old links, but the place had been pumped up to match its surroundings. And as for value—you could play links that were three times the price and have less to look at.

With eight miles left to Killorglin, I had to pass on the president's dinner and return to the road where I walked into town on fumes. I checked into the inn at the center of town and headed to a pub across the street to take in the Cork football semifinal against Tipperary.

The woman sitting next to me at the bar had big, black curls, and I doubted whether she could fit another swatch of Cork red anywhere on her body. I had been planning to put my tenner on Tipperary, but her county pride inspired me, not to mention the fact that she was of healthy stature and had been knocking down Coronas like milk bottles at the fair. By kickoff (or whatever the start was called), I had made up my mind that she could probably kick my ass, so I decided to root for her instead of against, and asked the bartender to call in 10 euros on Cork to win (did I mention that I loved the Irish bookkeepers?). He got the wager in just in time for us to watch the Rebels pound the favorites and earn for me a thirty-euro return on my investment. One hundred thirteen days, countless waste bins overflowing with my lost wagers, and in the magical pub of J. D. Favley's, I finally cashed a winner. I bought my friend a Corona with my winnings, a beer that almost lasted long enough for me to pay for it.

While few of us could hum a single note, "The Rose of Tralee" lingered in the imaginations of so many golfers, some unable to recall where they'd heard the phrase before, while some others who spent college watching *Caddyshack* played on a loop were more than able to recite the scene in which Maggie expressed her disdain for Lacey Underall, Judge Smails's niece from dreary old Manhattan: *She's been plucked more times than the Rose of Tralee. Biggest whore on Fifth Avenue, I'm told.* So I knew there was a song, a ditty popular with the pluckers, but as for the festival that song inspired, it was a whole new world to me.

The story went that a wealthy Protestant named William Mulchinock fell in love with his maid, the "lovely and fair" Mary O'Connor, a poor Catholic girl who would be immortalized in song as the Rose of Tralee. Their love was stymied by religion and class, and William was forced to leave his love and emigrate from Ireland. In a third act typical of all such feel-good Irish stories, William returned to Ireland many years later to find that his love had died from tuberculosis. And somehow that was the reason why girls came from Toronto to dress up in evening gowns and play the fiddle on Irish television.

I had been to Tralee on a previous memorable occasion, where my father at a feisty age sixty nearly came to blows with the town rummy in the pub in our hotel. This gentleman, with runny eyes and a tongue sloshing around in his mouth, didn't care for our accents, apparently, and teetered over to our table to let us know. He seemed intent on blaming us for his recent arrest in Los Angeles, where he was just helping out a lady in need by giving her a ride home, he explained. How was he to know she was a prostitute? The fact that we weren't cops, weren't from Los Angeles, and weren't prostitutes or purveyors thereof didn't impress him, as he barked at us about how he had been treated in our country, reminding us that we were now in his. He pointed his finger in my dad's face one too many times, Dad calmly explaining to me that he was two seconds away from breaking it off, until a table of locals stepped in and shooed the gentleman out of the pub, apologizing and sending us a round for our trouble.

I remembered Tralee as more of a town than a city, quiet with a few three-star hotels, lacking the restaurants and charm of Killarney, but a well-positioned hub for an Irish golf traveler. But when I walked into town in late August, I discovered a city bustling

with street vendors and live music. Drinkers spilled out the pub
doors, chippers and crepe stands lined the promenade, gypsy kids
worked the crowds peddling roses and plastic helicopters. Stages
were set in the town squares, acoustic bands and Disney dance
music echoing along the streets of Tralee. Banners hanging from
the pubs and shops advertised each establishment's Rose loyal-
ties: GOOD LUCK ROSE OF NEW ZEALAND! My hotel had gotten
behind the Rose of New Orleans, I would soon learn, when I
checked into the Grand and stuck my head out my hotel window,
and wondered what the hell was going on.

My Tralee festival research was conducted almost exclusively
in front of the television in a cozy rugby-centric pub off Tralee's
main street (Munster, Ireland's southwest province, was a proud
rugby stronghold), where I was aided by my assistant, one Paddy
just arrived from Kinsale. Apparently there existed Rose committees in cities all over the world who nominated girls of Irish heritage to compete in the big dance in August in Tralee. As Patrick
and I patiently watched the festivities, inquiring every ten minutes as to when the swimsuits would be making their appearance,
the lady Rose fans glued to the telly shouted us down, "No swimsuits, it's not a beauty pageant! It's about personality!" We were
lectured as to how the contest was aimed at identifying a young
lady who would best represent Ireland, Irish heritage, and the
Rose's idyllic qualities spelled out in the song. As the tune went:

> She was lovely and fair as the rose of the summer,
> Yet 'twas not her beauty alone that won me;
> Oh no, 'twas the truth in her eyes ever dawning,
> that made me love Mary, the Rose of Tralee.

While this 'twas the truth in her eyes business sounded a tad
disingenuous, like buying Playboy for the short fiction, the contest carried on without revealing a stitch of skin, Irish dancing in
prom dresses making up the meat of the competition. We shook
our heads and lipped our pints and indulged in a session I rarely
entertained, but that felt right that evening: all those things we
did better back home.

Pizza and interstates were easy pickings. USDA prime had no

Irish equivalent, you could fit four Irish refrigerators into an American one, and comparing our laundry technology to theirs was pure folly—easier to go beat your underwear on a rock by the river than try to get an Irish washer going. I was happy to concede chips, newspapers, bacon, and free text-messaging, because no rasher was ever as lovely as an electric shower was lame.

I once watched two foursomes of Texans in a pub on a Sunday night in Ballyliffin spend an evening engaged in a similar conversation—they couldn't get close enough to the television to see the end of the U.S. Open, and whined for most of the evening about Ireland's dearth of flat screens. *We'd have twenty TVs showing the Open back home. Twenty? Try fifty!* And they complained to one another how they were cramped in a corner while the family by the television wasn't even watching the tournament—God forbid, they were all actually talking to one another. I felt embarrassed, and after a Carlsberg, I felt mad, envisioning myself slapping the Longhorn off his head (*Get your damn hat off in the pub, you see anyone else wearing a hat in here? In the whole damn country?*), thus pinning the world's distaste for Americans on a guy in a polo shirt who couldn't comprehend why they served you vinegar with your french fries. So Patrick and I didn't talk about what we did better, or they did worse. We didn't sit in the pub in Tralee discussing what was inferior over here. But we did talk about what was different.

Patrick was a guy who you would guess could always make lemonade, but he told me that he struggled when he first moved to Kinsale. There was tightness to an Irish community that bordered on closed-ness, a reality I had been sensing as I made my way around—there was small-town-good to Ireland, and small-town-not-so-good. The Irish were quick to make you feel welcome, but if you endeavored to be more than a tourist, that welcome could turn suspicious as the locals might be eager to know what you were doing, where you were from, and when you would be going back. It wouldn't take long for the entire town to know the answers to those questions, Ireland being a country where all information was granted need-to-know status and all its citizenry given clearance. "Want something to get around in

Kinsale?" Patrick explained. "Three ways. Tele-phone, tele-graph, and tell-a-librarian."

From Donegal to Belfast to Dublin, I had encountered a great consistency to Ireland, the sort of reliability I suppose I craved and envied, the life that redheaded kids romanticized, imagining men with long memories sitting beside peat fires, telling us we'd come from royalty or, more romantic yet, come from nothing at all. Life was such yesterday in Ireland, and euros and satellite telly and Britney Spears be damned, it would be such tomorrow. But I sensed that such a consistent life was just a few steps removed from a claustrophobic one—I could sense it in a transplant like Paddy, and I certainly felt it myself, unable to escape an evening's indiscretions. Vegas this was not, and for a visitor on an extended stay, quaintness could feel like a closing-in. The more miles I logged, the smaller the whole place seemed.

If you were born a butcher's son in Ireland and grew up in the blue house, no matter if you went on to Irish dance on the moon, you would be known by all for eternity as the butcher's son from the blue house. If you were born in Kerry and moved to Cork when you were five, at age fifty they would still consider you a transplant, a "blow-in" as they called them. In the States, we didn't take the time to care as the Irish do, and I didn't believe that we respected one another nearly as much. I had tried to figure out what I so admired about the Irish, and why I grew up hyphenating my heritage. Frankly, the Irish were a little rough around the edges, they were professionally opinionated, and behind the laughter there was a sadness that filled whole jukeboxes, that you could see from time to time on a park bench or at the end of the bar—big hearts, easily broken. But I think I had figured it out in the four months shaking their hands and listening to their stories and watching them push through their day. Back home, our greatest American asset was that we had the chance to reinvent ourselves every morning, every minute. I was sure it had something to with why those women got on that boat in Westport a hundred years ago, for the right to be anybody. We believed that we had sold ourselves short in the States if we didn't take our shot at being someone better. But even in their modern success story, the Irish still possessed that most attractive of all qualities: They were content with themselves. They didn't appear pressured to be anyone they weren't—while we felt obliged to be otherwise, they felt entitled to be themselves. It was a quiet confidence, a contentedness that couldn't be faked. Sit around a table of Irish folks, and you'd sense it—just like the Rose, that truth in the eyes.

It seemed a pretty great way to live, unless you were from a place where you didn't mind not knowing your neighbors' names. Then it was time to go home.

On television, we watched the Rose of New York take the crown, and we toasted her with a patriotic pint. We headed back to the hotel as the pageant let out and the crowds clogged the streets. We missed most of the *craic*, but this was a night to sacrifice to the next morning. It was Patrick's first time in Tralee, so he didn't know it yet, but we would soon be visiting one of the most irresistible beauties in Ireland. There was no dreaming of swimsuits that evening, just two snoring Americans imagining the links of Tralee.

It was a few miles from town to the spot where the golfers of Tralee had taken their fourth stand in a hundred years. Since the club was first established in 1896, nine-holers around Tralee had suffered from high rainfall, until the membership finally took a gamble on some property in the dunes along Barrow Harbour in 1980, enlisting the design acumen of Arnold Palmer. The property had a lot going for it before it was ever imagined as a links— the beaches of Barrow were used in the filming of *Ryan's Daughter*, and nearby Fenit was the birthplace of Saint Brendan the Navigator, who legend tells reached the Americas a thousand years before Columbus.

The beaches below the Tralee links were also sight of yet another could-have, should-have moment in Irish history, and another example of Ireland's fate being tied to its European brethren. World War I presented an opportunity for Irish nationalists to court German favor in opposing the British. In 1916, returning from Germany where he had been rallying support and arms for their cause, Roger Casement's U-19 submarine landed on the beach at Tralee, where he was seized by Crown forces and eventually hanged for treason. A shipment of 20,000 rifles from Germany bound for the Easter Rising was seized by the British, and Casement was captured before he could warn his compatriots to call off the uprising, which would fail in Dublin a few days later. The long lens of history might not view the Easter Rising as a failure but as a first step, yet the missteps surrounding it led to the execution of Casement and fifteen other leaders. But it was hard to stand on any part of that duneland in Barrow and imagine that there was ever an angry or unpleasant word spoken anywhere on this island. There was a boulder beside the fourth fairway that local legend said had been thrown there from a nearby mountain peak by the Celtic hero Cuchulain, the crags in the stone described as Cuchulain's giant handprint. I told the story to Paddy as we passed the rock. It was too early in the round for him to consider it anything but typical Irish fare to roll your eyes at, but after the back nine at Tralee, Paddy might have believed anything.

Tralee was a tale of two nines—Arnold Palmer said he was responsible for the front, but credited God for the back. All over this golf course of Ireland, I'd played dozens of courses that had grown from an original nine holes to eighteen, making an uneven links a regular occurrence. Portstewart's outward holes outlegged its inward holes by a long stretch; Corballis's back nine wasn't on the same planet as its front. Placed on opposite corners of the beachhead, Tralee's outward nine was a stretch of very strong golf holes, but they were just a warm-up for the madness that would ensue on the way in.

I typically found celebrity stamps on a golf course to be silly time-share-selling stuff, courses branded a Nicklaus course as if Jack was driving the backhoe. But I didn't like a name in golf more than Arnold Palmer, and whoever got their shoes dirty in laying out Tralee, it was of no difference to me. Palmer was right, the back nine was all God's doing. The eleventh hole made the point, subtle as a sledgehammer—they didn't make earthmovers to shape that kind of incline, and when you finally reached the green the par-five that went on for a week—the hole had entire chapters to it, three different weather forecasts—He was the guy you were referencing, in a fit of thanks or something else.

The number-one handicap index twelfth was an outrageous par-four, driving blind into skyscraping dunes, avoiding a pit of despair to your left, then hurling your ball up to a green fronted by an abyss amid the sandhills, a yawning crevasse that was soon outdone by the gulf of nastiness separating you from the green on the par-three thirteenth. You would wish the ravine would have been filled with water, because a free drop would be an easier price than having to rappel down into that gorge should your tee ball fail to fly 150. Paddy's didn't quite make it, and after ten minutes without any sight of him, I half expected to get a text up on the green:

SEND HELP

Tralee just built from there—15, 16, and 17 were a rumbling crescendo of beachside target holes, plates of short grass cut into the dunes and calling for our golf balls. At low tide, the beach to our right seemed to stretch on to America, a chance for a caddy to tell a joke about the biggest sand trap in Ireland. But looking at the green and yellow peaks of the Tralee links, it was tough to make the turn out of the dunes and head up the eighteenth, no matter that it was an easy birdie downwind. There were a few special stretches I had found around Ireland where I could take someone who didn't know a links from a lollipop, and they'd walk a short while and say, "I get it." When you couldn't decide if you should play on or curl up like a sheep in one of the dents in the grass, lay there and watch the wind blow waves across the golden hillsides, forgetting all about those boxes on your score-card and using your course guide to scribble down your poetry—it happened in places, and Tralee was one of them.

Paddy offered me a ride as he always did, and I declined it for the last time. We promised to meet up over the holidays when he was back to visit the family in Philadelphia, and I set off up the road to a town called Ballyheigue. Two more nights to go, just one more stop after tomorrow, and as much as I would have enjoyed finishing off this Irish golf course with Paddy, who had been there from the start, I didn't offer him a spot. It wasn't just because I wanted to say good-bye to the Irish golf course in my own way, but Ballybunion had been this trip's beating heart, a links around which other Irish courses set their orbit, and I couldn't afford a faux pas at the finish line. Founded in 1893, Ballybunion was the match that sparked the golfing world's fascination with Irish links, a course that Herbert Warren Wind called "simply the finest seaside links in the world" in 1970, and the buses hadn't stopped since. Ranked among the world's premiere golf courses (only County Down outranks it on the island, and that's not in my book), it was Yankee Stadium, Churchill Downs, Madison Square Garden—you didn't play golf in Ireland and not play Bally-B. This also meant that they didn't really need my business, or my gushing review, so I figured it unwise to show up with a caravan as I did in Kinsale, asking to squeeze us out between the members.

There were other courses where, when they heard your accent, wouldn't let you leave without a folder full of promotional materials, extolling you to plunk down a deposit on an international membership. I learned that Ballybunion hadn't taken a new international member in years—*CEO? Own a football team? Sorry, all full.* They didn't even bother printing applications. They had more business than they could handle, they couldn't raise greens fees high enough, and despite my ruddy hair I would be just another American queuing up in the pro shop to buy souvenirs for the family. So I made a note to be on my best behavior the whole way into town. Last thing I needed was to end a four-month round of golf with another argument about my shoes.

I was able to do most of the miles to Ballyheigue on the beach, and I'd already started purging provisions as I went—I was down to one pair of boxers, one pair of socks, a lonely collared shirt. The inches-thick itinerary that I had taken months to build had been thinned down to just a few loose pages. It was a quick walk under bright skies as I watched the rippling water, spurred on by the knowledge that in short time the load I'd been living under for four months would be resting beneath those waves. I came upon a skeleton of an old boat on the beach, a wooden ribcage sticking out of the sand. I dropped my pack and looked at my clubs strapped to my backpack as they had been for the last four months, and I thought this a beautiful and quiet spot from which to send them sailing.

These sticks had been my companions not just in Ireland, but I had dragged them all over the world in my formerly golf-obsessed life. These clubs had given flight to golf balls on three continents; they had been gripped with sweaty hands at Q-Schools and U.S. Open qualifying and Nationwide Tour Mondays; they were bent and tweaked and doctored by the best club men in the business. For two years of my life, they hadn't spent a single night in a cold car trunk or an unlocked garage, my irons and woods and wedges never leaving my sight. I had spent more time with them over the last four years than I had with my wife. Seriously. We'd had good times and bad times, but overall, we'd had far too many times. If this trip had helped me get over Ireland, it had helped me get over them, too, and this Irish round would be their victory lap, my Mizunos' farewell tour. It wasn't going to be enough to stick them in a closet, not after what we'd been through. This breakup needed casualties and carnage, and the waves sliding past my shoes felt just final enough.

I would have let the Mizunos swim for it right there if I could have reconciled myself to playing Ballybunion with rentals, but I couldn't stomach that possibility so close to the finish line. I took off my shoes, which were now hard clumps, the padding all petrified like two crusted catcher's mitts strapped to my feet. I tied them to my bag and barefooted it along the hard sand, and in an hour I was turning heads on the beach in Bellyheigue, sunbathers trying to guess where this shoeless golfer had come from, wondering if I had just walked out of the sea.

My B&B was a modest one, where a kid in a beard and surfer trunks showed me a room befitting a beach town. I had a view of a strand that was crowded with families, and the place wasn't so nice that I'd have to worry about the sand stuck in my shoes.

I tried to pretend not to see it, but it was unavoidable, directly out the front door from the B&B, a sign that I couldn't miss.

BALLYHEIGUE CASTLE GOLF CLUB

I had planned on playing an Irish golf course that was 720 holes long. By the time I got on the plane in two days time, I would have played 954. What was nine more. And Ballyheigue to Ballybunion was a fair way to finish, I decided, golf on two remote ends of the Irish spectrum—from the town nine-holer to a course that made me wish I'd packed pants without cargo pockets (if noticed in Ballybunion, I had a Swiss Army knife ready to make them disappear). I put my last pair of wet, woolly socks over my sandy feet, grabbed my sack of sticks that had just barely survived the ocean an hour before, and headed for the clubhouse.

The course would have been more accurately described as the *last remaining bit of ballyheigue castle golf course*, because it was burned down by the IRA during the War of Independence, and what remained was the facade of the castle and a few turrets, sort of a backlot Hollywood set with nothing behind the windows. It was an adolescent nine-holer (born in 1996) and far from a true links—half the holes were treeless, and from its hillside location overlooking the water, it had a seaside feel, a fair community course with views through an old castle wall to the beach and Ballyheigue Bay. It might blossom into something more substantial, but as it was, Ballyheigue was a safe setting for kids on holiday to knock it around. And lucky for me, that's what I found as I dragged myself up to the first tee, three lads having just teed off ahead of me. They were each pulling golf bags bigger then they were and walking circles in the rough, looking like they had lost their mothers in the mall.

I took my time and played two balls, trying not to push the threesome, but on the fifth I wandered to the tee box and found a young boy sitting on a bench. He was wearing a soccer jersey and had short brown hair and a pale, freckled face. He couldn't have been ten years old, and there was no chance that he weighed more than my backpack.

"Do you want to play along?" he said, sounding confident. "It's slow today."

I had been used to getting waved through as a single, and was always disappointed when I wasn't asked to join a group—no matter if it was little old ladies or a pack of club-throwers, it was nice to be asked. His name was Eamon, and after watching their struggles over the opening holes, I was surprised to be asked to join up, but if he wasn't too shy to shank it in front of a stranger, neither was I.

I thanked him and headed for the back tee box, past where two lads were returning from the regular tee, headed for Eamon's bench. They were a couple years older, maybe twelve, both of them as skinny as six-irons, a kid named Colin in a Cork jersey and football shorts, and Eamon's brother Declan dressed in a collared shirt and spikes, the golfer of the group.

"You're teeing off from the blues," Declan noted. "What do you play off?"

"I don't know. Five, six maybe."

"Five handicap. Did you hear that, Eamon!" Declan announced. They hurried off the tee box and took spots behind the bench, eager spectators. I eyed the fairway of a bending par-four as the gallery carried on.

"I never played with a five handicap."

"Me neither."

"What's yer handicap?"

"I dunno. Maybe twenty."

"You're a twenty handicap on one hole."

"I am not."

"You had a twelve back there. On a par-four."

I hammered a booming cut down the right side of the fairway to a chorus of, *Whoa! See that? He hits it farther than your dad!*

"Where'd you get that driver?" Declan asked. "Can I have a look?"

I handed it over to him. "Colin, check it out," he said, showing it off like it was Excalibur, turning the blue shaft in the sunlight. "Gorgeous. How much did it cost?"

"I don't really remember," I told him.

"Where are you from?"

"He's from America, stupid."

"But where in America?"

"We've been to Disney World . . ."

For five holes the questions came, and I answered them coyly
with a smile, playing the reluctant celebrity for them. Declan had
an off-balance but consistent swing, and Eamon somehow got
the ball airborne with men's clubs—he looked like he was swinging a javelin. Colin was the quiet one, pipe-cleaner legs sticking
out of his white football shorts. He was struggling to keep it
moving and I could tell he was embarrassed.

"He's a better player than this," Declan whispered to me on
the sixth.

"He's been sick," Eamon agreed. "He's long off the tee. At
least I think he's long."

"Eamon's the putter," Declan said of his little brother.

"Love my putter. It's about the only thing I'm good at. Declan
can hit pretty much any shot."

"I like to play," Declan explained. "I practice a lot, too."

I had been of the opinion that Ireland was a country overrun
by its youngsters. It was an impression hard to shake after a summer bouncing from tourist town to tourist town, having to brave
packs of chocolate-fingered preteens, dodging their ice creams
and wasting hours of my life in line behind kids trying to figure if
they could squeeze one more piece of licorice out of their fiver.
Ireland was supposed to be an old place, wobbly canes and bushy
white eyebrows, a drafty old house my grandparents spoke about
as if it had been knocked down years ago. So where the hell did
all these kids come from? And why were they always in front of
me at the breakfast buffet?

When I was those boys' age, I'd like to think I wouldn't have,
but playing with three other ten-year-olds, I would have likely
laughed at my buddies' whiffs, thrown tantrums when they in
turn laughed at mine, and found a way to end the nine holes with
one of us storming off the course with a face hot with tears, all
friendships suspended for a minimum of twenty-five minutes. But
these lads cheered each other around the course. They stuck up
for one another, were quiet when they hit it sideways, told one
another to give it another go because they could do it better than
that. Golf took a lot of credit for teaching good manners, much
of it undeserved—I had met as many cheaters and jackasses on

the golf course as off. These boys had the respect their fathers showed for their friends, and that gave them a certain poise that I didn't expect from kids, a species I had previously considered the original four-letter word. Ireland was a changing place, a younger place, and the lads were all right.

Declan showed me how he hit his bunker shots: "I'm pretty good in bunkers. I've got a sixty-degree wedge," and from his little brother, "He's got a sixty-degree wedge, do you have one? They're amazing." On the last, I let them each take a swing with my driver, even Colin, whose struggles had his head hanging. He politely told me no thank you, but I wouldn't let him leave the ninth tee without getting up there in his sneakers and giving it a rip. I'd like to tell you he split the fairway, but he didn't, knocking a dribbler onto the ladies' tee. But at least he was laughing, and his friends were laughing, too.

His cheeks were red as he handed my driver back to me. "It's a good club," he said.

They had been around the nine holes three times that afternoon and had probably taken north of two hundred swipes each, but as we finished the final par-four in front of the stone facade of Ballyheigue, Colin looked down to the beach where the sun was still hanging above the ocean, and he guessed they had enough time to play nine more. So we said good-bye, and they kept going—they had plenty of excuses to quit, I was sure, Nintendos back in their beach caravans, and probably a half dozen blisters between them. They were stuck with hand-me-down sticks and bags big enough to take a nap in, but what did that matter when you were twelve and there was still light in the sky? I watched them tug their bags toward the first tee, sure they would be out there until dark. I used to play that kind of golf, and in Ireland or Philadelphia or anywhere, it was the best game I ever played.

The next morning, I woke with light feet. August 25th. Last day, last walk—last was a hard idea to embrace after subsisting on a routine where I tried to not let myself think about an end. I wavered from the routine, not taping up the heels of my shoes, forgetting about the chafing lube and the Band-Aids. Sixteen miles to my next tee box, five hours to a place where I would be sitting that evening, probably behind a tall glass of amber, and for the first time that summer, not having to worry about what my legs were going to feel like in the morning. I would soon be reunited with a former version of myself, the fatter, crankier, less pungent me, the guy who would honk at you to speed it up as he drove three blocks to pick up a pizza. I didn't necessarily want to be him again, but I sure missed hanging out with him. I hustled down to the breakfast table, and told the lady of the house to do her damndest. "Full Irish," I proclaimed. I asked for extra rashers, and nearly cleaned the place out of brown sauce.

I shoveled carbs into my gob and planned my morning's route. I faced the usual choice between the coastal route and the more direct national roadway. I asked the woman's husband which way he would recommend.

"You're playing Ballybunion?"

"I am."

"You're the lucky one. It's a special place, it is. Now what you're going to want to do is to go back down to the bottom of town, head on back out to the main road . . ."

I stopped him there. Psychologically, I found it far easier to walk two new miles than a mile I'd already covered. *Head back* was the wrong foot on which to start any directions, and the map seemed to suggest a route where I wouldn't need to backtrack.

"You could take that road," he said, looking at my map over the top of his glasses. "But it's an easier drive on the main road, that's the way I'd be recommending you go."

"That's fine. I'm actually going to walk it."

He cocked his head, and for a moment I could see it in his eyes—*This nutter slept in our house last night?*

"No. No, you can't walk it. It's far too long. You'll be out there all day."

I sopped up the last bit of lovely yolk with some toast and a bit of bacon, and told him, untroubled, "I probably will."

hole 928

612 over par

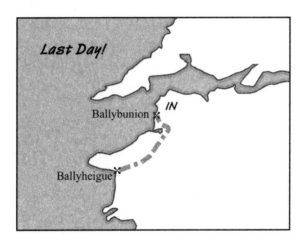

Last Day!

Ballybunion

IN

Ballyheigue

THE DOG WAS STILL GOING TO BE A PROBLEM.

I woke up that morning, believing that the course called Ireland had been beaten. There were 1,118 miles crossed, 1,967,680 yards played, and me passing signs that had only existed in my dreams, but were now posted there in front of me— BALLYBUNION, 7 KM. Through a month of rain, I had come out dry. I had walked away from a firing squad, unscratched. I put fried eggs in my pocket, I paid for a carpet, I looked hatred in the eyes—those bitter, green eyes—and I had still played through.

Twenty years of being humbled on a golf course by big numbers and putts that never had a chance, and I still hadn't learned that the precise moment you believed you had a firm grip on it, the game went to water on you, leaving you with empty hands and wet trousers. For a hundred days, I lived one slippery curve, one clumsy step, one distracted driver away from Ireland getting the last, last word. With just a handful of holes left, I was still standing, about to golf the whole island in one pair of shoes, until the course decided it still wanted its pound of flesh, and sent a dog the size of a wildebeest to collect it.

I knew all about nerves—first tees and jetways still pushed my stomach toward evacuation mode—but this was my first run-in in a very long time with pure fear. It felt as if my body had been cut loose from my throat, my lungs and heart going quiet and still, almost like they were trying to lay low, staying out of the fracas. I backed away from the dog, but he kept coming, eyes locked on mine, and in that moment, I didn't see my life flash before my eyes. I just felt tremendously, incredibly, irredeemably stupid. I was entirely alone on an unknown road in a foreign country staring a mauling in its bloodshot eyes, and it wasn't the dog's fault, or Ireland's. It was all my own doing. I was going to end my days looking at the rotten undercarriage of an anonymous Irish mutt because I was selfish enough to go it alone, to leave my wife at home for four months so I could go golf and drink and pillage our savings for the summer. Hell, when I put it that way, I almost sided with the dog.

As we continued our backward dance, the hound definitely leading, I reached into my pocket and pulled out my cell phone. It was my only hope. Now what to do with it? It seemed the wrong time to call home—*Hi, Allyson, can you do me a favor and Google "neck wound"?* Maybe I should throw the phone at him. Maybe if I held it up to his ear long enough, I could give him brain cancer. I ruled the phone useless and reached into my other pocket—passport, they'd need that to identify the leftovers—but in the cargo pocket on my thigh, wouldn't you know it . . .

A golf ball.

Now I didn't usually carry a ball in my pocket when I was walking, and I didn't remember how it had gotten there. There seemed an undeniable providence to it. If anything was going to save me today, my last morning on this golf course, it had to be a Titleist.

I put the ball between my thumb and forefinger and shook the white trinket in front of his eyes. "Here you go, good boy, here's a ball, look at the ball."

The dog sat back in his haunches and tilted his head. Praise God, the ball had his attention. I reached back, and launched the ball over him and down the road.

"Go get it!"

His head whipped around, but his paws never took their eyes off me. He turned back toward me, head cocked as if to say, *What was that for? You know how expensive those things are over here?* I watched the golf ball bound down the road before hopping into the deep weeds, growing my official lost ball tally to a hefty 129.

I got busy with my last resort, cutting deals with my maker— *If this dog could please just get bored with me, I swear I will never walk anywhere again. I'll ride a Rascal to the bathroom. I'll rescue and nurture a whole houseful of strays when I get home, if you can just send a truck to run this one over . . .*

The dog's attention suddenly turned away from my loins to where a mud-splashed SUV was headed down the road in our direction. I flagged the car down and saw two young women sitting in the front seat with a baby in the back. I didn't remember saying anything specific, dropping my jaw and squeaking out a few notes. My bloodless complexion and distended eyeballs told the story of my predicament, and while she didn't open the door— understandable with the toddler in tow—the driver was willing to drive slowly down the road, keeping her bumper between the dog's mouth and my ass. The dog didn't like gas-guzzlers, apparently, because it actually worked, the Range Rover escorting me down the road and around a bend until the dog was out of view.

I knew that I was in better shape than when I had arrived in Ireland, but for someone who had never run so much as a 1k, I was able to jog the next two miles at a steady clip with thirty pounds on my back and bear traps for sneakers. When I finally stopped, I was confused. I'd never run so far without going hands on knees and slobbering profanity, but I stood there looking behind me at a gloriously dog-free country road, and I wasn't so much as panting. I was unfamiliar with this athlete of ample wind. It was strange, and nice—and temporary, no doubt.

The homeward haul was a remembrance of roadside run-ins

past. I steered myself to the opposite side of the road when I came upon a gypsy camp, where a wire box full of muddy puppies fumbled over one another to yelp in my direction. I found a welcome sign for Ballybunion and stopped to take a picture of it, then didn't bother snapping a picture of the next Ballybunion signpost, telling me I still had five kilometers to go. And after those final five km, when I had finally drawn close enough to find a brown sign at a T-junction pointing me to the Ballybunion Galfchursa, it seemed fitting that the sign was twisted sideways, pointing me straight into a field of dairy cows.

I put my money on the road to the left, and a half mile later I could see I had gambled well, the top of the Ballybunion clubhouse rising out of the misty dunes. So I stopped. I dropped my bag and pushed it off the road, turned around, and started heading back the way I'd come. My end was in sight, but I had finally had enough.

I had made an effort that summer to be the uninvolved spectator, Ireland's inconspicuous guest, the outsider, the eavesdropper. Above all else, four months had taught me that I might feel a connection to this place, but it would always be just that—I was an American, impatient and obvious, of short history and of mottled lineage, and that was more than okay. The history and the brogue and the blarney were theirs, and no amount of miles could make that otherwise, and they didn't need to. But when it came to the signs, particularly the ones pointing to the golf course, those were mine. I had lived by them, put faith in them, taken more heart from a posted arrow than any soul in the island. They were the piece of Ireland I owned, and I was damned if I was going to leave the last one crooked.

I walked back to where the road began and hoisted myself up onto a mossy stone wall beside the sign pole, a horn blast from a passing tractor trailer nearly knocking me off my perch. I banged on the sign until the arrow had turned back around, pointing straight down the road toward the place I had been headed for since a far ago swing in Kilkee.

———

In *Ulysses*, Joyce's Irish hero called history a nightmare from which he was trying to wake, and in so many ways I had found an Ireland that was now wide awake—Eire was up and at 'em. Ireland had always read to me like a country that had never gotten its holiday. While the other kids were out playing in the sunshine at recess, Ireland was stuck inside, still learning its lessons. But after so many missed birthdays, Ireland had its cake now, and as if to reward her patience, she'd been served the biggest one on the block. Ireland was the envy of Europe, and not just with the golfers, but among the bankers and developers and shop clerks, too. And what had gotten the Irish there, through impassible mire and over unscalable walls, was something that had pulled me along through my own tiny trip. The story. The story could carry. In their songs, in their boasts, in the friends gathered around a torn-open bag of crisps, it was the story, sometimes a sad one, often a funny one, always a holy one, that gave Ireland its breath. Jokes about the widow Murphy or songs of Spancil Hill or words pressed into a tombstone in Sligo—it made the rain tolerable, gave history some levity. You could really get through anything if you convinced yourself there was still a third act, and Ireland's seemed to have finally arrived. Mine had, too, as I stood at the end of a 1,118-mile road, looking at a wall with the letters BAL-LYBUNION GOLF CLUB cut into the stone.

I took off my hat and stuffed it away, tried to un-flatten my hair, and wished I had shaved. I tucked in my shirt and left my bags out in the parking lot so as not to make a spectacle, trying to pretend I wasn't a golfing vagabond, at least until I found the first tee.

The glass doors to the clubhouse slid open, and in the lobby, a small group of people were standing there in a line, looking at me. A large man with black hair stepped forward and extended a hand.

"So tell me. How are the feet?"

An hour later, I was back out in the parking lot, sitting on a stone wall with my backpack and golf bag propped up next to me. The morning fog had lifted and there was a soft gray blanket of clouds over the golf course. The gentleman who had greeted

me in the clubhouse was the Ballybunion vice-captain, and though
I hadn't called ahead to tell them I was coming, alongside him
were the club captain, the club manager, and the ladies captain
who had brought along a camera to snap a picture of my arrival.
Upstairs in the lounge, they fed me a sandwich and chips and
welcomed me to their club, the manager introducing me to the
members who passed our table, most of them saying they had
been waiting for me, some inquiring about my shoes. I went outside and sat at the far end of the parking lot, away from where
anyone might overhear me. I took my phone out of my pocket,
and found a text waiting:

ALL THE BEST IN BALLYB! WELL PLAYED! PADDY

It was the time to call Allyson, but I wanted to call my dad
first. He had stood here before with Ballybunion waiting for him,
and if anyone was going to appreciate my news, it would be him.
They were just finishing up dinner back home when he answered
the phone.

"Are you safe?" he asked.

"I'm safe. I just walked into Ballybunion."

"Ballybunion? Ballybunion," he said, a memory in his voice.
"So that's it? All done?"

"All done. But I'm going to have to come back here sooner
than I thought."

"Go back? To Ireland? You've got to be kidding me."

"Back to Ballybunion, at least," I said. And then I explained
to my dad how, back inside, they had just made me a member.

Fifty-four logo balls sit in a crystal bowl on a shelf above my
desk. Mostly white, with two yellow ones from courses in Donegal, the pile looks like a bottomless bowl of ice cream scoops. My
shoes sit on the window ledge, and though I didn't wear them
once after that day in Ballybunion (it was Crocs on the flight
home), they look like they still have a few miles left in them. In a
Waterford frame, there's a picture of me shaking hands with the

captain of Ballybunion, my other hand holding the certificate they surprised me with, the one announcing my honorary membership. I haven't used it yet, but I plan to someday. There's a member-guest every fall, and Paddy has been texting.

The map on my wall has been covered up with Post-it notes and new business, to-do lists and a Phillies pennant (I got home just in time to see them win the division). Sundays watching Gaelic football games feels like a lifetime ago. I heard that Kerry beat Cork again. There were pubs in Philadelphia where I could have gone to watch the final match on satellite, but it didn't feel right. It would have been like drinking Guinness from a can, or ordering a cheesesteak in Cleveland. And there would have been a clash of personalities in that pub between the guy who was happy to be home and locked in his office now, who got out twice a day to follow his dog around the block, and the itinerant guy who never felt better than when he had his life strapped to his back, unaware of where he was headed but so damn fortunate to have spent those days ever hopeful for what was hanging around the next bend. In the year since I've been home, I haven't played a single hole of golf—not because I haven't wanted to, or had the opportunity, but because for the first time since I was eight years old, I don't have any golf clubs.

I'm not going to tell you much about the Ballybunion links. If you've played it, you know. If you haven't, I'm sorry. Other places I had visited were Irish links golf courses; to me, Ballybunion was Irish links golf. Bold but still subtle, grand without feeling pretentious, it was an ancient course where every inch still felt relevant. The second with its green tossed high above a hilltop; the seventh where the waves licked your cheeks and hopefully not your Titleist; the meanest 130 yards in Ireland covered with sand pits and uncharitable caroms on 8; and what about 11, a par-four rippling downward through the dunes, dollops of fairways spread here and there between the sand hills, or 16, where you fired over a ridge of dunes in search of a ribbon of fairway from which you would fight your way upward to a green floating on the horizon. Seventeen along the beach was hard to play as you fumbled for your camera, and if there was a better approach to a finishing hole than the second shot to the vaulted eighteenth at Ballybunion, the deep green set into a saddle of gentle humps and dune grasses, I had yet to play it. I'll stop there so as not to spoil the movie, because even if you're better with a camera than a pitching wedge, you should still go down to Kerry and see it.

It seemed a shame that golfers came to Ballybunion and didn't leave time for the Trent Jones designed Cashen course beside the old links—a little wilder with a few more quirks, if it wasn't attached to such a legend, it would be a destination course of its own. I played the Cashen course the afternoon I arrived, and the next morning, I teed it up on the Old Course with the captain, while the lady captain hopped around the dunes snapping pictures of my round, and I finished with a dozen or so members standing around that eighteenth green, where I knocked in a wobbly five-footer to finish Ireland with a par.

I had a few hours left before my ride came to bring me up to Limerick, and from the Ballybunion clubhouse, I had spied a path heading down to the beach. One of the caddies confirmed it for me, "Aye, that'll take you down to the sand," and while it wasn't the gnarled black cliff hanging over a dark and swirling sea that I had imagined in my daydreams, any beach would do. I removed my souvenir golf balls, my phone, and my wallet from my golf bag, threw the lightened sack over my shoulder, and headed for the water.

As I walked, I heard that familiar rattle of metal on metal coming from over my shoulder, five-iron clacking into seven, seven-iron knocking against the wedge. I loved that sound. It sounded like fourteen years old to me, hauling golf bags back toward a clubhouse where I would wait for my twenty dollars, sneaking out to squeeze in nine before dark, just the sound of crickets and the clicking of a hustling bag of golf clubs. We'd gone a thousand miles that summer, and that was as loud as they had ever complained. Freed from that backpack, they weren't very heavy at all, and maybe they deserved better than the ocean bottom. I thought of my young friends in Ballyheigue, how they'd handled my driver with such reverence, giddy about the chance to give it a lash. I should have handed my sack of clubs over to those lads then and there. That's what I wished I'd done, but maybe it wasn't too late.

I stopped at the top of the beach path, turned around, and I rattled my way back up to the clubhouse. By the first tee, I found the caddy master pouring over a clipboard busy with names and tee times. He looked up from the paperwork, and I asked him if he knew a kid who could use some golf clubs. He told he did, not sure what I was getting at. I took the bag off my shoulder and handed it to him, and I asked him to please do so when he had the chance.

Inside the clubhouse, I took advantage of my seven minutes of fame to enjoy a few Guinnesses on the house, shaking hands and looking out over the dunes in the bright afternoon sun, a restfulness washing over me that I knew I might never feel again. There was such a lightness—no clubs, no pack, no pages left—it felt like I almost wasn't there.

I sat there and smiled for an hour, then I said my good-byes and headed out to the parking lot to meet my lift to Limerick. And as I came out of the clubhouse, I saw a foursome of teenagers crowded around the first tee box. They were caddies, probably just returned from their morning loops and now loosening up to play the Old Course themselves. It wasn't unusual to see caddies out on the links—another of Ireland's charms, that club caddies were also often club members. But I stopped for a moment and watched them tee off, my focus on one of the boys in particular. He took a few extra practice swings with his new Mizuno driver, then stepped up to his ball and swung the club well, finding the fairway with a club that had just finished Ireland but wasn't finished yet.

I had always looked at that stick with a little worry in my heart. My clubs had plenty of power to provide joy or to pile on misery, and I regarded them with that respect, perhaps even that fear. But they never looked so good as they did that afternoon, heading out into the dunes on someone else's back. I hope they're still there and going straight for someone. I hope they're still going around.

COURSE: Ireland

DATE: 4/30/07–8/25/07

PLAYER A: Tom Coyne

HANDICAP: Backpack

Holes		Par	Score	Holes		Par	Score
1–18	Kilkee	70	85	550–567	Ballycastle	71	84
19–36	Doonbeg	72	80	568–585	Ardglass	70	84
37–54	Spanish Point	64	76	586–603	Royal County Down	71	90
55–72	Lahinch	72	82	604–621	Greenore	71	87
73–90	Connemara	72	85	623–639	Seapoint	72	87
91–108	Mulranny	71	76	641–657	Baltray	72	82
109–126	Westport	73	89	659–675	Laytown & Bettystown	71	85
127–144	Clew Bay	70	80	677–693	The Island	71	86
145–162	Achill Island	70	82	695–711	Corballis	65	78
163–180	Carne	72	77	713–729	Portmarnock	72	78
181–198	Enniscrone	73	86	731–747	Royal Dublin	72	83
199–216	Strandhill	69	83	749–765	St. Anne's	71	88
217–234	Rosses Point	71	89	767–783	Wicklow	71	78
235–252	Bundoran	70	79	785–801	The European Club	71	84
253–270	Donegal	73	94	803–819	St. Helen's Bay	72	78
271–288	Narin & Portnoo	73	86	821–837	Rosslare	72	81
289–306	Cruit Island	68	74	839–855	Old Head	72	89
307–324	Gweedore	70	80	857–873	Skellig Bay	72	90
325–342	Rosapenna Sandy Hills	71	83	875–891	Waterville	72	83
343–360	Rosapenna Tom Morris	70	82	893–909	Ceann Sibeal	72	89
361–378	Portsalon	72	90	911–927	Dooks	71	84
379–387	Otway	32	35	929–945	Tralee	72	79
388–405	Ballyliffin Old	71	81	947–954	Ballyheigue Castle	36	43
406–423	Ballyliffin Glashedy	72	82	965–972	Ballybunion Cashen	72	81
424–441	Buncrana	62	62	983–990	Ballybunion Old	71	85
442–459	North West	70	78				
460–477	Greencastle	70	79	IN	811,360 yards	1,745	2,056
478–495	Castlerock Mussenden	73	81				(+311)
496–513	Castlerock Bann	68	72				
514–531	Portstewart	72	79				
532–549	Royal Portrush	72	88				
OUT	1,156,320 yards	2,150	2,475				
			(+325)				

TOTAL 4,531 strokes (636 over par)
1,967,680 yards
196 pubs
129 lost balls

ACKNOWLEDGMENTS

I promised myself that I wasn't going to perpetrate another overwrought acknowledgments page, but after so many days spent enjoying the hospitality of the land of Cead Mile Failte—*a hundred thousand welcomes*—it seemed I owed at least as many thank yous.

My most exuberant thanks go to the best agent in the business, Dan Mandel, and to Bill Shinker and Patrick Mulligan at Gotham Books—with that name, Patrick was destined to edit an Irish golf book, and I was fortunate that this one landed in his lap.

I owe a special debt of gratitude to the staff at Tourism Ireland who proved to be an invaluable resource in making this trip come true. Thanks to Ruth Moran, Susan Bolger, and Maggie Lane in Dublin who worked magic arranging tee times for my unwieldy itinerary. Thanks to Bruce Riccio and all my friends at Mizuno for providing the best gear in golf to accompany me along the way, and thanks to Joe Gomes at Titleist/FootJoy, no matter that my shoes went home after thirty-six holes, and that the balls he sent were missing by week two. It wasn't the balls' fault.

Thanks to Brett Valley and Brendan Cahill who both helped bring this story to life. All the best to Nick Harris and Joe Quinlan. I am grateful to so many Irish friends who made this round a possibility, people like Gerry Burke, Jerry and Jo Quinlan, Tom Plunkett, Danny Brassil, Simon Duffield, John Slye, Anthony Byrne, Terry O'Doherty, Andrew Mawhinney, John Farren, Billy McCaul, Larry Byrne, John Farren, and especially Mr. Pat Ruddy. Thanks to Tony Leen at *The Irish Examiner*, Mark Jones and PJ Cunningham at *The Sunday Tribune*, and cheers to Morgan Treacy and Paul McGuckian for making a baggy-eyed ginger look like a golfer in the newspaper. Many thanks to Gary Perkinson, and all the best to Charlie Hanger and everyone at Golf.com.

To everyone who came over and joined me for a hole, I cannot thank you enough. There is no story here without your company, your shanks, and your shin-pain. I would have been home by June if forced to play this course as a single.

Thank you Eddie Hackett. Thank you Allyson. Thank you Ireland. And to Paddy from Kinsale, *go raibh maith agat*, a hundred thousand times.

AUTHOR'S NOTE

This book describes my experience while traveling and golfing Ireland and reflects my opinions, flawed and otherwise, relating to that experience. Events and conversations may have been reorganized for the sake of the narrative, and the names of some secondary characters have been changed. In researching the history of golf and Ireland, I borrowed information from golf club Web sites and course guides, and I utilized numerous online articles, including but not limited to material from the Links of Heaven and the Golfing Union of Ireland Web sites, Wikipedia, and the *Encyclopedia Britannica* online. Useful texts included Jim Finegan's *Where Golf Is Great*, *The Oxford Illustrated History of Ireland* (Foster), and *Teach Yourself History of Ireland* (Madden), the last of which won a place in my pack by being the lightest book in the history section. My most oft-consulted source, and potentially most inaccurate, was the gentleman seated next to me at the pub, thus all complaints and calls for retractions should be forwarded to St. James's Gate, Dublin.

The Course Called Ireland
COURSE GUIDE

THINK ABOUT BRINGING:

A rain hat

Something waterproof and stiff-brimmed. The overwide hat I overpaid for in the adventure store was not terribly handy in the wind, its floppy brim constantly slapping me in the ears. My nylon Mizuno baseball cap was much more helpful.

A knit hat

Even if it's August, pack a cap that will stick to your head in the breeze. It won't be ski-cap cold, but when the wind really blows, your ears will need the cover.

Rain pants

I played almost every round in rain pants worn right over my underwear. It saves you from falling over on every other tee box as you take your rain covers on and off and on again, and you avoid that steamy unpleasantness of corduroys encased in Gore-Tex. And even if it isn't raining, rain pants slip through the wind better than your khakis.

Suspenders
I wore rain paints fitted to be worn on their own. Your pair is probably a little baggy, and suspenders will save you from spending four hours hiking them back up over your belly. Don't worry, no one will see them under your wind shirt. Bring one of those, too.

Two pairs of golf shoes
An obvious necessity. I became accustomed to walking with damp, pulpy insoles, but Ireland will find a way into your Dry-Joys, and one night of drying time is never quite enough.

Sunblock
You don't think of Ireland as tropical (funny, thanks to temperate breezes from the Gulf Stream, the island is actually covered with palm trees), and you'll probably forget to lather up that first day in Lahinch. And you'll pay for it.

Lipitor
Handicap go up after ten days in Ireland? Wait 'til you see your cholesterol.

An open mind and an imagination
Though you might indeed find them, don't waste your trip waiting for idyllic conditions and immaculate layouts. Appreciate the wilds, and savor the silliness of golf holes squeezed into a dunescape. If you don't go into it expecting Florida, the place will blow you away.

Extra copies of *A Course Called Ireland*
Preferably in hardback.

THINK ABOUT LEAVING AT HOME:

The golf umbrella
Watching a golfer chase his tumbling umbrella across the whole of the Ceann Sibeal links was enough to convince me that I was right to leave mine at home. Rain suit and rain hat are all you need, leave the hang glider behind.

Shorts
Almost everyone that visited this summer brought a pair. And aside from Julian who was forced to change his at the turn in Baltray, they never left anyone's suitcase.

Rain gloves
I tried a number of different brands, but they all seemed to just soak up the water, keeping my hands damp and cold. Best way to play wet is to invest in new grips that will get tacky in the rain, and then play bare-handed.

The blow dryer
This is one for the wives. While I never fully embraced the necessity of a working hair dryer, wet hair was a crisis Allyson relived every morning. We couldn't find a converter in Ireland able to prevent her Conair from dying in a cloud of smoke. Stop at the first shop you see and spring for an Irish version. It was Allyson's favorite Irish souvenir by far; the Old Head sweater didn't even come close.

Cash
The exchange rate you're going to get through your ATM card is far better than what you'll get at the money changer.

Ball retriever
Aside from that thing called the Atlantic over your shoulder, water is an anomaly on a links. And if you actually do have a ball-scooper in your bag, you should think hard about whether your game is ready to go on the road.

Your Fighting Irish sweatshirt

Unless you want to see behind the scenes at Belfast International.

Your laptop

Golf. Pub. Food. Pub. Bed. Golf. Don't screw it up with your BlackBerry.

Prejudices regarding Ireland's culinary reputation

There is great food to be found around Ireland, especially if you're a seafood lover. Lovely soup and brown bread smeared with the world's sweetest butter are served in every clubhouse in the country, and along with the ubiquitous Irish toasted sandwich, they might be the perfect post-round meal.

Your ego

Links golf is a different kind of game, surprisingly punitive and far more fickle than the golf you're accustomed to. Accept that you are likely to shoot a few scores that you thought you had exorcised many seasons ago. I hated to watch Americans fret over their scorecards in the clubhouse, resenting a course because they didn't play to their handicap. If you can't let go of score and enjoy yourself, do as the Irish do and play a Stableford.

A Course Called Ireland
REDESIGNED

A biased and unscientific reordering of Ireland's golf holes, listed according to the courses I would walk back to first. *

Carne

Ballybunion (Old Course)

Old Head

The European Club

Cruit Island

Dooks

Ardglass

Portstewart

Tralee

Lahinch

Waterville

Rosses Point

Narin & Portnoo

Castlerock (Bann Course)

The Island

Mulranny

Laytown & Bettystown

Spanish Point

---

* I know, it's blasphemy that Royal County Down didn't make my list, but playing RCD the way we did, sans caddy or course guide, was like playing Marco Polo by yourself. We were lost, and there are numerous Irish rounds that I recall more fondly.

BEST GOLF VALUES

Dooks

Ceann Sibeal

Cruit Island

Donegal

Narin & Portnoo

Spanish Point

Skellig Bay

Laytown & Bettystown

BEST BETS FOR LINKS PURISTS

Rosses Point

Ballybunion

Portmarnock

Rosslare

Royal Portrush

Royal County Down

Narin & Portnoo

BEST BETS IF THE ONLY LAYOUT YOU REALLY CARE ABOUT IS THAT OF THE CLUBHOUSE BAR:

Lahinch

Waterville

Ardglass

Portsalon (visit the Stores Pub next door)

Rosses Point (Sligo Town is all craic)

Old Head (enjoy the view from the Lusitania Bar in the clubhouse, but have a pint with the caddies at the Speckled Door pub down the road)

THE OFFICIALLY DESIGNATED FOUR-PINT PUBS OF IRELAND:

The Beach Bar, Aughris Head

The Stores Pub, Portsalon

The Old Commercial Bar, Ardglass

THREE-PINT PUBS:

The Cornerstone, Lahinch

O'Connor's, Doolin

Keogh's, Ballyconneely

Matt Molloy's, Westport

Nevins, the Mulranny Road

Harry's, Rosses Point

Shoot the Crows, Sligo Town

The Pilot Bar, Enniscrone

The Grainne Uaile, Newport

The Wolfe Tone, Letterkenny

The Cottage Bar, Buncrana

Bittie's, Belfast

Culleton's, Rosslare

Doolan's, Waterford

The Mary B, Dungarvan

The Nook, Youghal

Mutton Lane, Cork City

The Spaniard, Kinsale

Baily's Corner, Tralee

PUBS FOR TRADITIONAL MUSIC:

O'Connor's, Doolin

Lowry's, Clifden

The Pilot's Bar, Enniscrone

The Bridge Bar, Bundoran

Dunnion's, Donegal Town

Jack White's, Brittas Bay

McManus's, Dundalk

Doolin's, Waterford

*Shoot the Crows, Sligo Town (if you consider
Tom Waits traditional music)*

FAVORITE GUEST HOUSES AND B&BS

Daly's B&B, Doolin

Boulevard Guest House, Westport

The Abbey B&B, Ballina

Oyster View B&B, Rosses Point

St. Ernan's House, Donegal Town

The Lake House, Narin & Portnoo

The Caldra B&B, Buncrana

The Strand House, Portstewart

The Carriage House, Dundrum

Lismar Guest House, Dundalk

The Red Bank, Skerries

Fernroyd House, Cork City

Desmond House, Kinsale

The Smugglers Inn, Waterville

MOST MEMORABLE MEALS:

Fishy Fishy, Kinsale

Vintage, Kinsale

The Tannery, Dungarvan

The Smugglers Inn, Waterville

The Kitchen Restaurant at the Mount Falcon Hotel, Ballina

The Grainne Uaile Pub, Newport

The Mourne Seafood Bar, Dundrum

Abrekebabra, all over Ireland, and thank God for that

COURSE: **Ireland**

DATE: _____

PLAYER A: _____

HANDICAP: _____

Holes		Par	Score	Holes		Par	Score
1–18	Kilkee	70		550–567	Ballycastle	71	
19–36	Doonbeg	72		568–585	Ardglass	70	
37–54	Spanish Point	64		586–603	Royal County Down	71	
55–72	Lahinch	72		604–621	Greenore	71	
73–90	Connemara	72		623–639	Seapoint	72	
91–108	Mulranny	71		641–657	Baltray	72	
109–126	Westport	73		659–675	Laytown & Bettystown	71	
127–144	Clew Bay	70		677–693	The Island	71	
145–162	Achill Island	70		695–711	Corballis	65	
163–180	Carne	72		713–729	Portmarnock	72	
181–198	Enniscrone	73		731–747	Royal Dublin	72	
199–216	Strandhill	69		749–765	St. Anne's	71	
217–234	Rosses Point	71		767–783	Wicklow	71	
235–252	Bundoran	70		785–801	The European Club	71	
253–270	Donegal	73		803–819	St. Helen's Bay	72	
271–288	Narin & Portnoo	73		821–837	Rosslare	72	
289–306	Cruit Island	68		839–855	Old Head	72	
307–324	Gweedore	70		857–873	Skellig Bay	72	
325–342	Rosapenna Sandy Hills	71		875–891	Waterville	72	
343–360	Rosapenna Tom Morris	70		893–909	Ceann Sibéal	72	
361–378	Portsalon	72		911–927	Dooks	71	
379–387	Otway	32		929–945	Tralee	72	
388–405	Ballyliffin Old	71		947–954	Ballyheigue Castle	36	
406–423	Ballyliffin Glashedy	72		965–972	Ballybunion Cashen	72	
424–441	Buncrana	62		983–990	Ballybunion Old	71	
442–459	North West	70					
460–477	Greencastle	70		**IN**	**811,360 yards**	**1,745**	
478–495	Castlerock Mussenden	73					
496–513	Castlerock Bann	68					
514–531	Portstewart	72					
532–549	Royal Portrush	72					
OUT	**1,156,320 yards**	**2,150**					

TOTAL   1,967,680 yards
PAR   3,895